Parliamentary Control and Government Accountability in South Asia

Parliaments or legislatures are the keystone of democratic governance and they are critical in securing government accountability. On the one hand, legislatures are representative bodies: they reflect the sentiments and opinions of the populace. On the other hand, they are the prime source of law by which a country is governed. This book presents a comparative analysis of the role of parliamentary committees in securing government accountability in the three largest and most important functioning democracies in South Asia: Bangladesh, India and Sri Lanka.

The author compares the nascent democracy of Bangladesh with the stable and vibrant democratic system of India since its independence from the British in 1947 and Sri Lanka's longstanding and established democracy. He argues that in each country, parliament has been able to survive and perform the key parliamentary tasks of representation, legislation, oversight of the executive, conflict resolution and regime maintenance. He concludes that parliamentary committees in Bangladesh, India and Sri Lanka do not perform as successfully as their counterparts in the Western world in controlling the government and holding it to account; however, their role in securing government accountability is not irrelevant.

This comparative research work is an important contribution to the study of parliaments in general worldwide and a useful reference for studying third world parliaments in particular.

Taiabur Rahman teaches Development Studies at the University of Dhaka, Bangladesh. His research interests are in the area of comparative politics, public administration and development studies.

Routledge advances in South Asian studies

Edited by Subrata K. Mitra

South Asia Institute, University of Heidelberg, Germany

South Asia, with its burgeoning, ethnically diverse population, soaring economies, and nuclear weapons, is an increasingly important region in the global context. The series, which builds on this complex, dynamic and volatile area, features innovative and original research on the region as a whole or on the countries. Its scope extends to scholarly works drawing on history, politics, development studies, sociology and economics of individual countries from the region as well those that take an interdisciplinary and comparative approach to the area as a whole or to a comparison of two or more countries from this region. In terms of theory and method, rather than basing itself on any one orthodoxy, the series draws broadly on the insights germane to area studies, as well as the tool kit of the social sciences in general, emphasizing comparison, the analysis of the structure and processes, and the application of qualitative and quantitative methods. The series welcomes submissions from established authors in the field as well as from young authors who have recently completed their doctoral dissertations.

1 **Perception, Politics and Security in South Asia**
The compound crisis of 1990
P. R. Chari, Pervaiz Iqbal Cheema and Stephen P. Cohen

2 **Coalition Politics and Hindu Nationalism**
Edited by Katharine Adeney and Lawrence Saez

3 **The Puzzle of India's Governance**
Culture, context and comparative theory
Subrata K. Mitra

4 **India's Nuclear Bomb and National Security**
Karsten Frey

5 **Starvation and India's Democracy**
Dan Banik

6 **Parliamentary Control and Government Accountability in South Asia**
A comparative analysis of Bangladesh, India and Sri Lanka
Taiabur Rahman

Parliamentary Control and Government Accountability in South Asia

A comparative analysis of Bangladesh, India and Sri Lanka

Taiabur Rahman

Routledge
Taylor & Francis Group
LONDON AND NEW YORK

First published 2008
by Routledge
2 Park Square, Milton Park, Abingdon, Oxon OX14 4RN

Simultaneously published in the USA and Canada
by Routledge
711 Third Avenue, New York, NY 10017

Routledge is an imprint of the Taylor & Francis Group, an informa business

Typeset in Times by Wearset Ltd, Boldon, Tyne and Wear

British Library Cataloguing in Publication Data
A catalogue record for this book is available from the British Library

Library of Congress Cataloging in Publication Data
A catalog record for this book has been requested

ISBN13: 978-0-415-40498-3 (hbk)
ISBN13: 978-0-203-94576-X (ebk)

In memory of my mother Rokeya Khatoon

Contents

Illustrations

Figures

Tables

Appendix

Foreword

As the frontiers of democracy have extended in recent decades, and the practice of actual, living popular representation has deepened in numerous societies across the globe, so academic interest in core institutions of this form of government has flourished. Standing at the very heart of democratic governance, legislatures have been the subject of a wide range of studies seeking to document and analyze how they are elected, how they are organized and how they function. In particular, the role legislatures play in monitoring and holding to account the core institution of contemporary democratic governance, the executive, has long been a developing area of scholarly inquiry.

At the same time, the growth of academic interest in legislatures has not been even across the realm of democratic governance, and it has not always mapped well on to the contours of contemporary democratic experience. India, the largest democracy in the world, has a bicameral legislature, the *Sansad*, elected from a population of more than one billion citizens. To date, however, the workings of its more powerful lower house, the *Lok Sabha*, have not been given the scholarly attention they deserve. In other parts of South Asia, shorter, more contested and more difficult democratic experiences have resulted in legislatures that do not have the prestige accorded to the Indian parliament. Nevertheless, the importance of the unicameral *Jatiya Sangsad* in Bangladesh, a country of 145 million people with a tradition of military involvement in politics, and of its counterpart, also unicameral, in Sri Lanka, a country of 20 million people with an experience of considerable inter-communal tension and violence, cannot be underestimated. These parliaments have also been understudied.

In this monograph, Dr. Taiabur Rahman fills a significant gap in the literatures on both legislative studies and South Asian politics by examining the parliaments of Bangladesh, India and Sri Lanka. He does so comparatively, using the common British parliamentary and colonial heritage of the three countries as the foundation for a study that is both grounded in history, and rich in contemporary analysis. He also does so on the basis of extensive fieldwork conducted in South Asia between late 2003 and late 2004. By constructing a clear theoretical framework and engaging in a comprehensive literature review, Dr. Rahman is able to generate a study that links to the mainstream of legislative studies, and advances many of its core themes and debates.

Dr. Rahman's focus is mainly on parliamentary committees, and in particular on the role they play in holding the executive to account in Bangladesh, India and Sri Lanka. His descriptions are presented in a common format, derived from his extensive literature review, which enhances the degree of comparative analysis in which he is able to engage. The evaluations that Dr. Rahman produces are contributions both to scholarship and to political debate, for he identifies clearly ways in which parliamentary committees in the three countries, and especially in Bangladesh and Sri Lanka, could improve their performance in the key realm of government accountability. In part, he encourages parliamentarians and analysts in South Asia's most vibrant democracies to learn from each other. In part, he points to lessons that emerge from wider literatures reflecting parliamentary experience across the world.

This pioneering study is likely to spark considerable interest in South Asian parliaments, and debate about the role they play in underpinning democracy in a critical region of the globe. It deserves to be widely read, and to be taken up by scholars who share Dr. Rahman's passion for democracy in South Asia, and determination to understand the key elements that enable it to function.

Ian Holliday
City University of Hong Kong

Preface

Parliaments or legislatures are the keystone of democratic governance and they are critical in securing government accountability. While parliaments were generally stronger in the 1990s than ever before, not all parliaments have been studied in depth. Parliaments in Asia, and particularly in South Asia, have been especially neglected. This study examines parliaments in South Asia by engaging in comparative institutional analysis of the three largest and most important functioning democracies in South Asia: Bangladesh, India and Sri Lanka. Within the broader functional jurisdictions of parliaments in these three countries, it focuses on the role of parliamentary committees in securing government accountability. The study is based on extensive fieldwork undertaken by the author in the parliaments of Bangladesh, India and Sri Lanka during the period from November 2003 to October 2004.

The book consists of eight chapters. The introductory chapter discusses research problems, research questions, rationale and significance of the study. Chapter 2 explores the core concepts, explains the major theories and discusses the research methods used in the study. Chapter 3 reviews the major literature on legislatures, in an attempt to figure out the factors determining the strengths of legislatures with regard to holding the government to account. Chapter 4 makes a review of global literatures on the institutional arrangements of committees to determine their strengths in securing government accountability. Chapters 5, 6 and 7 thoroughly investigate the role of parliament and parliamentary committees in Bangladesh, India and Sri Lanka respectively in holding the government to account in the light of the theoretical framework backed by primary and secondary data. The final chapter makes a comparative review of the role of committees in the three countries and reports the findings of the study based on the observations and results drawn from the previous chapters.

This study presents two major sets of findings. One is concerned with the extent to which parliamentary committees in Bangladesh, India and Sri Lanka have been able to hold the government to account. The other relates to the methodological approaches of studying parliaments.

In general, the research finds that parliamentary committees in Bangladesh, India and Sri Lanka do not perform at par with their counterparts in the Western world in controlling the government and holding it to account. They lag far behind other parliamentary democracies in Western Europe and Commonwealth countries in term of institutional arrangements and practical implications in securing government accountability. However, the role of committees in securing government accountability in these three countries cannot be overlooked. They are weak but not irrelevant. The mere existence of committees in these countries does matter. Committees are there to oversee the executive and they have been successful to some extent to make some impacts on holding the government to account.

India has got the most institutionalized and assertive committee system in South Asia. It is clearly ahead of Bangladesh and Sri Lanka with respect to institutional arrangements and real-world implications in holding the government accountable. In terms of ensuring government accountability, the role of committees is largely confined to the initiation and the recommendation stages of involvement with limited implications at the implementation level.

When comparing Bangladesh with Sri Lanka in terms of committee strengths to hold the government accountable, it is hard to judge which one is better in what respects. The role of committees in securing executive accountability in Bangladesh and Sri Lanka is largely confined to the initiation and the recommendation stages of their operations with unknown implications at the implementation level. The poor performance of the committee system in holding the government accountable in Sri Lanka emanates from the prevailing political system. In Bangladesh, it is the confrontational political culture which is causing problems for parliament and parliamentary committees to get institutionalized and perform to their potential.

This book also has implications for the study of parliaments worldwide. In contrast to the predominantly institutional approach of studying parliaments advocated by many Western scholars, the book argues that the point of departure for categorizing parliaments should be from society, economy and political regime to intra-institutional political system.

In order to investigate the ways in which scholars have sought to capture or measure parliamentary strengths in holding the government accountable, the study presents a series of basic typologies of legislatures. However, as these typologies are rather crude (to appreciate the variations and divergences within a specific category of parliament), it then focuses on additional factors (socio-economic, political and intra-institutional) that are relevant in determining parliamentary strengths to make the government accountable. Thus the study offers a blend of macro-societal and micro-institutional factors that determine parliaments' strengths in holding the government accountable. There are two additional observations that add value to the study of parliaments, committees and government accountability.

The first is that the more governing power is diffused and shared between and among contending veto players regardless of the system of government, the more the system bears the potential of having a strong parliament to hold the government to account.

The second is that a strong parliament is a prerequisite for a strong committee system and vice versa, and a strong committee system is a prerequisite for calling the government to account irrespective of whether the political system is parliamentary or presidential.

This study was basically undertaken to write my doctoral dissertation at the City University of Hong Kong during 2002–2005. I want to take this moment to put on record here my gratitude to several persons and institutions whose assistance – financial, academic, personal – has been essential to the production of this work. First of all, I want to acknowledge my indebtedness to my supervisor Professor Ian Holliday and associate supervisor Dr. Ahmed Shafiqul Huque for their precious, constructive comments and a thorough vacuum cleaning of earlier drafts of this manuscript and for being exceptionally nice to me throughout my Ph.D. studies.

Thanks are due to those honorable MPs in Bangladesh, India and Sri Lanka who had overwhelmingly responded to my questionnaire/interview and in turn cheered me up to carry this work forward. I am thankful to Mr. Qazi Tauhid Hasan of Bangladesh Parliament secretariat, Mr. Frank Christopher, Mr. S. Balshekar and Dr. Vinay, K. Bhatnagor of Lok Sabha secretariat and Mr. C. Kuruppu of Sri Lankan Parliament secretariat for their critical role in getting access to necessary information and documents in the respective parliament secretariat which were invaluable inputs to be included in my dissertation to give it a final shape.

I would like to record my gratitude to the City University of Hong Kong for providing me financial assistance to conduct the study. I also like to express my thanks and gratitude to Ms. Dorothea Schaefter of Routledge for taking her personal interest and care in the publication of this book.

Last but not least, my wife Sayka and our son Shadman deserve special thanks for their tolerance, understanding and emotional support throughout the study period. While, I have been greatly benefited by the help and cooperation of many people and institutions, I alone am responsible for any shortcomings of this work.

Taiabur Rahman
Department of Development Studies
University of Dhaka

Abbreviations and acronyms used

AO	Accounting Officer
AG	Auditor General
AIBP	Accelerated Irrigation Benefit Program
BAC	Business Advisory Committee
BAL	Bangladesh Awami League
BCS	Bangladesh Civil Service
BDT	Bangladesh Taka
BEC	Bangladesh Election Commission
BJP	Bharotio Janata Party
BJS	Bangladesh Jatiya Sangsad
BNP	Bangladesh Nationalist Party
BPLP	British Parliamentary Labor Party
CAG	Comptroller and Auditor General
CAO	Chief Accounting Officer
CBI	Central Intelligence Branch
CCOMOD	Consultative Committee on Ministry of Defense
CCOPA	Consultative Committee on Public Administration Management and Reform
CHT	Chittagong Hill Tracks
CIA	Central Intelligence Agency
COE	Committee on Estimates
CPA	Commonwealth Parliamentary Association
CPSU	Commonwealth Parliamentary Studies Unit
CNG	Concentrated Natural Gas
COPA	Committee on Public Accounts
COPE	Committee on Public Enterprises
COPU	Committee on Public Undertakings
CPI	Corruption Perceptions Index
CVC	Central Vigilance Commission
DCC	Dhaka City Corporation
DESA	Dhaka Electricity Supply Authority
DRDO	Defense Research and Development Organization
DRSCs	Departmentally-Related Standing Committees

DRSCOA	Departmentally-Related Standing Committee on Agriculture
DRSCOD	Departmentally-Related Standing Committee on Defense
DRSCOHA	Departmentally-Related Standing Committee on Home Affairs
EC	Estimates Committee
FPTP	First-Past-The-Post
GCEC	Greater Colombo Economic Commission
GDP	Gross Domestic Product
GOPRB	Government of the People's Republic of Bangladesh
GNI	Gross National Income
HC	House Committee
HDI	Human Development Index
HPC	High Post Committee
INC	Indian National Congress
IPU	Inter Parliamentary Union
IPS	Institute of Parliamentary Studies
JI	Jamat-e-Islami
JP	Jatiya Party
JS	*Jatiya Sangsad* (name of Bangladesh Parliament in Bangla)
LAFEAS	Legislative, Financial Committee, Executive and Administrative Service
LARRDIS	Library, Research, Reference, Documentation and Information Service
LS	*Lok Sabha*
MDSD	Most Different Systems Design
MP	Member of Parliament
MSSD	Most Similar Systems Design
NCG	Non-partisan Caretaker Government
NCTBB	National Curriculum and Text Book Board
NDA	National Democratic Alliances
NED	National Endowment for Democracy
NHRC	National Human Rights Commission
NICVD	National Institute of Cardio Vascular Disease
OSD	Officer of Special Desk
PAC	Public Accounts Committee
PC	Privileges Committee
PDB	Power Development Board
PR	Proportional Representation
PSC	Public Service Commission
RCC	Railway Convention Committee
RS	*Rajya Sabha*
SAC	Staff Advisory Committee
SCMs	Standing Committees on Ministries
SCOMOA	Standing Committee on Ministry of Agriculture
SCOMOD	Standing Committee on Ministry of Defense
SCOMOE	Standing Committee on Ministry of Establishment

TI	Transparency International
TIB	Transparency International Bangladesh
TNO	Thana Nirbahi Officer
UK	United Kingdom
US	United States
USD	US Dollar
UNDP	United Nations Development Program
UNP	United Nationalist Party

1 Introduction

The prime objective of this research work is to make a comparative analysis of the role of parliamentary committees in securing government accountability in the three largest and most important functioning democracies in South Asia: Bangladesh, India and Sri Lanka.

Parliaments or legislatures are the keystone of democratic governance and they are critical in securing government accountability. On the one hand, legislatures are representative bodies: they reflect the sentiments and opinions of the populace. On the other hand, they are the prime source of law by which a country is governed. The union of these two features qualifies their significance in democratic polities (Olson 1994: 1). In fact for Lijphart (1991: Ix), "Legislatures should probably be regarded as the most important institutions in a democracy".

Legislatures are pervasive: most countries in the world have one. They are resilient: once abolished they have a strong capacity to resurrect. They are also remarkable for their diversity. They vary in terms of structure, organization and function. Thus they differ in the consequence they have for their respective political systems. The fact that legislatures are so pervasive, diverse and resilient makes them a legitimate source of scholarly attention (Norton and Ahmed 1999: 1). What is of more importance is that legislatures, irrespective of government system, all over the world are the legitimate and representative institutions entrusted with securing public sector accountability.

In contrast to the false impression of a "decline of parliaments" which gave birth to an extensive scholarly literature in 1960s and 1970s, parliaments have in the past three decades become more influential bodies globally and this has been due particularly to their newly created or revived committee system (Strøm cited in Longley and Davidson 1998: 5). In general, parliaments are stronger in the 1990s than ever before. Commentators throughout the twentieth century bemoaned the decline of legislatures, yet the number shows no sign of declining: if anything the reverse. According to the IPU-Parline database, there were 180 national parliaments operating in September 2002. Today more than two-thirds of the world's population lives in parliamentary democracies (Copeland and Patterson 1998).

A phenomenon of the 1990s was the worldwide emergence of newly democratic or democratizing young regimes with their new democratic parliaments, developments which brought fresh dimensions and challenges to parliamentary research (Longley and Davidson 1998: 15). Their prominence increased in the 1990s because of developments in Central and Eastern Europe. In other parts of the world including Southern Europe, military rule and dictatorships have variously given way to elected assemblies (Norton 1999: xi). The increased prominence of legislatures has prompted a greater scholarly interest in their existence and functions (Norton 1998: xi). Norton (1999: xii) has drawn two principal conclusions on legislatures from his own observations. The first is that legislatures are worthy of study. Their sheer number and historical persistence deserve some attention. The second is that such study has to be undertaken on a cross-national basis.

Parliaments in Asia and particularly in South Asia hitherto have not been the subject of much cross-national study. That provides the rationale and basis of this study. Moreover, for the consolidation of democratic governance, the necessity of good institutions cannot be denied. Hence result-oriented parliamentary research concentrating on parliaments and their linkage to government on the one hand and to society on the other is of central concern for both understanding and promoting the process of democracy-building (Patzelt 1994: 431). Against this backdrop, it is worthwhile to examine parliaments in South Asia by engaging in comparative institutional analysis of the three largest and most important functioning democracies in South Asia: Bangladesh, India and Sri Lanka.

Post-colonial transitions to democracy in these three countries of South Asia have mixed experience of parliamentary government. Despite belonging to the most impoverished nations of the world, democracy in these three countries had some success, contrary to the thesis that economic development is a prerequisite for democracy. In each case, a crucial aspect of the functioning of democracy has been the ability of parliament to survive and perform the key parliamentary tasks of representation, legislation, oversight of the executive, conflict resolution and regime maintenance. There has been a new beginning in parliamentary politics in South Asia since the early 1990s. Not only did parliaments provide a means of peaceful transition to democracy from authoritarianism in Bangladesh and Pakistan and monarchical rule in Nepal, but also they appear to have the potential to hold the government to account in several countries in this region (Ahmed 2001: 18).

Bangladesh is a nascent democracy. After experiencing over one and a half decades of military and semi-authoritarian rule, it started its painstaking journey towards democratization in 1991. Since then, three parliamentary elections have been held under Caretaker Governments[1] and considered largely to be free and fair. Since early 1991, in an attempt to strengthen the role of parliament vis-à-vis the executive, some reforms had been brought into the formal arrangements of parliament in general and the committee system in particular in Bangladesh. These include a broadening of the jurisdictions of standing committees which are empowered to deal with legislation and oversight simultaneously, the establishment of an independent parliamentary secretariat and of an Institute of

Parliamentary Studies (IPS) for research support, the introduction of Prime Minster's Question Hour and the replacement of ministers as committee chairs by backbenchers.

India has been a stable and vibrant democracy since its independence from the British in 1947. Parliament has played a significant role in nation building and uninterrupted continuation of democratic governance (except the brief authoritarian interlude of the 1975–1977 national emergency) in India. Although India has met almost all the requirements associated with a mature and resilient democracy, it could not live up to the expectation of people in terms of providing effective governance. Lack of government accountability is thought be a key factor responsible for weak governance in India. Institutionalized financial committees had been in place to ensure executive accountability from the start of parliamentary democracy in independent India. In order to further strengthen the committees and secure administrative accountability in a far more effective manner, 17 departmentally-related standing committees (DRSCs) were introduced in 1993. Moreover, minority coalition governments were commonplace in the 1990s. The implications of these institutional changes in a new political framework provide a key context for government accountability.

Despite its ethnic conflicts, Sri Lanka has been a longstanding and established democracy in South Asia since it got its independence from the British. In 1947, the new parliamentary system, which came to be created on the traditional Westminster model, contained a traditional system of committees, which functioned effectively and served the intended purpose largely because of the fact that the parliament reigned supreme until it was devalued in 1978 by the introduction of executive presidency in the constitution. Since then, no major parliamentary reform for rationalizing or strengthening the committee system had been undertaken in Sri Lanka. However, 17 oversight committees (small in size and to be headed by the opposition MPs) were proposed by the Ranil Wickremasinghe Government in the fifth parliament (2002–2003). This proposal could not materialize due to the premature dissolution of parliament by the president, which put an end to Wickremasinghe regime. However, the debate over strengthening committees goes on and the proposed reform has a wide appeal still today. The role of the parliamentary committee system in holding the government accountable in a semi-presidential system is thus in prospect too.

Legislatures as a whole have been a relatively unexplored spectrum of research for the social scientists on South Asia. Very few authoritative research works have been conducted in the arena of parliamentary politics and development. Comparative legislative studies on South Asia are almost non-existent. A single article by Ahmed (2001b) is available on South Asian legislatures. This article is too general to grasp the role of parliamentary committees in holding the executive to account. However, there are some good works on parliament in individual countries. For instance, Ahmed's book (2002) is an excellent piece of scholarly work on the nature and working of parliament of Bangladesh in the 1990s. Likewise, a book edited by Malhotra (2002) is a comprehensive compendium on the working of Indian parliament for the last five decades.

Warnapala's (2004) book examines the relationship between the parliamentary financial control and government accountability in Sri Lanka.

Ahmed (1997a, 1997b, 1998a, 1998b, 2000, 2001a, 2001b, 2003) has published widely on different dimensions of Bangladesh parliament. Two scholarly articles (2000, 2001a) and one monograph (2001c) are available on the parliamentary committee system in Bangladesh. These are excellent reviews on the role of committees in making the government behave. No substantial survey/interview of the committee members or committee staffers was carried out earlier other than one by Rahman (2000) and another by Ahmed (2001c) to recognize their opinions regarding the functioning and efficacy of parliamentary committees in Bangladesh.

A volume of articles presented mostly by the MPs of the seventh parliament to a conference on the parliamentary committee system (BJS 1999) reports exclusively the formal arrangement of committee system in Bangladesh. Several articles (Norton 1998; Rubinoff 1996, 1999; Inter-parliamentary Union 1986; Kashyap 1973, 1979, 1997, 2000; Bhardwaj 1995, 1998; Malhotra 2000; Jain 1988, 1991, 1998; and Shastri 1998) on the role of parliamentary committees in India are available. However, the scope of the available articles is too general and broad to grasp the role of parliamentary committees in securing government accountability. The functions and role of committees are sketchy and cursorily depicted in almost all the articles.

No major scholarly article on the parliamentary committee system in Sri Lanka is available. However, two books, one by Warnapala (2004) and the other by Wijesekera (2002), are available on the Sri Lankan parliament and its role in securing government accountability. Both the books have covered committees but major discussions are confined to formal institutional arrangement. These books lack theoretical discussion and empirical data too. Not a single article on the comparative review of the role of committees in holding the government accountable in South Asia is available.

Hence, an in-depth analytical study on the role of parliaments and particularly parliamentary committees is in order and merits our attention to comprehend the implications of these new institutional arrangements and political developments in ensuring government accountability in Bangladesh, India and Sri Lanka.

Accountability which is complex and ever-changing is the core concept in this study. Likewise, it is possible to analyze parliaments from many different perspectives. The one that this book finds more interesting is the role of a parliament in general and its parliamentary committees in particular in securing government accountability. Accountability incorporates several typologies, dimensions or components, which are also inexorably intertwined and interdependent (Paul 1991: 5). Likewise, accountability has several aspects: financial accountability, transparency, responsiveness, regularity, participation, empowerment, decentralization, combating corruption etc. (Turner and Hulme 1997: 122–123; World Bank 1994: 14, 1996: 65; Dwivedi and Jabbra 1989: 6; Rosen 1989: 32–34, 1998; Uhr 1999). However, the focus of this study will be on financial accountability, regularity, transparency and the responsiveness aspects, for these dimensions cover in one way or another the remainder of the mentioned dimensions. In the following chapter, we have operationalized committee as an instrument of public accountability taking into account typology and aspects of accountability and its involvement in various stages of securing executive accountability.

In this research accountability has been analyzed from two broader perspectives: formal/institutional and informal/societal. Institutional/formal aspect of accountability is concerned with prevailing institutional rules of public organizations while societal/informal accountability emanates from the accountability values/norms of a society in which public organizations are nestled. A cultural-institutional approach that draws on broad cultural/institutional theory is adopted in this study as an analytical lens to address the issue.

Now it is imperative that the utility of parliamentary control of the executive and parliamentary committees' role in holding the government be established. In a democracy, there are three different branches of government: the executive, the legislative and the judicial. All these three branches are interlinked and interdependent. The power of these branches should be based on checks and balances. The executive branch has a management system of its own which is based on some principles of administrative science such as hierarchy, rules, division of labor and impersonality. These formal principles are not practiced by the bureaucracy in South Asia. Society in South Asia is mainly hierarchical and patrimonial where the application of institutional rules is not universal. Formalism, heterogeneity, overlapping (Riggs 1964) are widely prevalent in politics and administration in this region.

In a parliamentary system of government, power is fused between the executive and the legislative arms of the state. Even a considerable portion of the frontline members of legislative branch become members of cabinet and lead the executive branch. For instance, in the current Bangladesh parliament (the eighth), the ruling coalition has 220 members in a 300-member House. The present ministry size is 60 – so at least 60 – treasury bench MPs (who are ministers) are formally part of the executive. It may be assumed that many other government members aspire to hold one of those cabinet positions and hence more than 60 out of 220 government MPs are oriented to the executive in the legislative/executive dichotomy (Wiltshire 1982). Additional institutional devices must therefore be put in place to keep a watchful eye over the executive and hold them accountable for sins of omission and commission. Moreover, the executive usually dominates the legislative outputs while the bureaucracy dominates the legislative inputs by playing a determining role in preparing legislative bills in a parliamentary form of government. This contention holds that the executive in fact is not in control of all vital areas of public administration and therefore parliament must intervene and step in where executives fear to tread (Uhr 1982: 27, 1999; Evans 1982). The intention by parliaments to extend their ability to oversee, or scrutinize the government and ministers, is a major – perhaps even the central – factor explaining the increasing use of committees in parliamentary democracies (Longley and Davidson 1998: 4).

The main rationale for empowerment of parliamentary committees is the prevailing imbalance of power between the executive and legislative branches. To cope with the demands of modernization and complexity of society, the executive branches have expanded their departments and personnel. Thus the executive's possession of an expanded workforce with sophisticated technical and specialized knowledge has enabled the executive to become the dominant player in the governance system. In the legislatures, on the other hand, the number of members rarely rises. The result has been the steady decline in the ability of the legislature to fulfill its prime functions of legislation and oversight of the executive. This decline, coupled with rise of disciplined political parties, meant that the balance of power in most parliaments shifted decisively in favor of the executive. The only response the legislative branch can offer in order to effectively influence, scrutinize and control the executive is to improve the efficiency with which its membership is utilized. This includes the use of staff and experts but more significantly it means to rationalize and empower committees (Hazan 2001: 77–85; Mezey 1998: 791; Shaw 1998: 229).

In order to evaluate the role of parliamentary committees in ensuring government accountability in Bangladesh, India and Sri Lanka, a number of key questions are raised. These will be addressed in the subsequent chapters. The questions are:

1 To what extent are the macro and micro political contexts of the parliaments in Bangladesh, India and Sri Lanka conducive to influence/constrain the business of government?
2 How far are the parliaments in Bangladesh, India and Sri Lanka institutionalized with respect to their roles and functions?
3 What are the formal institutional arrangements in respect of structure, function, procedures and power of parliament and parliamentary committees in Bangladesh, India and Sri Lanka and to what extent are the institutional rules for the committee system exercised to make the executive accountable?
4 What are the key factors that affect the control of the executive by parliamentary committees in these three countries?

2 Concepts, theories and methods

This chapter explores the core concepts, explains the major theories and discusses the research methods used in the study. It is organized into five major sections. The first embarks upon the conceptual discourse on accountability, elaborating the concept, dimensions, typology and so on based on the available literature. The second section delineates and rationalizes the use of a cultural-institutional approach as a macro-analytical framework and its implications for the study. The third section explains the logic of adopting comparative analysis of a few cases. The fourth section reports the logic and method of case selection. The final section discusses about the data collection method of the study in a systematic manner.

Accountability

Accountability, which is the core concept in this book, is complex and ever-changing. Its meaning, typology, dimensions, mechanisms and perspectives are critical for conducting any study involving accountability. A clear understanding about using specific aspects and mechanisms of accountability and its linkage to the institutions and actors that will enforce accountability is necessary to operationalize accountability as an agenda of research. Likewise, it is possible to analyze parliaments from many different perspectives. The one that this book finds most interesting is the role of a parliament in general and its parliamentary committees in particular in ensuring government accountability. Hence knowledge about how I will establish a suitable linkage between various aspects, mechanisms of accountability and the pursuit of parliamentary committees to call and hold the government to account will be the focus of this section.

Accountability is at the heart of good governance and has to do with holding governments responsible for their actions. Governance incorporates two distinct but intimately intertwined dimensions: one is political (and relates to the commitment to good governance), and the other is technical (and relates to the issues of efficiency and public management). Both must be addressed. Without political commitment little can be achieved even with efficient public administration. And without an efficient public administration, no government can be effective, however benevolent (World Bank 1991: 307).

Accountability is a chameleon word (Quirk 1997: 580). It does not lend itself to neat, self-contained definitions (Pyper 1996: 1). Public accountability involves the methods by which a public agency or a public official (both political and administrative officials) fulfills its duties and obligations and the process by which that agency or the public official is required to account for such actions (Dwivedi and Jabbra 1989: 5). But accountability is not confined to mere responsibility to provide answers; it connotes the possibility of sanctions being invoked in cases where answers are unsatisfactory or problematic (Behn 2001).

The concept of accountability is complex and multifaceted. The creation of accountability relationships seeks to satisfy a range of aims (Pollitt 1999; Wolf 2000; Behn 1901). Most notably:

- Control of abuse, corruption and misuse of public power.
- Assurance of well-performing public institutions and that public resources are being used in accordance with publicly stated aims and that public service values (impartiality, equality and fairness in citizen treatment) are being adhered to.
- Improvement of the efficiency and effectiveness of public policies.
- The enhancement of the legitimacy of government.

The basic questions that must be taken into account in any elementary mapping of accountability are the following: accountability to whom? For what? How? The answers to these questions are not simple especially when administrators encounter multiple sources of legitimate authority and competing expectations for performance. The first question requires identification of the legitimate authorities for whom the relevant public officials work. The second requires clear specification of performance expectations. And the third entails identification of the various reporting relationships (institutional practice, procedures and strategies) that are available to hold public officials answerable for their performance (Romzek 2000: 416).

In the public sector, the public accountability process is largely determined by the legislation and the parliamentary system (Cameron 2004: 63). In a system of parliamentary democracy, the parliament represents the people and the government is accountable to the parliament. The government itself consists of the political executive and administrative executive. The administrative executive is accountable to the political executive, which in turn is accountable to the parliament. The administrative executive is arranged in hierarchical order and subordinate civil servants are accountable to their superior. Thoughtful analysis recognizes accountability as a two-way traffic suggesting that in addition to bureaucracies being held accountable by elected officials, those same elected officials also should be held accountable for their direction of the bureaucracy (Wood and Walterman 1994). These twin themes of accountability constitute government accountability (Mulgan 2000: 556; Pyper 1996).

In this research accountability has been analyzed from two broader perspectives. Public accountability has two interrelated aspects – formal/institutional and informal/societal. This relationship is like the head and tail of the same coin. These two aspects influence each other in a reciprocal way. Institutional/formal aspect of accountability is concerned with prevailing institutional rules of public organizations while societal/informal accountability emanates from people's perception of accountability in a society in which public organizations are nestled. Democratic institutions need to be supported by an enabling societal context to make them work.

Types of accountability

Viewed as a strategy for managing expectations, public administration accountability takes a variety of forms. The variety of possible mechanisms currently in use is suggested by a typology offered by Romzek and Ingraham (2000). They segregate four modes of accountability according to whether *the source of control* is (a) internal or (b) external and whether the *degree of autonomy* is (a) low or (b) high as illustrated in the following figure.

Hierarchical accountability

The functioning of hierarchical accountability system includes two simple ingredients:

1 An organized and legitimate relationship between a superior and subordinate in which the need to follow orders on the part of subordinate is unquestioned.
2 Close supervision of standard operating procedures or clearly stated rules and regulations. (Gouldner, cited in Romzek and Dubnick 1987: 228). The actual process of accountability within the executive branch takes many forms. It ranges from supervisory direction and review, through internal audit to evaluation by an external group (Rosen 1984: 32–34).

Professional accountability

Professional accountability relationships stress the individual responsibility of the administrator above all else as that individual exercises discretion on the job.

	Source of expectations and/or control		
Degree of autonomy		Internal	External
	Low	Hierarchical	Legal
	High	Professional	Political

Figure 2.1 Types of accountability relationships in democratic systems.

Underlying this system is the belief that administrators granted such discretion will monitor and regulate themselves through adherence to professional norms (Romzek and Dubnick 2000: 391).

Political accountability

Political accountability relationships afford public administrators the discretion of being responsive to the concerns of key stakeholders such as elected officials, clientele groups and the general public (Romzek 2000a: 27). Under political accountability, the administrator is the responsive actor and relevant stakeholders are the administrator's constituents. Periodic elections are the principal weapon in the hands of citizens to ensure political accountability and render the basis of legitimacy to govern. Numerous other instruments of political accountability include ministerial responsibility, parliamentary questions, vote of no confidence, budget appropriations and political parties.

Legal accountability

Legal accountability relationships involve detailed, external oversight of performance for compliance with established mandates such as legislative and constitutional strictures. Typically, the external party makes the laws and other policy mandates, which the public administrator is obligated to implement. These external reviewers, as independent actors, typically cannot take any disciplinary action against an errant administrator because the reviewers are outside the chain of command. However, reports by these reviewers can certainly trigger sanctions from the relevant supervisor for unacceptable performance (Romzek 2000: 419; Romzek and Dubnick 1987: 228–229). Legal accountability consists of two crucial subcategories (accountability through judicial system and accountability through legislative and supportive apparatus (parliamentary questions, various committees, Ombudsman, the Comptroller and Auditor General (CAG), etc.). The second category of legal accountability holds the executive accountable through monitoring, auditing and other forms of oversight. Figure 2.2 depicts different values and behavioral expectations emphasized by the various accountability relationships.

Parliamentary committees and accountability

As a distinct agency, the relationships parliamentary committees have with the executive can be characterized as legal and political. Legal accountability entails regularity and financial accountability:

- *Regularity* denotes bureaucrats' compliance with the formal rules and regulations of a bureaucratic organization (Turner and Hulme 1997: 122–123). We will see to what extent the institutional rules for committees are exercised in this regard.

Accountability	Value emphasis	Behavioral expectation
Hierarchical	Efficiency	Obedience to organizational directives
Legal (Legislative and Judicial)	Rule of Law	Compliance with external mandates
Professional	Expertise	Deference to individual judgment and expertise
Political	Responsiveness	Responsiveness to key external stakeholders

Figure 2.2 Values and behavioural expectations of different accountability types.

- *Financial accountability* entails improved budgeting, accounting and information system, building a professional cadre of accountants and auditors and strengthening the legal framework of modern accounting practice (World Bank 1994: 14). The parliament allocates money for all public sector organizations and oversees whether this money is spent with efficiency and economy to ensure financial accountability. Financial accountability is central to understanding the core of accountability since it underpins all other forms of accountability.

Political accountability entails responsiveness and transparency:

- *Responsiveness* for our study is more political than administrative. The committees make recommendations on different issues and ask the concerned public organizations and ministries to comply with them. Civil servants are usually expected to be loyal to their political masters i.e. the ministers. The implementation of committee recommendations depends largely on the goodwill of a minister and the incumbent government. He or she can direct the bureaucrats to act on committee recommendations and then follow it.
- *Transparency and access to information.* To be accountable, the operations of the government agencies need to be visible. On all but a handful of issues related to the security of the state, citizens should have uninhibited access to information. The wide dissemination of information on government policies provides for informed public debates, helps to improve policy design, facilitates wider acceptance and secures efficient implementation (World Bank 1996: 65). The incumbent government has a major role to decide which information is secret and sensitive to state security. Unless those calling subordinates (account holdees) to account have full access to the relevant people and relevant information their investigations and assessments will be frustrated (Mulgan 2000: 567).

An appropriate structure of accountability demands institutions, which will ensure that public officials are appropriately constrained. Indeed, if the central issue of democracy is to control the government so that it acts on the people's preference, then the entire complex edifice of modern democratic political system becomes in effect a system for ensuring government accountability (Day and Klein 1987). From this perspective, institutions of accountability include all institutions that are aimed at controlling or constraining government power, for instance legislatures, statutory authorities and courts. Devices of accountability then include separation of power, federalism, constitutionalism, judicial review, the rule of law, public service code of conduct and so on, all of which have an effect on the control of public power. Also added are the key extra-governmental institutions of a democratically effective civil society, which help constrain governments, for instance competitive markets, interest groups and the mass media (Peters 1995: 300–301).

Legislatures have a variety of functions – legislative, financial, investigative and so on – among which holding the executive publicly accountable is merely one, albeit extremely important, function. Within the overall operations of a modern legislature, accountability is associated with certain procedures such as committee enquiries or (in parliamentary systems) the questioning of ministers. But it may occur at any point, in legislative debate or financial authorization or committee hearings where members of the governments are required to explain their actions and take the consequences. Thus legislatures are pivotal institutions for securing public accountability (Mulgan 2000: 565).

Accountability and tripartite stages of committee involvement

The role of parliamentary committees as an instrument of securing executive accountability encompasses a three-step involvement:

- *Initiation.* It is about initiating the operation of committee. What are the formal institutional arrangements of committees? Do the rules of committees accommodate the opposition? Do the rules put the committees in a position to hold the government to account? Are the committees formed in time? Do they meet regularly? Do committee members attend the meeting regularly? Which sorts of agenda do the committees deliberate? Are the issues about routine matters of public organizations or those of government accountability? Are committees supported by well-equipped parliamentary secretariat?
- *Recommendation.* The committee members take decision over an issue at this stage. Do the committee members recommend penalties for errant civil servants when they are found indulged in misappropriation or abuse of public fund? Do they usually involve in mere discussion without making any specific decision?
- *Implementation.* This is the most vital stage of the whole committee process. Are the recommendations obligatory or advisory? Who are responsible to implement the recommendations? To what extent are these recommendations complied with? Is there any punitive measure in case of

non-compliance with committee recommendations? Are the committees provided with necessary documents from public organizations on demand or denied on security matters? Are the committees contented with mere acceptance of the recommendations by the government? Or do they like to go beyond that and see the recommendations implemented?

Cultural-institutional approach

A cultural-institutional approach has been adopted in this study as an analytical lens to explain the issue. This draws on broad cultural/institutional theory but it is also specific in various ways.

Historical and sociological institutionalism somewhat attend to the cultural aspect of political life (Hall and Taylor 1996). Rooted in a fourfold classification of cultures as institutions, Grendstad and Selle (1995: 6) consider cultural theory to be a dynamic typology of the new institutionalism. However, no institution can be properly comprehended without considering its wider social and cultural context (Selznick 1996). It has been emphasized by cultural theorists that the social contexts within which institutions operate shape the manner in which institutions behave and act (Thompson *et al.* 1990; Hofstede 2001). According to Putnam (1993: 8), "The Westminster-style constitutions left behind by the British as they retreated from empire had very different fates in different parts of the world." Therefore it may be said that context matters for institutional performance. Below we discuss some theories of culture in order to highlight societal culture that may have profound implications for institutional performance.

Cultural theory

Entering cultural theory is rather like walking in a maze because space and perspective never seem to be static and reliable. Cultural theory conceives of culture as a combination of values, norms (mental product) and social relationship. It may be succinctly capsuled by three distinct terms – cultural bias (shared values and belief), social relations (pattern of interpersonal relations), and ways of life (a viable combination of cultural bias and social relations) (Thompson *et al.* 1990: 1).

Grid-group theory

Grid-group cultural theory is an approach that has been developed over 30 years in the works of British anthropologist Mary Douglas and Michael Thompson, the American political scientist Aaron Wildavsky and many others (Douglas 1982, 1992; Wildavsky 1987; Coyle and Ellis 1994; Grendstad and Selle 1995; Thompson *et al.* 1990, 1999; Ellis and Thomson 1997; Rayner and Melone 1998; Ward 1998; Hood 1996, 1998).

The basic tenet of grid-group cultural theory is that the most important factor in people's lives is how they want to relate to other people and how they want others to relate to them (Grenstad 1995). The theory explains how people in a society derive a limited range of answers to basic social questions such as: How does the world work? What are humans really like? To whom are we accountable? (Wildavsky 1987: 6). Grid-group theorists argue that people's answers to these questions produce orientations towards two basic dimensions of sociality:

- *Group* denotes the extent to which people in a society believe that they belong to particular social groups.
- *Grid* refers to people's perception of the appropriate extent and variety of rules in a society. In other words, do people believe that social behavior should be (is) determined largely by rules (informal or formal) or is there greater leeway for them to determine which behavior is appropriate? (Christensen and Peters 1999: 138).

The answers to these two crucial questions: "who are we" (group) and "what shall we do" (grid), have profound consequences for major decisions people make (Wildavsky, cited in Grendstad 1995: 101). In any society, these two dimensions can vary from low to high, thereby resulting in four main ways of life.

- *Hierarchic*. This is characterized by strong group membership with strong systematic prescriptions. For hierarchists, stratification is an inescapable part of social organization (Coughlin and Lockhart 1998: 41). Order is the

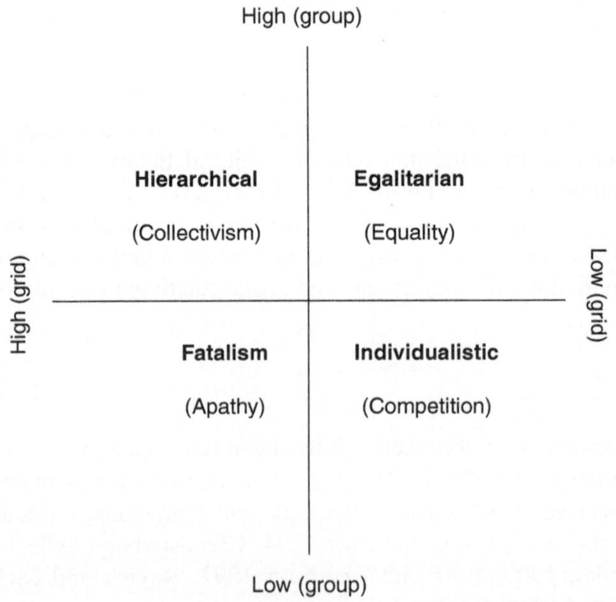

Figure 2.3 Four ways of life.

ultimate goal, which is sustained and upheld by wide application of rules and regulations (Lockhart 1999: 868).

- *Egalitarian*. This is characterized by strong group membership and few systematic prescriptions. The absence of effective and enforceable societal rules, in turn, appears to require consensual decision-making within the group (Christensen and Peters 1999: 139).
- *Individualistic.* This is characterized by weak systematic constrains and absence of binding group membership. Individualists view humans as self-interested and broad in capacities (Coughlin and Lockhart 1998: 38). Individualists therefore appear to correspond to the familiar model of economic man as utility maximizers relatively unconstrained by collective rules and norms (Christensen and Peters 1999: 138).
- *Fatalistic.* This is characterized by strong systematic prescriptions and no group membership. The fatalists have little control over their own life (Christensen and Peters 1999: 139). Fatalism is a passive way of life and experience of involuntary exclusion (Jensen 1998: 123).

In any society, all ways of life may coexist in a dynamic pattern of attraction and separation particularly at the individual level (Thompson 1996: 9). No way of life is entirely prominent in an individual's everyday life and idea of herself or himself and the world. However, most individuals find themselves inhabiting one way of life more than the others (Thompson *et al.* 1990: 267). The same is not the case with a society or a nation. The way of life of people (values, norms and culture) in a society or country is almost stable and enduring. One major constraint of switching from one way of social life to another is that varied modes of life not only produce different worldviews, but also produce and warrant different individual and social skills (Jensen 1998: 137–138). People who are predominantly accustomed to a hierarchical way of life cannot delete their social conviction and values overnight or over a year and switch to an individualistic way of life. So majority of the people in a society are used to inhabiting one way of life, which shapes and affects the institutions and institutional performance in that particular society.

Hofstede's four dimensions of culture

One of the most recent studies which addressed the question of influence of culture on organizational structure/performance was conducted by Hofstede (2001, 1991). In his investigations into the work-related attitudes and values of managers working for IBM in more than 50 countries and three regions, Hofstede was able to put together an impressive analysis of the cultural variations between nationalities (Tayeb 1988: 38–39; Handy 1993). He ended up with four cultural dimensions:

- *Power distance* is conceptually related to concentration of authority. It indicates the extent to which a society accepts that power in institutions and organizations is distributed unequally. Some national and regional cultures are characterized by large inequality, concentration of power in the hands of small and permanent elite, centralized organizations and restricted upward communication. Some national and regional cultures are characterized by small inequality, more social mobility, less concentration of power in the hands of a small elite, decentralized organizations with flatter hierarchies and relatively free upward communication.

- *Uncertainty avoidance* is related to structuring of activities and indicates the lack of tolerance in a society for uncertainty and ambiguity. The more active cultures tend to apply more specialization, formalization and standardization in their organizations. They put higher value on rules and uniformity and are less tolerant of and interested in deviant ideas. The less active cultures attach less importance to formal rules and specialization, are not interested in uniformity and are able to tolerate a large variety of different ideas.
- *Individualism/collectivism.* Individualism refers to a loosely-knit social framework in which people are supposed to take care only of themselves and their immediate families; collectivism is one in which they can expect their relatives, clan or work organization to look after them. More collectivist societies call for greater emotional dependence of members on their organizations.
- *Masculinity/femininity* is an equally powerful, yet often understated dimension. The predominant pattern of socialization in almost all societies is for men to be more assertive and for women to be more nurturing. Various data on the importance of work goals show near consistency on men emphasizing advancement and earnings as more important; women underpin quality of life and people higher. With respect to work goals, some societies are nearer to the masculinity end of the masculinity/femininity dimension, others nearer the femininity end.

If we endeavor to juxtapose these two pioneering works on the influence of culture on organizational and individual behavior we will find some sort of congruence between different dimensions of the works of Thompson and Hofstede. The society in which the degree of power distance and uncertainty avoidance is high, and masculinity coincide with collectivity, may resemble the hierarchic one. Where these dimensions of societal configuration are reversed (power distance and uncertainty avoidance is low and femininity coincides with individuality), the society seems to be close to individualistic one. The society, which contains masculinity and collectivity as dominant dimensions and is characterized by high uncertainty avoidance and long power distance, is compatible with fatalism. The egalitarian society shares the features of collectivity and femininity as dominant dimension followed by low power distance and low uncertainty avoidance.

Cultural theory has been used earlier in explaining political parties and can be used as a potential tool in legislative studies (Bale 1997). Grendstad (1995: 240) conducted a study on Norwegian political parties in the light of grid-group cultural theory and the results revealed that fatalism and hierarchy were pro-leadership cultures in that they correlated with party leadership tenure and experience, while individualism and egalitarianism were anti-leadership cultures in that these cultures correlated with the number of party chairs and inversely correlated with party leadership tenure and experience. Bale (1997: 37) also used grid-group cultural theory to explain why the British Parliamentary Labor Party (BPLP) had traditionally been more factionalized than its Conservative counterpart.

A superior–inferior (patron–client) relation, which is a key feature of a hierarchical society (most of the Third World countries are hierarchical), may profoundly affect prevailing accountability mechanisms. The relationship between father–children, teacher–student, senior official–subordinate official, husband–wife, housewife–maid servant, house owner–tenant, rich farmer marginal peasant, educated–uneducated, ruling part–opposition party, prime minister –leader of the opposition are based on the key notion of superior–inferior relations. Cultural values contain high deference towards superiors. Usually devising viable mechanisms is discouraged for ensuring accountability of the senior or stronger group/patron and hence no effective sanction is enforced even if found guilty. This discrimination is prevalent and accepted across the society.

The rank and status of a minister in a hierarchical society is quite high. He/she belongs to the elite strata of the society. A minister holds an extremely powerful position in a hierarchic society. The government backbenchers who constitute the majority membership of a parliamentary committee may find it awful and risky to call a minister and his/her executive ministry to account. The minister is treated as a father figure in party politics and backbenchers' attempts to interrogate the minister vigorously in committee sessions may be taken by the minister as an overt disregard towards him/her.

From the standpoint of prevalent cultural value of superior-inferior position of the executive and MPs, the MPs are lagging behind the political and administrative executives in almost all respects. Culturally, MPs are supposed to be in a better position to hold the executive accountable in a hierarchical society. The reality is not at par with the cultural expectation. In these circumstances, it becomes a formidable task for the committee members to make the executive accountable. The cultural value implies that the ruling party (government) is always superior to the opposition parties. The relationship between the government and the opposition is adverse and the government is suspicious about the opposition. The cultural value of domination and non-accountability of ruling regime is latent in the mind of the ruling regime. Hence it is cultural values which can profoundly influence and shape the ruling regime to devise institutional rules that could enable it to bypass accounting itself.

A hierarchical network cannot sustain social trust and cooperation (Putnam 1993: 174) for the whole society. Consequently, mutual trust and symbiotic relations loom in small coterie groups who have no incentive to work for the common well-being of the society and every incentive to indulge in costly and inefficient rent-seeking and pursuit of group interest only (Olson 1982). In a hierarchical society, the politicians, businessmen, parliamentarians and bureaucrats belong to a small coterie group who serve the interest of one another. They are symbiotically linked with each other and thus there is no interested party (barring the opposition) in the country that can strive to prevent the executive from indulging in corruption. Hence, being a partner of the small coterie group, it becomes a Herculean task for the committee members to arrest corruption and secure government accountability.

The case is reversed in an individualistic/egalitarian society (most Western countries) where the accountability relationship is reciprocal. Senior-junior relation is not prevalent. A son can point to the mistakes of his father in an individualistic/egalitarian society. Discrimination between and among people in terms of socio-economic status is minimal. The application of rules and laws is almost universal. Many institutions and mechanisms are in place in the society to check and balance the power and authority of divergent power-holders.

Third World countries by and large belong to hierarchical/collective culture. Hence, it may be assumed that there is a correlation between economic underdevelopment and hierarchical society. It is in this regard interesting to note that most of the Third World countries stand in the top of the Corruption Perception Index (CPI) launched by Transparency International (TI 2005). A causal relationship between corruption and hierarchical culture is therefore in prospect. And the prevalence of corruption in hierarchical/Third World societies can be largely attributed *inter alia* to the deficiency/absence of accountability (Klitgaard 1988).

Thus we can assume that the accountability mechanism is weaker in a hierarchical society than an individualistic/egalitarian society. We can also assume that it is easier for a legislature and its legislative committees to call the executive to account in a predominantly individualist/egalitarian society than a hierarchical/fatalistic society.

Institutional theory

In recent years, the focus on institutions as an important variable in political and organization science has gained substantial significance. In this tradition, institutions, more specifically institutional rules, norms and routines, are considered as determinants of politics and governance (March and Olsen 1984 1993, 1995, 1996) and at the same time they are shaped by history (Putnam 1993: 8). The new institutionalism contains a variety of different approaches to the institutional phenomena. In a seminal article, Hall and Taylor (1996) identified three new institutionalisms, i.e. rational choice, historical and sociological institutionalism.

Research works on US Congress and comparative legislative studies (British Westminster) have been accompanied by two distinct research approaches. Research on the United States Congress has been directed primarily at understanding the behavior of individual legislators. This research approach has depicted the legislator as a purposive political actor motivated primarily by electoral and constituency factors outside the institution and informational and bargaining process within it. Questions of institutional structure and performance are approached from the perspective of member's goal-seeking behavior. This paradigm has made extensive use of rational choice theory as an explanatory tool to interpret political behavior. Works on comparative parliamentary systems, in contrast, have been based on the party and state theories of comparative politics. This work has been more sensitive to the macro political context (rather than individual legislator) within which the legislature operates. It takes stock of the intra-institutional system as well. Institutional theory has been widely applied as a useful tool in this paradigm to explain political behavior (Mezey 199, 1994). As all of our cases belong to the comparative legislative studies paradigm and contain common hierarchical cultural attributes, we will be moving away from the rational choice institutional theory towards the direction of sociological institutional theory which tends to add cultural underpinnings.

Institutions differ among themselves on many aspects but on two fundamental points, they seem to agree (Putnam 1993: 7–8):

1 Institutions shape politics (Institutions as Rules): the rules and standard operating procedures (Hall 1986) that make up institutions affect political outcomes and behavior. Institutions affect outcome because they shape actor's identities, power and strategies.
2 Institutions are products of history (Institutions as History): history tells us about the extent and degree to which rules and standard operating procedures are institutionalized in organizations. The more these are ingrained in institutions, the more we can explain institutional behavior and performance on the basis of these aspects.

Institutions as rules/rule-based institutionalism

This perspective renders prominence on rules as the means of defining institutions and of governing behavior within those institutions (Peters 1999: 346). The rediscovery of rules and procedures as an important element for understanding legislative decision-making has become very apparent in recent summaries of research on Congress and European Parliaments (King 1995; Evans 1999; Cox 2000; Rasch 2000). The operation of the legislature in its various decision-making arenas is governed by a set of written and unwritten rules that determine how the institution does its work (Mezey 1993: 350).

Legislative institutions evince a high degree of formality. Obligations are formally understood; procedures and rules are well developed and to a considerable extent codified; the constitutional framework provides a relatively detailed foundation for organizational development (Patterson and Copeland 1994: 5). The legislative institution is strongly denoted by its formal rules-regulating representations, selection, procedures, decision-making and application (Patterson 1995: 12). The system of government, government's relationship with other branches, legislation-making, oversight power and above all the internal functioning procedures of legislatures, committee structures, power and procedures are imbedded in both formal rules and informal behavior. Two major sources of these vital rules are the constitution and the rules of procedures. These rules can constrain government. They may not constrain government as much as they constrain parliamentarians in a presidential system; they are nonetheless a constraint (Norton 2001: 30). A legislature's strength to call the government to account is largely contingent upon the rules and their proper application. However, sometimes these formal rules do not work properly in transitional legislatures due to weak informal institutional norms. These norms evolve over time, get institutionalized and are respected as convention in the Western world.

Likewise informal institutional rules can be every bit as important as in shaping actors' behavior as formally agreed procedures. The style and form of questioning in a UK parliamentary select committee for example may not be set down in writing; however, it is clearly identifiable as a "standard procedure" that structures political behavior whilst expressing particular values and power relationships. Moreover, informal conventions may reinforce formal rules. New rules about the separation of the executive and assembly function in British local government, for example, are influencing political behavior to a greater extent in those cities which already have a strong tradition of civic leadership (Lowndes 2002: 98, 103–104).

Institutions as history/historical institutionalism

Historical growth of a particular organization is crucial in identifying the degree of institutionalization. Institutionalization is something that happens to an organization over time, reflecting the organization's own distinctive history, the people who been in it, the groups it incorporates and the vested interests they have created and the way it has coped with the environment (Selznick 1957: 15–16).

An institution is, by definition, an organization that has been around quite a while; it has a life history. The US Congress became what it is today through an evolution of some 200 years. The British parliament took its current shape after a much longer evolutionary period than the US Congress (Patterson and Copeland 1994: 3). Institutions rely upon the logic of persistence or path dependency and once launched on that path they continue along until some sufficiently strong social/political force deflects them from it (Krasner 1984; Peters 1999: 63, 334).

Riggs (1975) emphasizes the connection between the conditions under which a nation's legislature first emerged and its current status in the political system. Decisions about US Congressional committee prerogatives taken in the 1990s reflect those made in the same legislature in prior decades. A particular institutional arrangement mirrors the interest of members and change depends on a change in these interests. Because of the dependency of present upon past arrangements, we cannot really understand institutional change in legislatures without observing a variety of examples of this institution (Kiewiet *et al.* 2002: 17).

New institutionalism

In order to evaluate parliament's power to constrain the executive in terms of formal power and consequences, one has to place parliamentary activities in its macro- and micro-institutional settings. Since the 1980s, political scientists have developed a renewed interest in the study of political institutions based on the assumption that "institutions matter" – that is a set of constitutional-legal rules and structural arrangements within which politics take place (as well as informal institutions) are crucial determinants of the shape of politics and policy outcomes (Lijphart 2002: vii). For others, institutions are rules or norms by which people live either abiding or breaching them (Lane and Ersson 2000: 213).

Most political action of real consequence occurs in institutions, so it is crucial to understand how these bodies act and how they influence the behavior of individuals working within them (Peters 1999: 150–151). A generation of work has shown that institutions affect various political outcomes. For instance, numerous scholars have shown that electoral systems shape the behaviors of parties, candidates and voters (Duverger 1964; Rae 1971; Riker 1982; Cain *et al.* 1987; Taagepara and Shugart 1989; Lijphart 1994; Sartori 1994; McCubbins and Rosenblurth 1995; Cox and Shugart 1996; and Cox 1997). Other scholars have demonstrated that different constitutional structures such as presidential or parliamentary systems affect regime stability, accountability, responsiveness and democratic durability (Lijphart 1991; Shugart and Cary 1992; Stepan and Skach 1993; Linz and Valenzuela 1994; and Shugart and Mainwaring 1997). Comprehending its significance, Rhodes (1997: 5, 64) has termed institutional approach as the "historic heart" of the political science discipline and "part of the toolkit of every political scientist".

Parliaments or legislatures are the keystone institutions in democratic polities (Patterson 1995: 10). Drawing on the political development literature in general and on Huntington (1965) in particular, Polsby (1968) used the concept of institutionalization to describe the process by which the House of Representatives became more complex, autonomous, coherent, adaptive and universal. The theme of institutionalization has since been pursued by Gerlich (1973) in a discussion of several European parliaments, by Opello (1986) in a case study of Portugal's parliament, by Hibbing (1988) in an analysis of the British House of Commons (Mezey 1993: 354), by Squire (1992) on California state legislature, by Patterson and Copeland (1994) in a collection of essays edited by them and by Norton (1998) in a book on governments and parliaments in Western Europe. For Norton, the more institutionalized parliaments have a somewhat greater capacity to constrain governments than less institutionalized parliaments. At the heart of institutionalization is specialization through committees (Norton 1998: 196).

For a political system to be viable, for it to succeed in performing tasks of authoritative resource allocation, problem solving, conflict resolution and so on, on behalf of a population of any substantial size, it must be institutionalized. That is to say, organizations must be created and sustained that are specialized to political activity. Otherwise the political system is likely to be unstable, weak and incapable of servicing the demands or protecting the interests of its constituent groups. Second, it is generally agreed that for a political system to be in some sense free and democratic means must be found for institutionalizing representativeness with all the diversity that this implies for legitimizing and at the same time containing political opposition within the system (Polsby 1968: 144). They are embodied principally in three main institutions: parties, elections and legislatures.

For Polsby (1968: 145), an organization becomes institutionalized when it:

1 becomes differentiated from its environment by developing and channeling career opportunities;
2 develops a division of labor in which roles are specified; and
3 becomes universalistic rather than particularistic in its methods of internal business.

The first two criteria are inexorably intertwined to the standing committees and sub-committees. Committees and sub-committees are made increasingly attractive to members as they gain greater seniority. And the division of labor in Congress is mostly one of dividing up the work among the various standing committees and their sub-committees. Universalism here refers to the emergence of automated decision rules that allow conflicts or dilemmas to be resolved "on the merits" rather than on the basis of particularistic criteria. The seniority rule (the tradition of granting privileges to those treasury bench MPs who have served the longest to a specific committee of a specific house) in US Congress is universalistic rather than individualistic (Froman and Lewis 1968: 523). The tradition of appointment of a neutral Speaker and "Question Hour" in the House of Commons and the allocation of the chair position of the Public Accounts Committee in British and Indian parliaments are universally applied.

On the basis of the discussion on the variants of institutional theory, it can be hypothesized that standard operating rules/procedures as well as the history of stability and continuity of institutions are vital for institutional performance. Institutional performance in this book refers to the role of parliamentary committees in ensuring executive accountability. A number of useful hypotheses may be drawn based on the preceding theoretical discussion:

- The more governing power is diffused and shared between and among contending veto players regardless of the system of government, the more the system bears the potentials of having a strong parliament to hold the government to account. The constitutional configuration of a political system along with other external political factors may be attributed to a large extent to provide a system of power fusion or diffusion.
- A strong parliament is a prerequisite for a strong committee system and vice

versa and a strong committee system is a prerequisite for calling the government into account irrespective of whether the political system is parliamentary or presidential. The standard rules originating from the constitution and the standing rules of procedures can indicate the strength of a parliament and its committee system to call the government to accounts

- The greater is the stability and continuity of politics in any society, the more likely it is that the parliament and its committees are effective institutions of ensuring executive accountability.

Comparative method

This work aims primarily at conducting a comparative study of the role of parliamentary committees in three major South Asian democracies: Bangladesh, India and Sri Lanka. Hence, it is imperative to link this study to an ongoing discussion about comparative method and analysis and find its relevance and use for the study. Comparing is learning from the experiences of others (Sartori 1991: 245). Comparison provides a basis for making statements about empirical regularities and for evaluating and interpreting cases relative to substantive and theoretical criterion (Ragin 1987: 1). Comparison plays a central role in concept formation by bringing into focus similarities and contrasts among cases. Comparison is routinely used in testing hypotheses and it can contribute to the inductive discovery of new hypotheses and to theory building (Collier 1993: 105).

Some analysts believe that political phenomena in general are best understood through the careful examination of a small number of cases (Collier 1993: 105). A single case study should not be given much weight in the evaluation of hypothesis and theory. Moreover, given the inevitable scarcity of time, energy and resources, the intensive analysis of a few cases may be more promising than a more superficial statistical analysis of many cases or an in-depth analysis of an unrepresentative single case (Lijphart 1971: 685–691). When using a small number of cases, each case is treated as a single case. Each case's conclusion can then be used as information contributing to the whole study, but each case remains a single case (Stake 1995; Simons 1980; Yin 1994). Keeping the merits of a small number of cases, we have confined our research to three cases only.

This is a comparative study of a few cases. The method of comparing a few countries is divided into two types of system design: Most Similar Systems Design (MSSD) and Most Different System Design (MDSD) (Przeworski and Teune 1970; Faure 1994). Through using the method of difference and method of agreement, comparing a few countries can lead to inferences that are better informed by the contextual specificities of the countries under scrutiny (Landman 2000: 34).

Based on J.S. Mill's (1843) method of difference, Most Similar Systems Design (MSSD) seeks to compare political systems that share a host of common features and subsequently study differences that exist between basically similar systems. Most Different Systems Design (MDSD), on the other hand, compares countries that do not share any common features apart from the political outcome to be explained and one or two of the explanatory factors seen to be important for that outcome. This system is based on Mill's method of agreement, which seeks to identify those features that are the same among different countries in an effort to account for a particular outcome (Collier 1993: 112).

Evaluating the essential features of the method of comparing a few countries, I have deliberately chosen the Most Similar Systems Design (MSSD) to conduct my study. Macro-systemic similarities and inter-systemic differences are the focus of the MSSD. Common systemic characteristics are conceived as "controlled for", whereas inter-systemic differences are viewed as explanatory/independent variables (Przeworski and Teune 1970: 32–33). A researcher who engages in cross-country systematic comparison with no "control purpose" in the forefront of his mind is missing something important (Sartori 1994: 16). For this study, culture (and socio-economic status) is the common systematic factor which is taken as a control explanatory variable while institutional factors are taken to explain inter-systematic variations.

Case selection

Most Similar Systems Design is used in the selection of cases in this study. It is particularly well suited for those engaged in area studies (Przeworski and Teune 1970: 33). My study concerns a region – South Asia – that appears relatively homogenous. A geographical area can indeed delineate a culturally, economically and historically similar milieu appropriate for discovering causal relationships noting similarities and differences between countries (Dogan and Kazancigil 1994: 7). For our study, culture broadly is implied as the matching factor between the cases. Socio-economic development is also used as a factor to identify the similarities between cases. The macro-systemic commonalities among the three cases in my study as well as the inter-systemic variations are depicted in the following paragraphs:

As Sri Lanka was not included in Hofstede's (2001) cross-cultural study, we do not have quantitative data on Sri Lanka. However, I have used qualitative data to bridge the data gap during my field work in Sri Lanka. All the respondents invariably termed Sri Lanka as a hierarchical society. This was also confirmed by Perera (2000). All South Asian countries are predominantly hierarchical. Moreover, based on Sri Lanka's somewhat identical regional, socio-cultural and historical background with Bangladesh, India and other South Asian countries we can assert that Sri Lanka is also a hierarchical society.

In short, according to Hofstede's features of national culture, Bangladesh, India and Sri Lanka appear to be collective, somewhat masculine societies with high power distance and uncertainty avoidance, which resemble to hierarchic one as posited by Thompson *et al.* (1990).

Now, it is imperative to explain the reasons behind the selection of three countries (Bangladesh, India and Sri Lanka) among the eight countries in South Asia. Bangladesh is one of the three biggest functioning democracies in South Asia. Bangladesh, which is a third-wave democracy, is younger than India and

Table: 2.1 Cultural differences between nations according to Hofstede

Cultural dimensions	*India*	*Bangladesh*	*Index (score)*		
			Highest	*Lowest*	*Mean*
Power distance	77	80	104	11	58
Individualism	48	20	91	06	48
Masculinity–femininity	54	55	95	05	50
Uncertainty avoidance	40	60	112	08	60

Source: compiled by the author from Hofstede (2001: 500–502).

Note
The higher the score, the stronger the dimension.

Table 2.2 Commonalities between Bangladesh, India and Sri Lanka

Criteria	*Description of the criteria*	*Examples/characteristic features*
Culture	Presence of dominant cultural	Predominantly hierarchical
Area/region	Countries which share many characteristics in terms of colonial heritage, culture, political institutions	South Asian nations, members of SAARC
Socio-economic status	Level of economic development	Third World nations
Systemic characteristics	Nature of Political regime/system	Multiparty democracies written constitution judicial review
Natural groups or families of nations	Countries that constitute a relatively homogeneous group on the basis of a common heritage	Westminster adapted/British colonial heritage

Source: prepared by the author.

Sri Lanka (second-wave democracies). Bangladesh is also among the very few countries in the world which combines Western democratic institutions and Islam simultaneously. After the restoration and resumption of parliamentary democracy in Bangladesh since 1991, change of government has been through regular free and fair elections. Since 1991, in order to strengthen parliament, some parliamentary reforms have been introduced in Bangladesh, which have made some impacts too. The selection of India as one of the cases is obvious. India is not only a stable and strategically significant democracy in South Asia but also the biggest democracy in the world. India has got the strongest parliament in South Asia too. It is a plural and multiethnic society where democracy has been in place since its inception and emancipation from the British. It is also the biggest Hindu-dominated polity in the world. The influence of religion is enormous on politics and society in India and the emergence of the BJP (Bharotio

Table 2.3 Comparative socio-economic and political development indicators in Bangladesh, India and Sri Lanka

	Development indicators	*Bangladesh*	*India*	*Sri Lanka*
Social indicator	Area (in sq km)	144,000	3,287,590	65,610
	Population (in million)	141.3	1065	19.9
	Population growth	2.08%	1.44%	0.81%
	Life expectancy	62	64	73
	Literacy rate	43%	59.5%	92.3%
	Infant mortality	6.4%	5.8%	1.5%
	Urban population	25.6%	27%	23%
	Human Development Index	138 (177)	127	96
Economic indicator	GNI, per capita (USD)	360	460	880
	GDP growth	5.3%	8.3%	5.5%
	Inflation rate	5.6%	3.8%	6.3%
	Population below poverty line	35.6%	25%	22%
	Unemployment rate	40%	9.5%	8.4%
	Index of Economic Freedom	141 (155)	118	79
	Corruption Perception Index	145 (1.5)	90 (2.8)	67 (3.5)
Political indicator	Freedom (civil liberty and political right, election) score (the lower the better)	Partly free (4)	Free (2.5)	Partly free (3)
	Bertelsmann Democratic Transformation	SI-45 (116)	SI-29	SI-37
	Index (BTI) two index-Status Index (SI) and Management Index (MI) (the lower the better)	MI-51 (116)	MI-43	MI-24

Source: World Bank (2004); Transparency International (2004); UNDP (2004); Freedom House (2005); CIA (2004); The Asian Wall Street Journal (January 4, 2005); Center for Policy Research (CAP) 2005.

Janata Party), an extremist Hindu religious party, as one of two major political parties in India testimonies that statement. Despite its trouble with ethnic conflicts, Sri Lanka has been the most stable democracy in South Asia since its inception as an independent nation and tops the HDI (UNDP 2004) in this region. It is also the single Buddhist nation in South Asia and the influence of monks on the state apparatus is substantial. The parallel sketch of the committee system in Bangladesh with two other former colonies (India and Sri Lanka) of Britain – one modeled on the Westminster parliamentary system and the other on the French hybrid model will be interesting to portray the variations deriving from the replicated models.

Although the study is on the parliaments in South Asia, Nepal, Pakistan, the Maldives and Bhutan are excluded from the purview of this study on logical grounds. The legislative history of Pakistan is intermittent and it never finds an opportunity to evolve and last, let alone function effectively. In fact democracy could not thrive in Pakistan due to recurring military intervention and the failure of the elected civilian rulers to govern. Parliaments in the Maldives, which is a

Table 2.4 Divergences between Bangladesh, India and Sri Lanka

	System of governance	*Electoral system*	*Ethnicity*	*Political history*	*State format*	*Cameral structure*	*Religious affiliation*
Bangladesh	Parliamentary democracy	Majoritarian	Homogenous (Bengali – 98%, tribal groups and others – 2%)	History of military intervention	Unitary state (six divisions)	Unicameral (330/5)	Muslim (83%, Hindu – 16%, others – 1%)
India	Parliamentary democracy	Majoritarian	Heterogeneous society (Indo-Aryan – 72%, Draviadian– 25%, Mongoloid and others – 3%)	No history of military intervention, history of state emergency (1975–1977)	Federal state (28 states and seven union territories)	Bicameral 545/6 245/5	Hindu (81.3%, Muslim – 12%, Christian – 2.3%, Sikh – 1.9% Others – 2.5)
Sri Lanka	Semi-presidential democracy	Proportional	Heterogeneous society (Singhalese– 74%, Tamil – 18%, moor – 7% and others – 1%	No history of Military intervention	Unitary state (eight provinces)	Unicameral (225/6)	Buddhist (70%, Hindu – 15%,Christian – 8%, Muslim – 7%

Source: CIA (2004)

one party state, and Bhutan, which is an absolute monarchy, are not worth serious academic attention. Nepal had a short-lived experiment with parliamentary democracy in 1950s before becoming a constitutional monarchy in 1990. It has seen 11 governments in as many years since the transition from absolute monarchy to multiparty democracy in the spring of 1990. Currently no parliament is at work in Nepal. Nepal's parliament was dissolved on May 22, 2002 and elections were scheduled for November 13, 2002 and postponed eventually. Parliamentary democracy is still at its infancy in Nepal and needs time to get institutionalized. Since I have already included three major South Asian countries in my work, including one more will be too ambitious and unwieldy to manage.

Data collection methods

The study is an overall review of the parliaments of the three South Asian countries (for Bangladesh see Chapter 5) since their independence from the British in 1947. However, the role of parliaments and parliamentary committees in these three countries in securing government accountability is largely analyzed based on the real-world working of parliaments in the 1990s. This study was based on extensive fieldwork undertaken by the author in three parliaments of South Asia from November 2003 to October 2004. A questionnaire survey of 72 MPs (30 MPs of seventh and eighth JS in Bangladesh, 27 MPs of the thirteenth *Lok Sabha* in India and 15 MPs of the fifth parliament in Sri Lanka, more than 5 percent of the total MPs in each country has been questionnaire surveyed/interviewed)[1] was conducted, followed by a face-to-face interview of the majority of them to know their views on different aspects of parliament and parliamentary committees to make the government accountable. The nature of questionnaire was semi-structured/open-ended which gave the respondents the leeway either to choose answer from among a set of predetermined options or add new ones. Furthermore, a rich pool of data has been collected from all three parliament secretariats (both primary and secondary) in South Asia while conducting fieldwork.

Regarding the questionnaire survey of MPs, a good number of questions (on context, structure, functions, procedures, resources and so on) was formulated which narrated statements on various dimensions of parliament and parliamentary committee system to hold the executive accountable. Questionnaires were sent to some hundreds of MPs in three countries by air mail with a prepaid envelope printed with return address. The response was poor and disappointing. Hence, I went to the field with the questionnaire and got as many questionnaire as I could filled in. The selection of respondents thus became random to some extent. Later I conducted an in-depth face-to-face interview of most of the MPs who filled in the questionnaires in three countries. The interview really helped me to obtain invaluable qualitative information from MPs and committee staffers regarding the real-world functioning of parliaments and parliamentary committees in three countries. To ascertain which preferences were prominent among the MPs in Bangladesh, statistical analyses such as percentages and means were carried out. For each statement there was a four-point answer scale ranging from "agree completely", "agree partly", "neither agree nor disagree" (0 for this option), "disagree partly" to "disagree completely" in which 4 indicates the highest value and 0 the lowest. The higher the mean score, the stronger is the preferences of MPs in favor of the institutional overhauling of the committee system.

Data collection method of the research was in part documentary too. The first three categories of data mentioned in the following analysis were documentary. Documentary data were both primary and secondary. A rich pool of data had been collected from parliament secretariats of all these three countries while conducting fieldwork in South Asia from November 2003 to October 2004. Moreover, I had also interviewed a good number of parliamentary officials (in total 50 in three countries) who were concerned with committee works. They rendered useful qualitative data regarding the operation of committees.

It was simply impossible for me to use observation (being a part of the research population) as data generation for the research since committee meetings were exclusively closed to committee members and concerned civil servants and committee officials and no one else was permitted to witness the operation of a committee session in person.

Documentary data can be further divided into three precise categories:

1 Data/information on the formal arrangement (legal basis, number and types, functions, membership and chairmanship, power authority etc.) of committee system in Bangladesh, India and Sri Lanka were collected from the Constitution (1996), Rules of Procedure (1997) and Parliament Secretariat of the country concerned (1999).
2 Data on the basics of parliament (its longevity, sessions, numerical strength of position and opposition members etc.), and the background characteristics of the MPs (education, profession, experience, prime minister's question hour, loan-defaulting MPs etc.) required for illuminating the resource strengths of bureaucracy vis-à-vis parliament were collected from Rashid (1997), Ullah (1992), Ahmed (1997a, 1997b, 1998a, 1998b), Maniruzzaman (1992), *Sangsad Bulletins* (1991–1999), parliament secretariats and different dailies of three countries.
3 Data on selected parliamentary committees to explore the real-world operations of committees in securing executive accountability in three countries were collected from the parliamentary *Bulletins*, the summary of the proceedings of three parliaments, different reports and proceedings of committees, annual reports of the office of CAG (1997, 1998, 1999) and official documents stored by the law section of all parliament secretariats. The summary and the bulletin were the major sources of information on the precise and concise operation of parliamentary sessions. The reports of different committees contain valuable data on the detailed functioning of the committee system including the discussants, agenda of deliberation, debates and recommendations. As the parliamentary committees (in Bangladesh and Sri Lanka) were not regular in publishing their reports, I had to go through the minutes of meetings of several committees in two countries. I sought the

permission of the concerned authority to do the same and got it. The minutes are not public materials unless, and until, they are published as reports. I collected the data on the operation of the committee on the Ministry of Defense from several dailies in Bangladesh and Sri Lanka because I was not allowed to go through the minutes of the committee for state security reason. The national daily newspapers in three countries were also useful sources of data on plenary sessions and the functioning of different committees.

This study is about the legislative oversight of the executive. Hence, I chose to collect data on selected watchdog committees – the Public Accounts Committee (PAC), the Committee on Public Undertaking (COPU), the Committee on Estimates (COE) and three other ministerial committees (Standing Committee on Ministry of Establishment and Standing Committee on Ministry of Agriculture and Standing Committee on Ministry of Defense) which seem to play a significant role in exerting a check over financial scrutiny and overseeing the operation of government.

As the Committee on Ministry of Establishment (Standing Committee on Public Administration in the case of the Sri Lankan parliament and DRSC on Home Affairs in the case of the Indian parliament) deals with the problems and issues of the public personnel system in Bangladesh, it has a major role in implementing committee decisions, particularly related to disciplinary action against delinquent civil servants, along with all other dealing ministries. Moreover, it also deals with Bangladesh Civil Service (BCS administration), the dominant civil service cadre in Bangladesh. Most of the secretaries who are the principal accounting officers of different ministries belong to BCS (administration) cadre. They attend committee meetings to account on behalf of their ministries. Hence the operations of the Committee on Ministry of Establishment are worth scrutinizing for finding the committee's role in ensuring executive accountability.

The Committee on Ministry of Agriculture (in India and Bangladesh) is selected deliberately in order to see the variation of committee role between a general and a specialized ministry with regard to ensuring executive accountability. I did not look into the working on Consultative Committee on Agriculture in Sri Lanka due to unavailability of sufficient data on it. But I had included the High Post Committee (HPC) which was concerned with examining the suitability of high officials in Sri Lanka. Standing Committee on Ministry of Defense in all three countries was selected to assess the committee's role in ensuring *inter alia* the transparency and information dissemination component of executive accountability in these countries.

For the three heads of data stated above, I have developed several benchmarks (the institutional formal structure, composition, the function, the power, the nature of deliberation of committees etc.) for committee operation in three countries and analyze the data collected against those benchmarks. I have also collected data about the key background characteristics of MPs of the three countries to assess the resource strengths of parliaments.

3 Parliaments and accountability

In analyzing parliamentary committees, a critical context is parliaments themselves. A strong parliament is believed to fare better to hold the government to account. Here the relevant literature has built up over many decades and has become particularly extensive in recent years. This chapter reviews that literature as a necessary first step in examining parliamentary committees. It begins by investigating the ways in which scholars have sought to capture or measure parliamentary strength and weakness. On this basis, it presents a series of basic typologies of legislatures. However, as these typologies are rather crude, it then focuses on additional factors that are relevant in determining parliamentary strength to control the government and hold it to account for its actions. In this regard, an essential point to remember is that parliament cannot be insulated from the effects of wider social, economic and political contexts and that in a democracy the functioning of parliament is inexorably linked with the functioning of other key institutions. In this way, the chapter is able to generate a broad analytical framework focused on parliaments within which the subsequent analysis of parliamentary committees can be set.

Analyzing parliament: a policy focus

The most common comparative statements about legislatures focus on the strength or weakness of particular legislative institutions. By parliamentary strength or weakness we usually comprehend parliament's command of political resources for the purpose of influencing public policy (Edelman and Zelniker 1973: 2). Such statements usually refer to the importance of legislatures in the policy-making process relative to the importance of non-legislative institutions, commonly those operating through the executive branch of government (Mezey 1979: 23). The strength of the legislature's policy-making role is most frequently connected to its capacity to resist or modify policy initiatives emanating from the executive branch (Polsby 1975: 277; Mezey 1979: 26–27). When the legislature has no such capacity, its policy-making role is obviously weak; in contrast, legislatures with strong policy-making roles can say no to the executive and stick to it.

Strong legislatures are those that can and do make decisions and take actions independently from the executive. Access to information and expertise on policy from sources independent of the executive, generally through a stable and specialized system of legislative committees, is widely regarded as a necessary condition for legislative strength regardless of regime type (Carey 2002; Norton 1994; Schuttemeyer 1994; Strøm 1998). Classifying legislatures on the basis of their policy-making significance is not as easy as it may seem to be (Mezey 1979: 23). However, almost all major works on classifying legislatures to date have invariably been conducted by keeping public policy as the focus of analysis.

Beginning in the late 1960s, legislative scholars began to develop a more sophisticated sense of what legislatures did and how they affected public policy. While admitting that most legislatures seldom made the major policy decisions and usually followed the lead of other institutions, more subtle ways by which legislatures influence public policy were detected. Through public debates, the private interaction of their members with the executive, the linkage activities that they perform on behalf of their constituents and their activities in regard to oversight, legislatures as collective bodies and their members individually seemed to have a greater impact on the contours of public policy than had been perceived by the earlier generations of scholars (Olson and Mezey 1991: 1).

Although this more refined image of the legislature emerged first in the study of minimal legislatures of the Third World (Mezey 1985), those studying European legislatures soon began to utilize this expanded framework. Thus instead of beginning and ending discussion of the British House of Commons by noting the prevalence of straight party-line votes, studies began to look at the lobbying activities that British MPs conducted on behalf of the constituencies, the nature of the questions asked on the floor and the impact of public parliamentary deliberation on the plans of the executive (Leonard and Herman 1972). And even in the US, where the constitutional claim of the Congress for a central policy-making role was beyond dispute, attention began to shift towards the linkage activities that legislators performed for their constituencies (Meyhew 1974; Fiorina 1977) and towards their oversight activities (Saloma 1969).

Some questions of public policy do not come to parliaments at all depending on the constitution of each country. In Britain, for example, the government does not need parliamentary approval for some foreign policy, capital expenditures or even many aspects of economic policy (Ryle 1988: 232). While it may be an exaggeration to say that we have witnessed a convergence of scholarly opinion on the policy-making role of the legislature, it is probably accurate to say that most political scientists today look at legislative policy-making activity with fewer and less rigid preoccupations regarding what the proper policy-making role legislatures should be and are willing to consider the impact of a variety of legislative activities on public policy (Olson and Mezey 1991: 2).

Arguments that place high value on the representation of societal diversity (Lijphart 1984, 1994), those that emphasize deliberation as a means of honing policy alternatives and producing consensus (Miller 1993) and those focusing on regime stability (Shugart and Carey 1992) all imply the significance of legislatures as fora for making key policy decisions.

The legislature is the most authoritative and legitimate among the sources of decisions about public policy within a political system (Olsen 1994). Even the executive president in a presidential system has to depend on the legislature for approval of the legislative proposals. A legislature's function to decide government policy stems from the historic power of the purse of English parliament as the basis for its representative character. (Mezey 1991: 6). Moreover, an aspect of policy-making activity found in almost every legislative setting is the legislative oversight of the executive (Kornberg 1970; Agor 1970; Packenham 1970; Singvi 1970; Lees 1977). In both parliamentary and presidential systems, legislative committees call executives (both political and administrative) to account for their actions, conduct investigations of policies and make recommendations either to the legislature or to the government (Mezey 1979: 8). The goals (Dodd and Schott 1979: 156; Aberbach 1979: 494) of legislative oversight of the executive are:

1 to see that policy is implemented in accordance with the intent;
2 to determine whether policy is effective and its impact in accord with legislative standards;
3 to prevent waste and dishonesty and assure efficiency;
4 to prevent discretionary abuse; and
5 to represent public interest by monitoring and constraining agency-client group relations.

The effectiveness of a legislature in scrutinizing government and public sector issues really depends on its commitment to its core business of legislating. The more responsible is its legislating, then the more effective will be its supplementary scrutiny of government activities (Uhr 1997: 51). In other words, an active legislating/policy-making legislature usually becomes an effective reviewer of the executive activities.

Policies are the principal outcome of a political system. People participate in a political system in order to promote the outcomes (policies) that they prefer. Political actors propose different policies and are elected on the basis of the policies that they recommend. Politicians or parties are replaced in office when the policies they propose lead to undesirable outcomes or when they do not apply the policies they promised before an election (Tsebelis 2002: 6).

Usually the executives take over power by winning an election with a host of electoral pledges and policies. To turn those electoral pledges and policies into reality, they must come up with legislative proposals and turn to parliament for its approval. The executive must win the nod of the legislature in allocating budget for an existing institution or establishing a new one for implementing public policy or law.

Public policy does not grow in a vacuum. The ability to get legislative proposals enacted by parliament to see its effect on public life is one of the crucial policy resources at the disposal of government (Rose 1984: 63). In fact public policy is a broader term and the multiple stages of policy proposal, policy deliberation, policy approval and policy oversight take place in legislatures during its consideration of legislative proposals.

Legislative influence on the content of the policy tends to be the influence of legislative committees, of a special subset of legislators who have special knowledge and special interest in a particular policy area. Legislative influence on the pace of policy-making tends to be the influence of party groups or factions within the legislature. And legislative influence over the implementation and oversight of policy tends to be the influence of the minority or the opposition parties (Loewenberg and Patterson 1979: 278).

Policy-making is macroscopic which incorporates the core functions of legislatures (representation, legislation-making and oversight). Policy-making tends to stress on specialization which is at par with the establishment of subject-matter committee system which can play a pivotal role in making legislations as well as exercising oversight functions and thereby ensure executive accountability. Moreover, public policy process can be a linchpin between the elected representatives, the bureaucracy, interest groups and the citizens. In a more general sense, legislatures, because of their composition and organization, are concerned that policies should be acceptable to the general public. Because of legislatures' sensitivity to the acceptability dimension of policy, this appears to be the distinctive contribution of legislature to the policy-making process (Loewenberg and Patterson 1979: 279).

A legislature's policy-making role is a function of the degree to which it can constrain the actions of the executives depending on the political system in which it is found (Mezey 1979). The ability of a legislature in a parliamentary system is, in theory, in a strong position to make policy since the executive is drawn from it and responsible to it. In practice, the legislature does the task of legitimizing policies (through deliberation, amendment and approval), in other words turning executive decisions into laws (Derbyshire and Derbyshire 1999). Thus the legislature does the most important task of recruiting executive leaders (the cabinet) who in turn play the key role in making policies in a parliamentary system. As Copeland and Patterson (1998: xxii) note, "the most important decision of many parliamentary bodies is the selection of the executive".

Where the overlap between the membership of the legislature and the executive is great, as in Britain, the parliament influences the pace of policy-making and effectiveness and efficiency of policy implementation rather than the content of policy. It defers to executive leadership in policy formulation (Loewenberg and Patterson 1979: 278).

In presidential regimes, policy-making is by definition characterized by a separation of power; it is very often characterized as well by a separation of purpose. The separation of powers inherent in presidentialism has consequences for policy-making even when it does not produce divergent partisan control of the assembly and executive (Shugart and Haggard 2001: 64–66).

The United States Congress primarily exerts its influence not by recruiting the executives but by controlling them once they are in office through the exercise of law-making, appropriations and investigative power. The US president holds the office for a fixed term, regardless of the legislature's attitude towards him. Only an extreme case of impeachment can allow Congress to remove an executive from office. But in the course of governing, he is subject to the day-to-day constraints, which the legislature imposes on him by its exercise of policy-making and oversight power (Loewenberg and Patterson 1979: 54–55). Thus taxonomy of legislatures based on public policy-making seems useful and instrumental to determine the strength of parliament to influence or constrain government.

Typology of legislatures

Riggs' (1975) work on the origin of legislatures suggests the need to develop categories of legislatures reflecting the different positions that the institution might occupy in a political system. Traditionally, such classification schemes have focused on the legislative role in making policy and more specifically on its formal relationship with the executive. Thus the presidential-parliamentary dichotomy has been with us for sometime, as have more sophisticated gradations of legislative-executive relationships based on constitutional provision (Blondel 1973).

The fragility and formality of constitutional provisions led some to look at what the legislature does rather than at what the constitution says about the legislature. Thus Polsby (1975: 281, 291–292) constructed a continuum of legislatures ranging from arena to transformative legislatures based on the degree of a legislature's independence from external influences. He noted that the contrast between the two ends of the continuum captures the distinction between the British (arena) and US (transformative) legislatures with others falling either in between or at the arena end of the spectrum. The more independent the legislature is making decisions, the more it is a transformative legislature; the more the legislature defers to or is subject to the influence of another body, the more it is an arena type legislature.

Transformative legislature is best exemplified by the US Congress (both chambers). The tasks of a transformative legislature are to create, amend and adopt legislation (that may originate from the legislature or the executive). At the other end lie arena legislatures where social differences are represented and articulated. Public policies are debated from different perspectives and government actions are assessed by different criteria. For many years, the British House of Commons has been a leading example of an arena or "legitimizing type" of legislature. It legitimizes but does not legislate. Over three decades, a bedrock feature of the British political system has been the almost unfailing willingness of the House of Commons to defer in the end to will and authority of the government (Schwarz 1980: 23).

Polsby (1975) notes that the two different types of legislatures are fundamentally different in terms of what drives them and what controls their activity. In particular, arena legislatures are controlled externally, generally by the national political party organizations. Transformative legislatures are controlled from within through the committees and parliamentary party apparatus (Polsby 1975: 141). To determine where on the arena-transformative axis a legislature lies, Polsby suggests three variables:

1 Homogeneity of controlling group in the legislature: the more homogeneous and smaller the controlling group (party or coalition) the less transformative the legislature.
2 Hierarchy: the more hierarchical the internal party structures (and in particular control over electoral lists) the less transformative the legislature.
3 Consistency: the more consistent the voting coalitions/majorities that pass successive legislative proposals the less transformative the legislature.

The basic categorization of some European legislatures, according to Polsby (1975) is depicted in Figure 3.1.

In his landmark study of *Comparative Legislatures*, Mezey (1979: 27) developed a classification scheme based on the policy-making role of the legislature with "the degree of support accruing to the institution" as the second dimension and with support defined as "a set of attitudes that look to the legislature as a valued and popular political institution".

Mezey's definition of parliamentary power and influence was built upon even earlier work, notably that of Blondel (1970) who had argued for the influence of a chamber on policy to be understood in terms of "Viscosity" – the degree to which the legislature could impede the "flow" of proposals advanced by the executive. Based on the constraints that a legislature is capable of placing on policy-making activities of the executive, Mezey (1979) presents a rough but workable three-fold categorization of legislatures:

1 Legislatures with strong policy-making power: these legislatures are able to modify and reject executive proposals.
2 Legislatures with modest policy-making power: these legislatures have the ability to modify but not definitively reject executive proposals.
3 Legislatures with little or no policy-making power: these legislatures can neither reject nor modify executive proposals.

Distinguishing the policy-making strength of legislatures is a valuable exercise. But to focus solely on policy effect is to lose sight of the wider con-

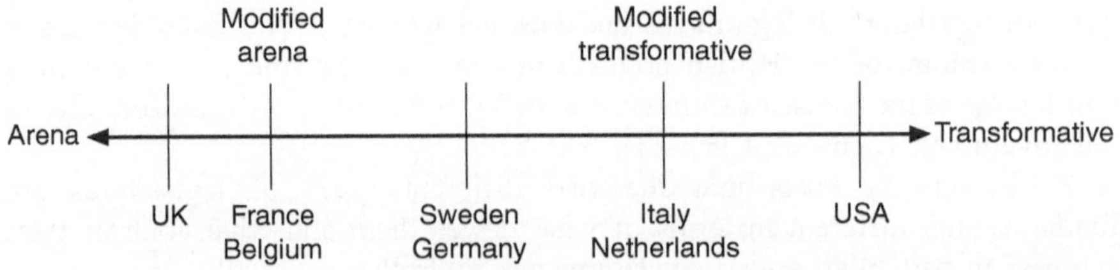

Figure 3.1 Categorization of some European legislatures.

sequences of parliament for the political system. There is more to legislatures than their relationship to the executive in the policy cycle. There is, for instance, the relationship of the legislature to the citizenry. Hence the value of Mezey's stress upon support aspect is justified (Norton 1990a: 5).

Not satisfied with just the explicit political power of the legislature Mezey adds an additional axis upon which legislatures can be measured and this is support largely determined by their popular legitimacy. Support is significant because the degree of support enjoyed by a legislature lends a certain degree of predictability to the policy-making dimension. This argument has been starkly illustrated by the example of the Philippine Congress. This was one of the most powerful legislatures in the world right up until the time in 1972 when President Marcos suspended the institution, with hardly a murmur of domestic dissent to be heard (Mezey 1979: 27).

Many comparative scholars have observed that parliaments can play a highly significant role in the legitimization of a political system (e.g. Packenham 1970). Parliaments, which enjoy higher levels of support, are more secure in their long-term status, either from challenges to their status within the political system, or from broader challenges to the system as a whole. As regards operationalization of the concept of support, Mezey (1979: 29) advocated thinking of it as involving a combination of three major indicators:

- Institutional continuity: how long has the institution been around and has it been able to weather "difficult times"?
- Attitudes of government elites: whether or not there is broad inter-institutional support for the legislature among the other relevant political institutions (may include military, civil society, bureaucracy).
- Attitudes of the public: the extent to which the public supports and believes in the legitimacy of the legislature (corruption scandals etc.).

Because of the inherent difficult in adequately and consistently measuring these variables Mezey resorts to merely dichotomizing the "support" variable into the categories "more supported legislatures" and "less supported legislatures". This results in a 3×2 table within which legislatures can be categorized (Table 3.1).

Mezey finally classified legislatures principally into five – active, vulnerable, reactive, marginal and minimal – on the basis of a cross tabulation of two major variables – policy-making power (strong, modest, little or none) and the degree of support mass/elite support they enjoyed (less or more). From Table 3.1, one can observe categories of legislatures that match to different classifications along the two dimensions of power and support. A more comprehensive discussion on the legislative categorization as propounded by Mezey is required for better clarification and comprehension.

Table 3.1 Mezey's typology of legislatures

Policy-making power	*Support (elite/mass)*	
	More	*Less*
Strong	Active legislatures: USA, Costa Rica	Vulnerable legislatures: Italy, France – third and fourth republics and Weimar Germany, European Parliament
Modest	Reactive legislatures: UK, Sweden, Denmark, Finland, Norway, Belgium, France – fifth republic, Ireland, India Austria etc.	Marginal legislatures: Colombia, Jordan, Brazil, Malaysia, Bangladesh Sri Lanka
Little or none	Minimal legislatures: Soviet Union, Communist Poland, Singapore, former Yugoslavia	Inconsequential (?)

Source: Mezey (1979: 36).

Active and vulnerable legislatures

Active and vulnerable legislatures are involved in all phases of the policy-making process. As a prerequisite for such involvement, these legislatures have highly developed committee systems, which enable them to divide the legislative labor in such a way that a degree of legislative expertise is generated in most policy areas. Plenary arenas are more likely to be involved in deliberative than in proposal or oversight activities. The differences between active and vulnerable legislatures emanate from the lower level of elite support accruing to the latter.

An active legislature can make or break executives and reject, amend or ignore policy proposals initiated by either the executive or its own members. It can even initiate and pass its own legislative proposals. The best example of an active legislature is the US Congress.

A vulnerable legislature can modify and reject policy proposals but its support base is fragile and thus vulnerable to extra-constitutional attack, i.e. military intervention. The legislature's institutional continuity might be marred earlier. The legislators may be elected through free and fair election but their images to citizens are opaque. The Congress of the Philippines (during 1946–1972) belongs to this category. The European parliament increasingly resembles a vulnerable legislature – a chamber wielding considerable powers but lacking deep-rooted wider support to legitimize that authority (Scully 1999).

The primary arena for legislative deliberation in active and vulnerable legislatures is the committee. The committees can modify, amend, pigeonhole or even reject the proposal and legislative proposals are invariably referred to committees immediately after they are introduced. For the two active legislatures – the US Congress and the Costa Rican Assembly – committees are quite independent of party influence but for most of the vulnerable legislatures, partisan influence on committee deliberation is a more significant variable. Significant deliberative activities take place in caucus in vulnerable legislatures and the final decision is reached in plenary sessions. Moreover, the committees are the prime parliamentary arenas for exercising oversight activities in both active and vulnerable legislatures. Some additional oversight activities are carried on in the plenary arenas of vulnerable legislatures (Mezey 1979: 60–86).

Reactive legislatures

A reactive legislature can amend and/or veto executive proposals. The British parliament and major European parliaments are offered as examples of reactive legislatures. Though a reactive legislature has the capacity, sporadically exercised to modify and even reject executive proposals, the legislature usually does not have the capability to generate alternative policies.

Reactive legislatures have a less influential policy-making role than active or vulnerable legislatures particularly during the proposal phase. Consequently a good deal of policy-making activities in these political systems goes forth in extra-parliamentary or leadership arenas. Most reactive systems are controlled by relatively strong governing parties that resist the establishment of independent sources of legislative expertise. A reactive legislature is dominated by the prime minister and his/her cabinet who, working through a disciplined majority in parliament can regularly produce a majority vote in the parliament and pass its own sponsored bills and programs. As a result, committee systems are weaker than in active and vulnerable legislatures, while party causes are normally stronger. Much of the oversight activities take place in the plenary sessions of reactive legislatures (Mezey 1979: 57–58).

Although a reactive parliament like the House of Commons does not have the effective power to say no to the government, the influence of the government backbenchers in the policy-making is substantial. For instance, governments may be put under pressure at private party meetings by their own supporters either to introduce or to drop measures (Mezey 1979: 21–44). The years since 1970s have seen a notable increase in the willingness of MPs to vote against their own side. The incumbent government suffered one defeat in each parliament in the period from 1945 to 1990 because its own supporters voted either with the opposition or abstained from voting (Norton 1997a: 161–163).

But the ultimate result in the UK is a parliament with a practical policy role considerably more limited than its formal prerogatives would suggest. Although there are numerous other avenues for influence – informal lobbying by parliamentarians, the use of private members' bills, and free votes over conscience issues (Marsh and Read 1988; Cowley 1997) – and despite a growth in dissent from the party line since the 1970s (Norton 1975, 1980; Cowley and Norton 1996), the parliament remains a moderate influence on policy-making.

Marginal legislatures

Although marginal legislatures are not the primary engines of policy-making in their political systems, they remain critical actors. Much of politics and political debate eludes these chambers, who have a limited role but little connection to, or support from, the rest of the polity. The rules of the game still require that the legislature pass bills for them to become laws. Examples of marginal legislatures include various one-party states like China, Iran, Maldives, North Korea, etc. Most policy-making activities takes place in extra-parliamentary arenas or occasionally in leadership arenas; committees and caucus are generally weak. Therefore whatever legislative constraints exist are exercised in plenary sessions.

Committees in marginal legislatures are weaker than those in reactive legislatures. They are somewhat more effective in deliberating than in formulating public policies but that activity is also impeded by the institutional instability, the lack of legislative experience and expertise of committee members, the fluidity of membership and the absence of competent professional staff. An impediment to effective parliamentary oversight is the fact that ministers in most marginal systems are responsible to the executive leadership rather the parliament and thus the legislature has few sanctions that it can exercise against ministers whose performance they find wanting. More importantly, legislators may be dependent on administrators for a variety of personal and political favors and therefore may be reluctant to call them to account (Mezey 1979: 113–131).

Minimal legislatures

The minimal legislatures simply endorse choices made elsewhere in the society. They can neither reject nor amend policy proposals. The most frequently cited examples are those drawn from authoritarian and totalitarian countries where legislatures are largely symbolic bodies assenting the decisions of leaders. Former USSR and East European countries belong to this category.

Minimal legislatures are dominated by executive-centered elites whose influence permeates the entire policy-making process. The base of this influence is a dominant political party whose control extends not simply to public policy-making but through the entire society. Minimal legislatures have only the most peripheral role to play in the formulation and deliberation of public policy. Some oversight of executive activities takes place in minimal legislatures primarily in committee arenas.

In plenary sessions, some mild dissent is permitted but it takes place within very strict limits. Criticisms are usually confined to technical problems and issues of economy and administration. Legislative debate does not bring forth a substantial change in legislation. Discipline and strong penalty measures mean the party legislators refrain from voting against party.

A great deal of deliberative activity takes place in committee arenas of minimal legislatures, as committees meet more frequently and regularly than the House does (Modelski 1973: 76). Committee sessions sometimes do result in modifications of pieces of legislation. Committees are private and can therefore affect policy without embarrassing the government. Committees, however, have no sanctions power at all at their disposal to enforce compliance with their requests or recommendations. Usually committees lack competent staff and must rely on the bureaucracy for the information they require to oversee its activities (Mezey 1979: 132–141).

Mezey's work is useful in providing a broader analytic framework for legislative activities by taking beyond an exclusive focus on policy-making. Despite the presentation of the most sophisticated and useful classification of legislatures by Mezey, one problem is clear in his definitions of strong and modest policy-making power. Legislatures with a capacity to modify and reject executive proposals are deemed to enjoy strong policy-making power, whereas those that can modify but not reject are deemed to have modest policy-making power. In the 1970s, the British parliament exercised, and in the 1980s continued to exercise, its power to reject various government proposals. On the definition propounded by Mezey, this would place British parliament in the category of an active (rather than a reactive) legislature and on a par with the US Congress, which is misleading and untenable. The power to reject, especially if only occasionally exercised, does not render a legislature a policy-making body (Norton 1990: 128).

If one takes Polsby's classification as providing a continuum the British parliament conforms neither to an arena nor transformative legislature rather ranks somewhere in the middle veering more towards an arena than transformative assembly (Norton 1990: 177–178). Hence, Norton (1984) came forward with a new wide-ranging trichotomy of legislatures.

In terms of their impact on public policy, three types of legislature are evident: policy-making, policy influencing and those with little or no effect. The US Congress stands as an exceptional instance of the policy-making legislature. The British parliament, along with majority of the Western European countries, falls within the same broad category of policy-influencing legislatures. The third

Table 3.2 Typology of legislatures

Types of legislatures	*Features*
Policy-making legislatures	Have the capacity to amend or reject policy brought forward by the executive and the capacity to formulate and substitute policy of their own.
Policy-influencing legislatures	Have the capacity to amend or reject policy brought forward by the executive but lack the capacity to formulate and substitute policy of their own.
Legislatures with little or no policy effect	Lack the capacity both to amend and reject policy brought forward by the executive and to formulate and substitute policy of their own. They confine themselves to assenting to whatever is placed before them.

Source: Norton (1984: 198–202).

category of legislature with little or no policy effect comprises legislatures in erstwhile communist and one-party states, i.e. former USSR, China and the Central and Eastern European countries (Norton 1997a: 156–157).

Taking the key stages of the law-making process as essentially four in number – initiation, formulation, deliberation and assent and implementation – a policy-making legislature has the capacity to be involved in all four stages whereas other legislatures are principally involved in the later stages. Policy-influencing legislatures become central at the stage of deliberation and assent, and legislatures with little or no policy influence get involved only in the stage of giving assent (Norton 1994: 19).

The categories are broad. Furthermore, policy-influencing category is increasingly crowded. When Mezey published his comparative study, there were already many examples of reactive legislatures: he included most of the legislatures of Western Europe as well as the leading countries of the Commonwealth (UK, Canada, Australia, India and New Zealand). The number has escalated after the collapse of communism in Russian and Eastern Europe. We thus have a large number of legislatures with modest policy-making power. But still there are differences and variations between them in terms of their capacity to affect policy outcomes. They may share the basic relationship to government but they differ in the extent to which they can actually constrain government (Norton 1998: 3). Norton has noted (1994: 19) the variations between European legislatures in a study. According to that study, Italy and Denmark border the categories between policy-making and policy-influencing legislatures. In contrast, Ireland and France come close to occupying the category of legislatures with little or no policy influence. For most of the twentieth century, the British parliament has come close to this category albeit moving away from it in recent years. The German Bundestag appears a good example of a solid policy-influencing legislature.

While not, as Norton acknowledged, a radical reordering of Mezey's framework, this is a useful amendment and clarification. But the problem of categorization is yet to be resolved. The categorization of legislature as modified by Norton is too crowded to demarcate reasonably between and among the legislatures. Norton's policy-influencing category is more relevant and useful in classifying the Western European legislatures. The legislatures in Western Europe are largely confined to this category. But a good number of the Third World legislatures tend to swing between the marginal and minimal categories although electoral democracy is the practice in these democracies. At least one Third World legislature could be found in each of the five categories, most Third World legislatures were either marginal or minimal (Mezey 1985: 762). Hence we can turn back to Mezey's categorization taking the refined definition of policy-making and policy-influencing as proposed by Norton. Thus the typology of legislatures advanced by Michael Mezey (1979) and later refined by Philip Norton (1984) still retains a relevance to current legislative research (Norton 1990), while offering a well-established basis on which general comparisons of legislatures can be constructed.

Thus the aforementioned framework takes us beyond an exclusive focus on policy-making and has proved particularly useful in offering a broad outlook. But as Gladdish (1991) reminds us, it does not help us appreciate the variations and divergences within a specific category. The essential point is that there are differences between and among legislatures within a category and we need to explore some of the key variables that help determine the degree of differences. Many of the differences emanate from the nature of the institutions themselves and the environment they inhabit (Norton 1990: 141).

Before going to embark upon the factors determining parliamentary strength in controlling the government, it is essential to briefly know how the three parliaments under review have been discussed in the literature. All the three parliaments in South Asia belong to Third World legislature. India was categorized as a reactive legislature by Mezey or policy-influencing legislature by Norton. Bangladesh and Sri Lanka were categorized as marginal by Mezey. However, it is difficult to categorize Bangladesh and Sri Lankan parliament in the light of Norton's classification of parliament. They may fall in between parliament with little or no policy effects and parliament with major policy effect categories.

Legislative strength: determining factors

The political context within which the legislatures exist as well as their internal resource strength and organization enormously affects the formation, development and work legislatures as well as committees. The fundamental relationship between the legislature and the executive – in other words whether the legislature in Mezey's terminology – active, vulnerable, reactive, marginal or minimal – are believed to be determined by the interplay of a number of social, economic, political and intra-institutional factors (Olson and Mezey 1991: 19; Olson 1994: 132–151; Olson and Norton 1996: 5–13). These are:

- Social factors
    - Civil society, political history and culture;
    - Media;
    - Interest groups.
- Economic factors
- Political factors
    - The constitutional dimension;
    - The party dimension;
    - Intra-institutional factors;
    - Chamber;
    - Members.

While the policy power dimension of Mezey's categorization of legislatures demonstrates the centrality of politico-institutional elements of a polity to determine the strength of a legislature, the support dimension entails the complementary significance of social forces for the legitimacy and continuity of a strong legislature. This approach is more suitable for analyzing parliaments in the Western industrialized countries where socio-economic disparity among citizenry is minimal. The case tends to be diametrically opposite to the Third World nations. Socio-economic and cultural factors in Third World democracies may prevail over the politico-constitutional factors in explaining the role of legislature in Third World countries. These social factors can be critical to weigh the degree of a parliament's ability to hold the government to account.

The starting point for categorizing Third World legislatures is unlikely to be the same as the Western industrialized nations due to the diametrically opposite socio-cultural, politico-economic atmosphere prevailing in the Third World compared to its Western counterparts. Pursuing the Western approach in term of categorization of Third World legislatures runs the risk of being flawed methodologically. The point of departure for categorizing Third World legislatures tends to be the other way round as to the Western world. Nature of society (individualistic/hierarchical), economy (poor/rich) and political regime (democratic/non-democratic) should precede the intra-political institutional features in an effort to fathom the strength of legislatures in Third World countries. In the Western countries, the first three prerequisites of strong parliaments are already in place. Hence while studying the strength of legislatures of the world; the Western scholars start looking at the intra-institutional political factors without taking into account the crucial three broad prerequisites of strong parliaments in any society. This is a myopic approach, which takes into account the context of 30 industrialized countries and imposes it on the remaining 150 nations in the globe. The approach asserted by this book advocates that the starting point for categorizing parliament should be from society, economy and political regime to intra-institutional political factors. This approach bears the potential of being a generally acceptable way of categorizing parliaments and thereby determining its strength in holding the executive accountable.

Social factors

These social factors include civil society, institutional history, political cultures, media, interest groups and the like.

Civil society, political history and culture

A flourishing civil society provides important checks and balances on governmental power. Civil society can channel people's participation in economic and social activities and organize them into potent groups to influence public policies. An informed civil society can ventilate their opinion and dissatisfaction over the maladministration of the public officials through the electronic media and identical means.

The civil society obviously has its root in the history and political culture of the respective country. Just as citizens must understand the legislature in order to influence it, so must civil society groups. In countries with a limited history of legislative democracy, civil society organizations tend to lack knowledge of legislative processes even though they may be well organized around a particular issue and/or at implementing programs to address their particular concerns. And yet, in legislative systems, civil society organizations have a critical role to play whether in lobbying legislators for policy change or in representing the aspirations of their constituents at public hearings.

The political culture, the amalgam of attitudes built up over time towards society and the running of that society will shape both the constitution and how people behave politically. Attitudes derived from the experience of British rule motivated the founding fathers in the US to craft a political system that diffused political power (Norton 1998: 6). An ideological consensus in the US – believed to result from the absence of a feudal history – has militated against the emergence of parties with strong ideological bases (Hartz 1955).

The distinctiveness of parliament's history and constitutional practice of a polity is relevant to any study of the present position of the institution (Norton 1990b: 10–11). The legitimizing authority of parliament has been strengthened by virtue of longevity – there is no recollection, no recognizable history of any alternative form of legitimization – and now by virtue of the election of the House of Commons (Norton 1990b: 12).

Each legislature has to be analyzed in the context of the political culture in which it nestles. That political culture determines or rather defines elite and mass orientation to political rule. Where there is a strong attachment at both elite and mass levels to parliamentary institutions, there will be a stable system. The extent to which the legislature can influence the government will be determined by elite and mass expectations of the institution. Where there is a subservient or apathetic population and elite imbued with a desire for power and little or no attachment to parliamentary institutions and norms, then the legislature will have little or no capability to constrain government and may indeed have a discontinuous existence. For instance, in South Korea, there is a homogenous and conformist culture, the citizenry being submissive to those in power. There have been low support at both mass and elite level for parliamentary institutions and, although there have been some changes, a low level of public support remains a problem in empowering the Korean Assembly (Norton 1999: 186). A deferential political culture is often assumed as more conducive to the evolution of strong parliament and committee system than a culture that promotes and sustains distrust (Ahmed 2001: 64).

The political culture of a country – the sum of its citizens, acquired history, attitudes and experience – contributes to the extent to which citizens do possess the willingness and ability to hold the executive to account for their actions. In countries of the former USSR and Eastern Europe as well as in the countries formerly ruled by military, decades of political repression and consequent lack of civic engagement by citizens may make them naive and hesitant to make their rulers answerable. Conversely the newly elected executives who are accustomed to such a quiescent culture may be willing to skip being accountable to the citizens. Furthermore, clientelism prevails in large parts of Latin America and

Asia. Throughout long periods of military rule, the ruling elites were able to hold onto elected office by extending patronage and privileges to specific groups. These political cultures of repression and clientelism are enduring and difficult to overcome in the short run. In essence, a culture that suppresses accountability can cripple legal and institutional arrangements. Conversely, a culture that favors and supports accountability can overcome legal and institutional weakness (Coghill 2001).

Media

The media can serve as a civic watchdog for the public and also as a voice in helping cultivate an informed citizenry. A free press can play a decisive role to hold the executive accountable by exposing misfeasance, malfeasance and nonfeasance in government. Investigative reporters have given the news media vast leeway in holding the executive accountable (Rosen 1998). The degree to which the media is independent is the degree to which it can perform an effective watchdog function on the conduct of the executives.

In countries with publicly funded mass media, one of the decisions to be made is how to regulate the media. The incumbent party in a fledging democracy may desire to obtain favorable treatment in the media. Consequently the mass media cannot play its due role to keep the government on its toes. The print media – newspapers and journals – have a greater opportunity than the electronic media to provide analysis and commentary but they are often affiliated with one party or least express one point of view (Olson 1994: 128). They can help in building public opinion and disseminating information about the operations of government. But this potential can be highly diluted by the constraints of low literacy and low purchasing power of the common people in a transitional polity.

A free media can report on the use of public funds and the exercise of power. Its sources may include the activities of others such as MPs and its committees, reports to the parliament, or its own reporters' investigations. Media reports are very often the people's quickest and easiest source of information and are therefore absolutely central to meeting the objectives of good governance. Where the media failed to investigate and report information critical of the misuse of public funds and powers by government it thus helped allow that to occur (e.g. WA Inc.). In other instances, the media played an important public role in exposing corrupt conduct (e.g. Queensland under the former Bjelke-Petersen Government) (Coghill 2001).

Citizen understanding and impressions of legislatures are, to a great degree, shaped by media coverage given to the legislature. The viewpoint of the media (government controlled, opposition controlled or independent), the style of political reporting (skeptical, sensational), and the level of knowledge and professionalism of reporters largely affect legislative coverage. In many developing countries, legislative coverage, where available, is provided by state-run media. And in most new democracies, where independent journalists do exist, they often lack the skills to professionally report on parliamentary or legislative affairs (UNDP 2000).

Open access for the media to report parliamentary operations is a prerequisite for building trust between citizens and parliament. Observations of open parliamentary debate, access to parliamentarians, transparent coverage of deliberations and committee meetings and decentralized dissemination of information all contribute to citizen's ability to call the parliamentarians and government to account.

Interest groups

Private organizations of persons, communities or businesses often attempt to influence the decision of government and when they do they are termed interest groups (Truman 1981). The diverse activities of interest groups may serve as an empirical foundation for pluralistic theory of democracy, which many scholars have argued, involves pluralistic interest groups serving as a counter to any monopoly of power in a developed democratic society (Kolobov *et al.*, cited in Kolobov 1994: 108).

The effect of interest group activity on the nature of the legislature's involvement in policy-making process depends in part upon the characteristics of the group/groups, in part upon the institutions with which these involved groups interact and in part upon the degree of consensus and desensus that characterize the groups that are activated by the particular policy. Where interest groups are numerous, functionally specialized and homogenous and in conflict with administrative agencies, then we would expect parliamentary activity to increase and for that activity to follow a reasonable pattern. Where there is a virtual absence of interest group activity, then we would expect the activity of MPs to be shaped by other influences (Olson and Mezey 1991: 11–12).

In the absence of agreement between groups, and between groups and the relevant agencies, the more likely groups are to seek allies in the legislature. Certain internal characteristics of the legislature, such as a specialized and active committee system, may further encourage groups to seek to encourage and influence parliamentary activities (Olson and Norton 1996: 9).

In those political systems in which central political direction tends to be strong and parties are characterized by high level of cohesion, notably parliamentary systems, interest group activity is less likely to have less effect than systems like that of the US where the dispersal of power enhances the influences of interest groups (Rush 1998: 814). In corporate-style government-interest relations, interest associations licensed and empowered by the state play a prominent role in structuring public policy (Greenwood and Thomas 1998: 498).

Although interest group activity has generated the criticism of privileged access to policy-making, it has provided committees of the House and MPs individually with an alternative source of information other than the government and thereby reinforced the capacity of the House of Commons to challenge government and helped generate a more open institution (Norton 1994a: 27–28).

Economic factors

Since the 1950s, the quantitative comparison of country cases across space and time has achieved a strong consensus about the positive linear relationship between economic development and democracy (Rueschemeyer *et al.* 1992: 12–39; Landman 2000: 61–71). This relationship suggests that those countries with high levels of economic development tend to be democratic, while less developed counties have never been democratic or have experienced democratic breakdown on one or more occasions. In sum, the richer a country, the greater are its chances of sustaining democracy (Lipset 1959). More recently, it has been claimed that when democracies attain an income level of US$6000 per capita or above "they are impregnable and can be expected to live forever". On the other hand, poor democracies, particularly those with annual per capita income of less than US$1000 are extremely fragile although the faster the economy grows the more likely democracy is to survive especially if growth is accompanied by a moderate rate of inflation. But once established in a developed country, democracy endures regardless of how it performs (Przeworski *et al.* 1996: 4).

Generally speaking, economic development fosters and leads to democratic governance with few exceptions. All Western industrialized nations today belong to the most advanced and mature democracies in the world. This is evident from the Corruption Perception Index (CPI) of Transparency International (2005) as well that corruption is higher in poor democracies than in wealthy industrialized ones. Economic underdevelopment and corruption in poor democracies can be attributed *inter alia* to inadequacy or lack of accountability of the ruling elites. This is substantiated by renowned corruption analyst, Robert Klitgaard (1988: 75) who has given a formula regarding the scope of corruption. The formula is:

Corruption = Monopoly + Discretion – Accountability

In short, government accountability tends to be weaker in poor democracies than wealthy democracies. This logic is explained and elaborated in the following paragraphs.

The established wealthy liberal democracies outperform the electoral democracies by measures of accountability and representation, as well as civil rights and rule of law. The poor electoral democracies are more successful in meeting the formal constitutional requirements of electoral democracy than implementing the rule of law and effective protection of individual and group liberties (Foweraker 2001: 355–365; Diamond 1997). In poor electoral democracies, elections are relatively free and fair, they are held regularly and their outcome does decide the composition of the government. But the effectiveness of the electoral rules is seen as an exception to a patchy and often ineffective rule of law. On the one hand, the electoral process is protected by the degree of accountability implicit in political party competition; on the other hand by international monitoring and international conditionality of credit, investment and trade (O'Donnel 1997: 49). Government accountability is then preferably secured by the incumbent political party and the international donors rather the common masses. The opposition in the parliament, who virtually oppose everything regardless of its merits or demerits, may be the most effective party to hold the government accountable but is silenced by virtue of government majority. Thus parliaments in poor democracies emerge more as legitimate means of regime change rather than authoritative fora to call the government to account.

If the majority of the common masses in a polity live under the poverty line and keep struggling for their subsistence and in turn cannot afford to educate themselves and their children, consequently, they lose the willingness and ability to adopt various measures to call the government to account. The ruling elites take the advantage of the ignorance and poverty of the poor citizens. Poverty and illiteracy hinders the gradual growth of a vigilant civil society willing to keep a watchful eye on the operations of government.

Due to scarce resources, in poor democracies, a small coterie or rich elite group consisting of the ruling politicians, civil and military bureaucrats, business community, union leaders and other professional interest groups become allies and develop symbiotic relations with one another to deter and squeeze the access of common people to state resources for the pursuit of their own interest and reap the fruits of developmental initiatives in the country. The influential elites do not intend to be in conflict with the government, which virtually monopolizes the state resource delivery and distribution system and get benefit out of this. On the contrary, the government has to depend on these elites for finance to cover electoral expenses and run its political party. In order to ensure government accountability, the relationships between and among these groups has to be competing and conflicting, and that is missing to a large extent in poor democracies.

Political factors

The constitutional dimension

The policy-making role of a legislature is in the first instance dependent upon its relationships with other political institutions and actors, most notably executive-centered elites in the bureaucracy, chief executives in presidential system, cabinet members in parliamentary systems and party elites in those systems characterized by strong political parties. To the extent that legislatures are subordinate to these institutions – to the extent that the members of legislatures are constrained from acting autonomously by political actors situated in these external institutions – the legislature's policy-making role will be restricted. On the other hand, the legislator's claim to a significant policy-making role may be bolstered by its relationship with broader public outside government. The strength of the legislature's connection with the constituencies and groups that its members represent may be directly related to its capacity to achieve a strong policy-making role (Olson and Mezey 1991: 6).

The type of governance system under which a country operates fundamentally influences the structure and tenor of legislative-executive relations. Each system assigns certain fundamental privileges and responsibilities to the legislature and executive, respectively, while additional factors encourage cooperation or confrontation between the branches.

The constitution of a country tends to stipulate the relationship between different parts of the political system at both the horizontal level (a presidential or parliamentary system or some variant) and the vertical level (a unitary or federal state). It will determine the form of the legislature (unicameral or bicameral) and adumbrate the power of the legislature. It will stipulate the mode of electoral system to be employed as well as the categories of people eligible to participate. It will delineate the role of judicial branch in constitutional and statutory interpretation. The constitution thus institutes the place of the legislature in the nation's formal political structure (Norton 1998: 6).

The working of a political structure is influenced more or less by such principles, an example being the separation of powers. Specifically, it is useful to look at the political systems in terms of whether they are parliamentary or presidential. Of note, these categories are ambiguous and within each category, there are variations that sometimes result in qualified designations (Shaw 1979: 398–399).

System of governance: the parliamentary and the presidential

Generalizations about the magnitude and character of structural effects are difficult to make because government structures vary considerably within and between types. Some portions of apparent differences are due to other factors (including the state of the party system, the number of parties, how competitive, institutionalized, or centralized they are), and the partisan balance (in parliamentary systems the state of coalitions, in presidential systems the extent of "divided government" if and when different parties control the executive and legislative branches).

One way to summarize some of these differences is to compare features of the UK's parliament with those of the US Congress. The UK sees less conflict between the executive and legislature than does the US. Parliament in the UK, compared to Congress, has a less developed internal structure of committees, and rank and file members have less power and less capacity for independent action. The parliamentary role is one of an arena for national debate whereas Congress plays that role along with larger law-making and oversight roles (UNDP 1999).

Aside from the US, presidential systems are most common in Latin America while parliamentary systems are typically in practice in Western Europe and the former British colonies (including Bangladesh and India). There is a third model usually referred to as French hybrid, which is usually identified with the Fifth French Republic. Countries that have adopted the French model include former French colonies in West Africa – such as Cote D'Ivoire, Gabon, Mali and

Senegal – and a few Eastern European states, such as Poland and Bulgaria. Sri Lanka also has a hybrid system, with similar elements as the French model. This hybrid model features an independently elected presidents sharing executive power with prime minister and cabinet selected under the procedures of a parliamentary system. Although the hybrid system appears to incorporate elements of both parliamentary and presidential systems, it has been argued that in practice, it operates as one or the other depending on whether the president and the parliamentary majority are of the same party (Mezey 1998: 781; Lijphart 1994; Sartori 1994).

In fact it will be more convenient to make a two-way breakdown on the parliamentary thus producing a trichotomy. Thus the categories of constitutional system now become:

1 parliamentary (Westminster);
2 parliamentary (continental/Paris model);
3 presidential/Washington model.

In terms of relationship between legislature and executive, the models can be further delineated as follows: constitutional systems based on the Westminster model presuppose that political executives operate within the legislature and lead it; constitutional systems based on the Washington model presupposes that political executives will be separated from the legislature; constitutional systems based on continental model presuppose a range of parallel executive-legislative relationships tending to fall at various points between fusion and separation (Shaw 1979: 398–399).

The works of Lijphart will be of relevance in this respect. In his latest book *Patterns of Democracy: Government Forms and Performance in Thirty-six*

Table 3.3 Lijphart's characteristics for describing democracies

Majoritarian	*Consensus*
Executive-parties dimension	
Single-party majority cabinets	Multiparty executive coalitions
Executive dominance/Parliamentarism	Executive-legislative balance of power/ Presidentialism
Two-party system	Multiparty system
Majoritarian electoral system	Proportional electoral system
Pluralist interest group system	Corporatist interest group system
Federal-unitary dimension	
Unitary and centralized government	Federal and decentralized government
Unicameral (or asymmetrical bicameralism)	Symmetrical bicameralism
Flexible or "unwritten" constitution	Rigid constitution
Legislative sovereignty	Judicial review

Source: Lijphart (1999).

Countries Lijphart (1999: 3) described and analyzed the institutional features that form his two broad patterns of democratic polities – majoritarian and consensus – and made the performance of these democracies in terms of policy-making and democratic quality contingent upon their institutional arrangements. The two major patterns of democracies are summarized in terms of nine variables.

The majoritarian principle emphasizes that democracy is majority rule and is based on a concentration of power. Majoritarian democracy can create sharp divisions between those who hold power and those who do not, and it does not allow the opposition much influence over government policy. The consensus principle, on the other hand, promotes the idea that democracy should represent as many citizens as possible and that a simple majority should not govern in an unfettered fashion. Consensus democracy disperses power so that there are multiple poles of decision-making and multiple checks and balances, thus limiting the power of the central government while providing for the representation of a broader array of interests (Lijphart 1999: 170). The UK and India belong to the majoritarian democracy. Switzerland and Belgium are examples of consensus democracy.

In terms of measuring the balance of power between the legislature and the executive, Lijphart distinguishes between three categories of systems:

- those with legislative dominance;
- those with executive dominance;
- those that are relatively balanced.

Lijphart (1984, 1999) then strives to establish patterns or correlations between his different models and tendency toward executive or legislative dominance. There are some clear patterns:

1. Single party executives in parliamentary systems tend to have executive dominance (UK).
2. Minority and super-majority coalitions in parliamentary systems have legislative dominance (Italy, Germany).
3. Standard presidential systems with separation of powers systems tend to have executive–legislative balance (US).

Lijphart's model includes as one element executive institutions, where he makes distinctions between majoritarian executives and consociational ones which strictly speaking applies to the set of parliamentary regimes. How about presidentialism? One could interpret presidentialism as a majoritarian institution, given obvious need in such regimes for majoritarian election formulas for the election of the head of the state. However one could also interpret presidentialism (US presidential system) as institutions for power sharing, especially if power of the president is limited by various additional institutions. But power-sharing implies the consensus model with Lijphart. It would thus seem natural to argue that presidentialism entails a division of powers between the executive, the legislature and the judiciary. After all consensus model is about diffusion of political power (Lane and Ersson 2000: 216).

The majoritarian democracy as a general rule is characterized by a pattern of executive dominance and the concentration of political power into the executive branch of government. The consensual model is characterized by pattern of legislative dominance or by a more balanced executive-legislative relationship.

In order to understand how parliament in a parliamentary system actually runs, one must understand the fusion of power between the executive and the legislature (Dickerson and Flanagan 1998: 272). In a parliamentary system, prime ministers and cabinets, because of their selection by the parliament and their control of a partisan majority, are quite likely to see their policy initiatives pass the parliament. In a parliamentary system, the defeat of the government usually results in the resignation of the cabinet or the dissolution of the parliament. Hence, unlike presidential systems, parliamentary parties tend to be more disciplined and serve as a links between the executive and the ruling government (Olson and Mezey 1991: 8).

In parliamentary systems it is the government that controls the parliamentary agenda. One of the major reasons is its capacity to associate a vote on a bill with the question of confidence (Huber 1996). Such a government initiative forces the parliament either to accept the government proposal or replace the government. As a result, as long as it is in power is it able to impose its will on parliament. Some simple statistics suggest that the general assessment that governments control the agenda in parliamentary democracies is correct. In more than 50 percent of all countries, governments introduce more than 90 percent of the bills. Moreover, the probability of success of these bills is very high: over 60 percent of bills pass with probability greater than 0.9 and over 85 percent of bills pass with probability greater than 0.8 (Inter-Parliamentary Union 1986: Table 29). The actual practice more often begins with 60 percent as the minimum of government bills introduced, with at least 80 percent of them adopted (Peters 1991: 79–80).

The parliamentary system today has become what some observers refer to as cabinet government or prime-ministerial government (Dickerson and Flanagan 1998: 268). The cabinet determines legislative priorities and sets the legislative agenda. Cabinet decisions supported by a majority in a parliament ultimately become the laws and public policies of the land. Cabinet ministers initiate almost all legislative proposals using the civil service as a primary source of information and ideas. The cabinet has aptly been called a combining committee – a hyphen, which joins a buckle, which fastens the legislative part of the state to the executive part (Bagehot, cited in Dawson 1970: 168). It is the institution that most clearly distinguishes the modern parliamentary system from the presidential form of government. The potential for concentration of power can be especially high in those parliamentary systems where a prime minister has a firm majority in the legislature, has no constitutional requirement for cabinet consultation and is surrounded with weak and compliant ministers. Under these circumstances, a prime minister may simply choose not to consult (Crossman 1985: 175–194).

At base, parliament in a parliamentary democracy has two inherently contradictory roles – first, to sustain the executive which it would appear to do well and, second, to hold the executive accountable between elections, which it does rather less well (Flinders 2001: 23). The governing party chosen by the electorate is the major medium of democratic control in the parliamentary system (Mulgan 1989: 58). Nolan (1996) noted, "the role of sustaining the government does not match well with the task of challenging it and holding it to task".

Accountability, that is the ability to compel governments to account for their actions, is an adjunct of responsibility, the ability to remove ministers or governments from office. As the thesis of parliamentary deliberation has it, governments are no longer responsible to parliament but only to the electorate at election time. Accountability therefore focuses on the mechanism of responsibility. It essentially consists of public exposure of matters that affect public perception of a government. Such exposure can have an effect if a great deal of public noise is made about it. Government tries to avoid accountability to the maximum extent, that is, they try to avoid public exposure of their blunders and misdeeds because such exposure may erode public support or at least public acquiescence, of their holding office. If governments have the power to do so they will avoid accountability by weakening or even removing, rather than strengthening, accountability mechanisms (Evans 1999: 87–88).

Parliament in a parliamentary democracy has a weak capacity to constrain the executive because it is unable to match the policy expertise of the government and the bureaucrats who work for it (Mezey 1998). Cabinets in a parliamentary system have very high workloads, which result in decisions being driven downward into cabinet committees and individual departments (Mackie and Hogwood 1985: 1–15). Thus bureaucracy is likely to become the principal fountain of policy advice. In addition, high levels of party discipline in parliament, due to costs of defying the party lines, enable party leaders to push the government program through the legislature (Gallagher *et al.* 1992: 20).

Political institutions in the US are constructed to minimize or, if possible, avoid the exertion of concentrated power. Power and authority are separated and shared across all aspects of political life. This principle of fragmentation is carried within institutions (e.g. bicameral legislatures and separation of authorizing and appropriations functions within the legislative branch) as well as across most level of government (shared power between a state governor and a state legislature or between a city major or a city council). Consequently, unlike parliamentary system, there is no institutional actor with authority to look at the government as a whole (Radin and Boase 2000: 67–68).

The principle of separation of power and the lack of responsible government set the presidential system of government from the parliamentary system. In the US presidential system, there is no vote of confidence and thus no principle of responsible government. The tenure of the office of the president and members of Congress is specified in the constitution. No matter how votes go on the floor of either house, there is nothing comparable to the non-confidence motion or dissolution of parliament. Barring death, resignation or removal for misconduct, the president is in office for four years, members of the House of Representatives for two years and senators for six years. Since the executive is not responsible to the legislature, there is less need to exercise party discipline and party solidarity is not crucial for survival (Dickerson and Flanagan 1998: 281–287).

One of the results of the divisions of power in the US is that in most others states, every year is an election year; that is, during each year some municipal, county, state or federal offices are filled by election. This means that the citizen has the opportunity to go to the polls twice each year: first, in the primary election, to choose the candidates of his or her party; and, later, in the general election, to choose among the candidates of the various parties. As a practical matter, this means that government is subject to constant scrutiny, and, thus, is subject to an ongoing process of accountability (Baker 2000: 9).

In the US, presidential and congressional tenure are almost totally independent of each other. The independence of presidential and congressional tenure reflects the American notion of the separation of powers. However, all other top executives are appointed by the president, usually to serve at the president's pleasure, but subject to confirmation by the Senate. A simple majority suffices. Moreover, the president is responsible for the general conduct of foreign affairs and in particular is authorized to negotiate treaties with other states. But these treaties must also receive the advice and consent of the Senate – in this case a qualified majority of two-thirds. This procedure constitutes one of the checks and balances which attenuate the separation of powers and it provides one branch of national legislature considerable influence over executive appointment (Loewenberg and Patterson 1979: 239; Dickerson and Flanagan 1998).

The checks and balances system of potentially competing executive and legislative branches also provides incentives for each branch to develop its own technical expertise. This limits the ability of the executive to demand blind obedience along party lines or mislead the legislature, as possible in parliamentary regimes. Thus presidential regime may produce not only more innovative but better policies because bad ideas do not survive the gauntlet of committee staff and legislators (Feigenbaum *et al.* 1993: 45)

Thus the space of policy activity of legislatures is greater in presidential than in parliamentary systems. In the latter, parliamentary parties are the major actors in policy-making and particularly if parties are concentrated by a cohesive voting pattern, there is not much room left for independent policy activities. In contrast, the presidential model clearly reflects the American political process and involves far greater independent policy roles (Olson and Mezey 1991: 201–202). In a presidential system where the separation of powers exists, the legislature is by definition intended to be strong and independent. Of course, a legislature cannot have this strength without having strong committee system serving as "counter-bureaucracy". The US, with the strongest policy-making strength, has a presidential system, a formidable counter-bureaucracy in its generously staffed committees and sub-committees (Shaw 1979: 401).

On the whole, the strongest parliaments are less assertive and powerful as legislatures than are the strongest congresses. There is, however, considerable variation among parliamentary and congressional legislative bodies. The decision to choose a parliamentary or Westminster form does not automatically foreclose the exercise of a degree of independent power. While the strongest legislatures – those capable of transforming societal demands made upon them and channeling them in new directions – are found in congressional systems, there are rubber-stamp congresses as well as powerful parliaments (UNDP 1999: 9).

The functioning of parliaments is certainly affected by the major institutional variations. However, it would be unfair to reduce the variation in parliamentary control to any sort of simple distinction or any other dichotomy (presidentialism vs. parliamentarianism or majoritarian vs. consensus democracy) (Pennings 2003). It is rather logical to interpret this issue through a broad number of institutional factors as we do in the later discussion.

Electoral system

Among the most important constitutional choices that have to be made in democracies is the choice of the electoral system, especially majoritarian election methods versus proportional representation (Lijphart 1994: 202; also Taagepara 1998; Merkel 1998). Through the electoral process, the citizens can alter the composition of the legislature, the party that controls it and the public policy agenda that parliamentary and executive elites will pursue (Olsen and Mezey 1991: 9–10). Electoral systems shape party systems, which in turn have a strong causal effect on the formation of cabinets (Lijphart 1999: 181).

The plurality and majority single-member district methods are winner-takes-all methods – the candidates supported by the largest number of voters wins and all other voters remain unrepresented. The system tends to produce highly disproportional and manufactured results. In sharp contrast, the basic aim of proportional representation is to represent both majority and minority instead of over representing or under representing any party to translate votes into seats proportionally while producing a higher party fragmentation (Lijphart 1999: 143).

Duverger (1964: 217, 226) posits that the plurality method favors two-party systems and proportional representation and two-ballot systems encourage multipartism. Politicians are also less likely to engage as third parties candidates and they seek a position in one of the two major parties. Furthermore, legislative rules in majoritarian electoral system render the parliamentary majority the more or less unfettered capacity to implement its policies, while rules in proportional democracies favor the dispersion of power and enhance the opposition's influence (Powell 2000). The plurality-majority system drives the competing parties to stiff competition, rivalry and adversities between two major parties. In contrast, proportional representation leads to compromise, coalition governments, multiparty political systems and minority-inclusion.

In those political system where parties dominate the electoral process (by nominating, candidate financing and organizing election), the policy-making activities of the legislature is likely to be controlled by party elites rather than individual legislator. But in those systems where elections are largely decentralized and candidate-centered (in term of nomination, finance and organizing), legislators are more independent to pursue their own policy ideas (Olsen and Mezey 1991: 9–10). Although the plurality system provides stronger links between legislators and their constituents since legislators represent particular geographic areas rather just the party, party control and discipline compel them to sacrifice their own policy choices in favor of the party elites.

Electoral systems affect indirectly the fusion or diffusion of political power between the executive and the legislative branch of government since in parliamentary systems the degree of cabinet stability is closely connected to the structure of the party system. For instance, Taylor and Herman (1971: 37) have shown that there is a strong inverse correlation between cabinet stability and fragmentation of party systems. Electoral systems can also influence the "dispersion of political power" between cabinet and legislature between the two chambers of parliament in presidential systems and/or in bicameral systems (presidential or parliamentary). This is mostly the case when staggered elections and different electoral formula are used in presidential and legislative elections.

Although majority-plurality electoral system is in force in both the US and the UK, the output is different. The American constitution with its separation of executive and legislative branches produces a very different form of political party system to that which exists in the UK. Whereas in the latter a single electoral process usually produces a single outcome for both the composition of the legislature and the formation of the executive, in the US the executive and the legislature are formed by separate electoral processes. Thus the executive cannot directly control and use the constitutional power of the legislature; it operates with, rather than through, the legislature. Parties are necessarily structured to reflect this and this result in them being more election machines than ideological or policy-making bodies. This contributes to an apparent paradox in the Congress in that party is the fundamental determinants of distinguishing between the majority and minority but may not be so crucial in determining the legislative actions and outcomes of Congress and its individual members (Winetrobe 2000: 24).

Unicameral/bicameral legislature and unitary/federalism

The cameral structure of a legislature has a major impact in the public policy process upon the ease or difficulty with which any one element can exercise control over the whole institution. In short, a single chamber is easier to control than two. Since in most systems, the executive is the central actor in the policy process, the practical effect of legislative bicameralism is to dilute the ability of a chief executive to control the legislature and thus to control one of the central institution of the regime (Longley and Olson 1991: 12).

Most of the upper houses have no formal power to remove the government, yet they have the potential, through rejection or repeated delay of government legislation, to bring the government to its knees. Second chambers have more time and better suited for the work of investigations and scrutiny of bills and can make a major impact on government policy. (Russel 2000: 176, 203). Moreover, the second chamber can ensure adequate representation and in a presidential system, where a virtue is made of checks and balances between the executive and the legislature, a strong second chamber can be viewed positively as providing a further dimension to such checks and balances. (Shell 1998: 850)

For the organization of legislature, the majoritarian principle of concentration of power means the legislative power should be concentrated in a single chamber. The pure consensus model is characterized by a bicameral legislature in which power is divided equally between two differently constituted chambers. (Lijphart 1999: 200)

Two major features of bicameral parliaments determine the strength and weakness of bicameralism. On the basis of the two criteria – the relative formal powers of two chambers (is it subordinate to the first chamber or not) and the democratic legitimacy (directly/indirectly elected or nominated) of the second chambers-bicameral legislatures can be classified as either symmetrical or asymmetrical. Symmetrical chambers are those with equal only moderately unequal constitutional powers and democratic legitimacy. Asymmetrical chambers are highly unequal in these respects (Lijphart 1999: 205–206)

The highly asymmetric bicameral system (based on heredity and appointment) in Britain may also be called near-unicameralism. The only power the House of Lords retains is the power to delay legislation: a financial bill can be delayed for one month and all other bills for one year (Lijphart 1999: 18). Weak bicameralism at least represents a degree of legislative power while unicameralism means complete concentration of power. Since the 1999 House of Lords Reform Act the second chamber has displayed a new and combative confidence. The government suffered 36 defeats in the Lords in the 1999–2000 session and in February 2000 the Lords rejected a piece of delegated legislation for the first time since 1968 (Flinders 2001: 35).

The symmetrical category has chambers with formally equal power. Colombia, Italy and US have directly elected second chambers while most of the members of Swiss and Belgian second chambers are popularly elected. In the US, all bills passed by the first chamber (Congress) require the approval of Senate. Even the second chamber (the Senate) can initiate its own legislations.

The most drastic method of diving power among multiple centers is federalism. Strong bicameralism is typical for federal systems because it enables power sharing between the federal state and the territorial units (Tsebelis and Money 1997; Derbyshire and Derbyshire 1999). Strong bicameralism affects working and lifetime of government as it may impair the "room to maneuver" for government when one House supports the government and the others does not (a divided parliamentary government). The chance of keeping the executive under surveillance is brighter where there are upper houses in which governments do not have party majorities. Those houses can conduct inquiries not supported by governments and amend or reject government legislations (Evans 1999).

A blend of federalism (for Switzerland and the US) with a dual structure of national-level governmental power are the attributes of the strong bicameral states (Lijphart 1984: 99–101). The question of formation of governing executive was a major factor, which ultimately led to the elimination of bicameral systems in Sweden, Denmark and New Zealand. Germany on the other hand evades this potential conflict through the provision that the government is clearly accountable to the Lower House whilst the Upper House exists to review legislation. In short, bicameralism at best rests uneasily with parliamentary government (Olson and Longley 1991: 221).

Bicameralism and coalition governments enhance the separation of the legislative from the executive (Tsebelis and Money 1997: 98–109). Multiparty systems typically make coalition governments necessary, an arrangement those too often foster unstable cabinets of short duration. Consequently, the cabinet and the parliaments, although theoretically linked, often behave as though they are distinct entities (Austen-Smith and Banks 1988: 407). Conceiving of parliament and the executive as separate players much like legislatures and executives in presidential systems is justified in many European contexts. Cohabitation is now as common in France (1986–1988, 1993–1995, 1997-present), as are presidential majorities and bicameral negotiations involve the separately elected Senate in all law-making (Tsebelis and Money 1995); the German Bundesrat must concur in many laws and may be dominated by a majority different from that of the Chancellor.

Flexibility/rigidity of constitution

Whether a constitution can impose restraints on the ruling majority is likely to be associated with the flexibility of a constitution. The degree of flexibility of a constitution can be determined on the basis of how easily a constitution adapts to changing circumstances. An unwritten constitution suggests great flexibility. After all there is no formal, legalistic procedure for making a change. If the political will is there, then a change can take place, probably by introducing a new constitutional convention or usage or discarding an old one (Derbyshire and Derbyshire 1999: 15).

The fact that the constitution is unwritten has two significant implications. One is that it makes the constitution completely flexible because it can be changed by the parliament in the same way as any other laws by regular majorities instead of supermajorities, like two-third majorities required in many other democracies for amending their written constitutions. The other important implication of an unwritten constitution is the absence of judicial review: there is no written constitutional document with the status of higher law against which the courts can test the constitutionality of regular legislation. Although parliament normally accepts and feels bound by the rules of unwritten constitution, it is not formally bound by them. With regard to both changing and interpreting the constitution, therefore parliament that is the parliamentary majority can be said to be the ultimate or sovereign authority (Lijphart 1999: 20).

The British have tended to reject a formalized code of conduct for their political elite. The system has relied on the good moral character and patriotism of the politicians (Simms 1999: 35). Usually a written constitution is a single document containing the basic rules of governance that can be changed only by special majorities. If a change has to go through some elaborate formal procedure, such as in the United States where an amendment to the constitution has to be proposed by two-thirds votes of both Houses of Congress and then ratified by the legislatures of three-quarters or 38 of the 50 the states of the Union, it seems reasonable to assume that a lightly conceived change will get a thorough consideration before it is finally accepted. Thus there have been only 27 amendments to the US Constitution since 1789 (Derbyshire and Derbyshire 1999: 15).

Judicial review

An independent, impartial and informed judiciary can hold government accountable through their power to review the actions of the legislature and the executive. Judicial review is above all treated as a means of guarding against legislative encroachments on the constitution. In some instances, its jurisdiction of review extends to cases protecting individual liberties against the undemocratic action and abuse of governmental power (Deener 1956). By adding an additional intra-governmental veto point, judicial review may influence a number of governmental capabilities for example, decreasing government's ability to impose losses, raising obstacles to rapid legislative innovation and inhibiting coherence among policies (Weaver and Rockman 1993: 31).

A written and rigid constitution cannot ensure a sufficient restrain on parliamentary majorities unless accompanied by an independent body (through judicial review) that can test the constitutionality of laws passed by the national legislature. If parliament itself is the arbiter of the constitutionality of its own laws, it can easily be tempted to resolve any doubts in its own favor (Lijphart 1999: 233; Lane and Ersson 2000: 146). Both rigidity and judicial review are anti-majoritarian devices and that completely flexible constitutions and an absence of judicial review permit unrestricted majority rule (Lijphart 1999: 228).

All federal states require a judicial review (Russia and Switzerland are exceptions) for federal constitutional arrangements tend to be more elaborate than in many other states (Riker 1975; Lane and Ersson 1997). Therefore, federal systems rely strongly on formal rules regulating power sharing (Elazar 1995; Lijphart 1999). However, in many unitary states, the judiciary is primarily involved in the external reviewing process. Yet, the exceptions to having an external review are more interesting (Israel, New Zealand and the UK). Here it is the parliament and no other power that can decide upon the constitutionality of governmental actions (Hague *et al.* 1993: 279). These can easily be explained by the fact that there is no written constitution in these polities.

In the classic Westminster model, the parliament is supremely bound only by convention and traditional rights rather by a written constitution (Weaver and Rockman 1993: 31). Parliamentary sovereignty dictates that judicial review is a secondary form of accountability. Any adverse court ruling can generally be overturned by a minister introducing new legislation (Zellick 1985; Rawlings 1986). On the contrary, in the US, judicial review can declare the acts of Congress or the president, state or local government or lower courts unconstitutional that is incompatible with the constitution (Jillson 2002: 349). Thus, in the American presidential model, it is the constitution, which is sovereign, rather the president, or Congress. The US experience of the functioning of judicial review reveals that the real effect of judicial review is akin to the proverbial "gun behind the door". It keeps the other branches of the government and states honest with threat that the courts could judge their actions unconstitutional and unacceptable (Bosso *et al.* 2000: 488).

The party dimension

The state of a nation's political party system is more important than any other factor in understanding the manner in which the legislature and the executive interact in the public policy-making process (Mezey 1998: 785; Ball and Peters 2000: 181; Bobbio 1989). Even in the US Congress with less party discipline than most of its European counterparts, party members stand out as the most reliable indicator of congressional voting (McSweeney and Owens 1998).

The role of parliaments varies according to the structure of party system. In a power-sharing system, the parliament is more likely to be a policy-making arena, while in a parliamentary system,; it is more likely to be one of competition between the party or parties in power and the opposition. But we also find diversities in different parliamentary regimes. In some countries with a predominantly two-party system, like in the United Kingdom, we have a talking parliament. The opposition has little or no chance at all to directly influence legislative proposals advanced by the government. What is left for the opposition is to publicly point out what they believe to be the major drawbacks with the government's proposals and expect that public opinion will compel the government to change its mind. In countries where the government is often of a minority type the situation is somewhat different. Here the opposition at least gets a chance to directly influence new policy presented by the government. We may also get parliaments in these countries that is more focused on negotiating behind close doors with government – a working parliament as opposed to a talking one (EIPA 2000: 73).

The policy activities of parliaments will be greater in party systems in which parties are numerous and in which no one party or coalition is dominant rather than in a system in which there are few parties and in which one party or coalition is dominant. The parliament can play a greater role in policy-making where the parliamentary parities are weakly organized or fragmented rather hierarchically organized (Olson and Mezey 1991: 206–207).

Party is crucial to political life and indeed central to the Westminster form of government (Norton 1900: 8). Effect of party discipline has been a virtual destruction of parliament as an institution and of parliamentary democracy as a process (Jaensch 1994: 238). The dominance and competitiveness of two-party system is so intense that all significant aspects of parliamentary activities including parliamentary committees are likely to be dominated by the majority party. Party considerations have come to dominate appointments; even the Speaker of the parliament changes regularly with the change in government (Palmer 1992).

In the parliamentary system, the lifeblood of the government is party loyalty. The exercise of power hinges upon the government's ability to maintain the confidence of the house (Dickerson and Flanagan 1998: 275). It is inevitable that for most MPs, the party role is their primary concern; MPs rely on the party for selection, election and re-election. They rely on the patronage and support of the party hierarchy if they are to develop a career in government. Scrutiny, in short, is a job for the opposition. In some parliaments, sanctions against members breaking party discipline are draconian. In India and Bangladesh, it entails expulsion from parliament.

Unlike the congressional system where the political party lines are less defined the legislature has more autonomy in setting the agenda, the Westminster model encourages members to vote along party lines, which weaken the power of the parliament to hold the government to account (Barnhart 1999: 8). One can have a weak party system if the constitution allows a government a long period in office, as in the US. Under the constitution the parties can behave almost as they please (Ornstein ed.1981: 118).

In the US, central party organizations play a weaker role in candidate recruitment and campaign financing. Legislators therefore have much more leeway to build a "personal vote" for themselves through constituency service and by voting the interests of their districts over that of the party. Legislators' job security and career advancement also rely less on cooperation with party leaders. As a result, incentive to cooperate is lower (Weaver and Rockman 1993: 13–14). The American political parties, each a coalition of heterogeneous interests, do not command the discipline and cohesion of parties in the legislatures of Britain and Germany (Fenno 1973; Loewenberg and Patterson 1979: 128).

Loyal opposition

In ways a democracy can be almost be defined in terms of the existence of an effective opposition (Arthur 1991). In fact, when suggestions are made to empower or extend the influence/strength of parliament, the suggestions are normally either in favor of increasing the power of the opposition or parliamentary backbenchers of the ruling side. Today, parliaments do not control the governments; this is done by the political opposition with the assistance of interest groups, the citizen and increasingly by the media (Beyme 1993: 278–285).

"Loyal opposition" means, in essence, that all parties share a common commitment to basic values and principles of democracy. Political competitors do not necessarily have to like each other, but they must tolerate one another and acknowledge each other's legitimacy. Opposition days are days on which the subject for debate is chosen by one of the opposition parties. Twenty days are allocated per parliamentary session – 17 to the largest opposition party and three among the other parties in British parliament. In the same way that the prime minister forms a cabinet, so the leader of the opposition forms a shadow cabinet, which acts as a "government-in-waiting" and consists of the leading figures from the official opposition. The Speaker and his Deputies are drawn from the Labour and Conservative parties – they do not vote. These formal and informal practices restrict absolute government power.

In the US system of separated but shared powers, it is possible to have a situation where the government is divided between two competing groups or parties. There is no true loyal opposition which is excluded from formal power. Rather, two rival parties face each other from positions of strength (controlling either the presidency or Congress) in a struggle for control over the development of public policy (Unekis 1998: 195).

Since it is government that needs to get its business through, obstruction by the opposition can be a considerable embarrassment. Prolongation of the debate in the House will upset government's timetable. So the government has a real interest in ensuring that its relations the opposition are harmonious as can be expected and that the opposition is given as little opportunity as possible for obstruction (Griffth *et al.* 1989: 287). In transitional democracies, the opposition can shift the politics from parliament to street and disrupt public life and resources that can lead to political turbulence and instability if it is forcefully handled instead of accommodating and providing some room to vent its grievance and opinion both inside and outside the parliament.

Intra-institutional factors

The extent to which a legislature is well organized and well equipped greatly affects its ability to participate in the policy process. While a legislature's relationship with external institutions and actors may empower it with a potentially strong policy-making role, it may not be able to realize that potential if it has no efficient way of dealing with policy questions and it has not adequate resources and professional staff to assist it (Olson and Mezey 1991: 6–7).

It is worth mentioning that if a parliament is strictly controlled externally, it hardly makes difference how it is organized internally. But if has some latitude for independent thought and action, its ability to take advantage of those opportunities is affected by the extent to which it is internally organized (Olson 1994: 137). The main internal components with which a legislature functions include its members and resources available to the whole chamber as well as its structure of committees. Chapter 4 will be devoted to discussion on committees. Resources will also be discussed in this chapter.

Chamber

The ability of a parliament to meet for a good part of a year and to set its own agenda is an important, if elemental resource in the development of autonomous legislatures. Most established democratic parliaments meet more frequently than an ineffective one. A chamber which can determine its own agenda will be able to constrain the executive to a greater extent than a chamber which exert little or no control over its own agenda. Although the government usually sets the bulk of legislative agenda, some parliaments have latitude to select their own issues as well (Olson 1994: 141; Norton 1998). Even the British parliament protects a portion of the legislative timetable for private members' bills; several significant social reforms have been enacted through such legislations (March and Read 1988; Norton 1993).

The amount of staff, research facilities and even secretarial support are basic to independent legislature and its members (Olson 1994: 141). The US Congress has considerable research, library and support staff and exerts a notable viscosity in the legislative process. Resources should have some impact on the capacity of the legislature to engage in scrutiny of the executive. For members to question effectively the actions and policies of government, very often they need precise information from specialized sources on which to engage in such questioning. Those sources may take the form of researchers at the disposal of the members individually (personal staff) or collectively either through committees (committee staff or expert retained by committees), libraries or research units (Norton 1998: 12–13). A member of the House of Representatives has 17 assistants while a senator has 40 (Wilson and DiIulio 1995: 313). Resources have to combine with other variables to provide significant degree of viscosity to constrain government.

Members

The parliament is only as effective as its members. The members are the basic component of a legislature and of its internal institutions of party and committee. The more knowledgeable and capable individual members are, the greater their capacity to develop and facilitate the operations of an active and powerful legislature and thereby act independently of the chief executive. A high turnover of members coupled with low degrees of organization helps build a subservient parliament (Longley and Olson 1991: 16; Olson 1994). A salary sufficient to attract and maintain a membership willing to devote its time largely or wholly to parliamentary duties is also essential.

The more prominent the legislature, the larger are the number of full-time professional legislators. The presence of such legislators, in turn, will create further pressure for an even stronger, more active legislative role. They will advocate strong committees, they will be more disposed to question and even oppose the government and their party leaders and they will wish to pursue public policy initiatives of their own (Mezey 1994: 437).

Conclusion

A typology of national legislatures advanced by Mezey and eventually refined by Norton based on policy-making power as well as support is discernible from the legislative literature review which facilitates our comprehension of the capability and ramification of the legislatures to hold the executive accountable. But this categorization is too crude to appreciate the variations and divergences within a specific category which prompts us to go further and explore some of the key political and social variables stemming from Mezey's two dimensions of legislative typology to measure the variations. The interplay of political and social factors will determine the place of legislature in the political system – whether it is in Mezey's categorization, an active, reactive, vulnerable, marginal or minimal legislature.

It is apparent that the political context in which a legislature operates predominantly matters in order to measure the strength of parliament to constrain the executives. Where the political power is diffused and fragmented either vertically between and among different branches of government or horizontally between and among different state legislatures and local government units or due to sharing of power with coalition partners, legislatures appear to be stronger. In this respect, the constitutional structure of a polity seems to be the most crucial factor.

In a presidential system where the separation of powers exists, the legislature is by definition intended to be strong and independent. Political institutions in the US are constructed to minimize or, if possible, avoid the exertion of concentrated power. Power and authority are separated and shared across all aspects of political life. Even in a parliamentary system, the parliament has the potential of being a strong legislature if it is accompanied by a written constitution, a proportional electoral system with a low threshold requirement, federalism and symmetrical bicameralism and judicial review.

The party system is a resultant outcome of a country's electoral system which in turn has a strong causal effect on the formation of cabinets. Lack of party control resulting either from non-cohesion or multipartism tends to be correlated with strong parliament regardless of system of governance. Two-party systems tend to generate single-party governments where the parliament runs the risk of being relegated to a rubber stamp of government activities while multiparty system generate more influential parliaments.

Bicameralism and coalition governments enhance the separation of the legislature from the executive. Multiparty systems typically make coalition governments necessary, an arrangement that too often fosters unstable cabinets of short duration. Consequently, the cabinet and the parliaments, although theoretically linked, often behave as though they are distinct entities and can turn into strong parliaments.

While the political variables demonstrate the centrality of politico-institutional elements of a polity to determine the strength of a legislature, the support dimension also entails the concomitant significance of socio-economic forces such as civil society, institutional history, political cultures, media, interest groups, the economic condition and the like, for the legitimacy and continuity of a strong legislature. In fact the socio-economic and cultural factors can go a long way in explaining functioning of parliaments and their strength to hold the government to account in Third World countries. But looking into the macro- and micro-political institutional factors will certainly help find the factors responsible for the divergent level of legislative performance within the Third World countries.

Ultimately an analytical framework springs from this literature reviews on legislatures which will guide the subsequent chapters and in turn pave the way to interpret the role of parliamentary committees in holding the executive accountable in Bangladesh, India and Sri Lanka.

4 Parliamentary committees and accountability

An exclusive focus on the macro-contextual ecology of legislatures may appear misleading as well as lopsided with the plausible conclusion that parliaments play a marginal role in holding the government accountable. External contextual determinants may affirm that most legislatures in parliamentary system belong to the reactive rather the active category, but within the same category there are considerable variations which prompt us to dig further into the internal organizational arrangements of legislatures. This chapter aims at delineating parliamentary committees, which are generally believed to be the most significant internal instrument of a legislature to oversee the activities of government and hold it to account. By focusing on the contextual political-institutional aspects, which do have direct bearings on the functioning of committees as well as intra-institutional arrangements of committees, this chapter strives to explore the factors that help determine the strength of committees which in turn maximize their capacity to call the government to account.

Parliamentary committees

By broad consensus committees are considered one of the most significant internal organizational features of modern parliaments (Mattson and Strøm 1995: 303). Parliamentary committees figure significantly in all continents and in most countries of the world, increasingly serving as the main center of both legislation and parliamentary oversight of government (Longly and Davidson 1998: 2).

A legislative committee is a sub-group of legislators, normally a group entrusted with specific organizational tasks. Committees are typically found among the most privileged groups in modern parliaments. Like other legislative areas, a legislative committee is designed to promote majority rule but also to protect minority rights. In this way, as in many others, committees are microcosms of the larger assembly (Mattson and Strøm 1995: 249).

Strong committees are a necessary condition for parliamentary significance (Rommetvedt 1998). Parliamentary committees are among the most important features of legislative organizations in contemporary democracies (Strøm 1998: 21). Governments today have become more complicated and their jurisdictions have also widened. Due to paucity of time and adverse atmosphere in the floor, detailed parliamentary business obviously cannot be transacted by plenary sessions. That is the very rationale for the parliamentary committee system followed by most parliaments of the world today. Most committees are also a vehicle for specialization that essentially meets the professionalism and expertise critical for legislative phase of policy-making process involving ever more complex policy issues. Thorough scrutiny of government activities occurs at committees. It is committees where public officials give hearings and answer questions about their performances and policy intentions. Committees also ensure government accountability through enquires, investigation and financial reviews. All committee devices are ultimately geared to securing government accountability.

There has been a growth of the centrality of committees, not only in a few parliaments, but also as a global phenomenon, increasingly serving as the main organizing center of both legislation and parliamentary oversight of government. The most frequently quoted statement in the studies of parliamentary committee systems, that of Woodrow Wilson that "Congress in its committee-room is Congress at work" was originally written in 1885 and, while less valid then, became the hallmark of scholarly understanding of US congressional committees in the century to follow. Committees are an efficient means of dividing up the growing legislative workload. They are also convenient, freeing the chambers from the chore of constantly choosing committee members. In the US, eventually committees prove to be a powerful antidote to the rising influence of presidents and their cabinet members in framing the legislative agenda. This intention by the parliament to extend their ability to oversee, or scrutinize the government and ministers is a major – perhaps even the central – factor explaining the rising use of committees in parliamentary democracies (Longley and Davidson 1998: 1–4).

Literature review on committees

There remains a dearth of academic literature on parliamentary committees. There is an abundance of research on the most powerful committee systems, that of the US Congress. Yet, when one searches for published materials on committees in legislatures other than the US Congress, one becomes aware of a body of grotesque imbalance of systematic information (Lee and Shaw 1979: 5). The lack of a body of comparative literature for the purpose of carrying out a proper analysis of parliamentary committees is a flagrant deficiency in the political science literature (Hazan 2001: 2).

The first substantial attempt to analyze parliamentary committees cross-nationally came in the late 1970s, capped by the publication in 1979 of *Committees in Legislatures: A Comparative Analysis* edited by Lee and Shaw. Lee and Shaw (1979) sought to assemble empirical materials on the committees in eight national legislatures: parliaments in Britain, Canada, Germany, India, Italy and Japan and the Congress in the Philippines and the US. They also aimed to construct a comparative analytical perspective in order to integrate their country studies and foster research on committees in other parliaments. This work endorses a thoughtful, multifaceted conceptualization of the structures, purposes and consequences of various parliamentary committee systems and plays a crucial role in establishing the importance of committee research and its scholarly tradition.

Nowadays, almost every major work on cross-national parliaments contains a section on committee although the number of such work is meager and sporadic (Olson 1994; Döring 1995; Kurian 1998). In the middle of the 1990s, a turning point was reached in the study of Western European parliaments in general and in that of their committees in particular through the multinational substantive collection of studies, *Parliaments and Majority Rule in Western Europe*, edited by Döring (1995). This is a truly comparative analyses of key dimensions of West European parliaments and in chapters by Mattson and Strøm (1995) and by Damgaard (1995), important studies focus on parliamentary committees. This comparative works reveals that in 16 countries of Western Europe (Britain and Ireland being exceptions to the 18 countries considered) parliamentary committees deal meaningfully with legislation and executive oversight.

A more inclusive attempt to collect empirical materials on parliamentary committees emerged in the 1990s under the aegis of the Research Committee of Legislative Specialists, one of the research entities of the International Political Science Association. In 1996, the committee convened an international conference on parliamentary committees in Budapest and the leading papers from this conference were published in 1997 as *The Changing Role of Parliamentary Committees* (edited by Longley and Agh). Covering a wide range of committee-related topics, these contributions provided information on committees in some 19 national parliaments. In their wide-ranging enquiries, the contributors of this volume elaborate and investigate the explosion of parliamentary committees in the 1990s. These studies provide rich new information about the structures of parliamentary committees – their organizational bases, the number of committees in various systems, the sizes of committees, committee jurisdictions. They also spell out varieties in parliamentary committee procedures – how parliamentarians are assigned to committees and chairs chosen and the ways in which committees conduct their legislative works. Finally, these studies add to our understanding of committee power, particularly the power of committees as they engage in policy-making. Strong committees, it appears, are at least a necessary condition for effective parliamentary influence in the policy-making process. Whether they are also a sufficient condition is less obvious (Mattson and Strøm 1995: 250). In his recent book on committee reform in Israel, Hazan (2001) initially dissects the committee systems of four European parliaments: in Britain, Germany, Italy and the Netherlands because of the particular cogency of the committee systems in these parliaments for analysis of the Israeli case. This book also reinforces the primacy of external political environment of parliament as the key factor in making the committees work.

It is difficult to achieve a global perspective on committees without taking into account their role in Third World legislatures which amount to over 100 countries, in Africa, Asia and Latin America. Smith (1996: 16) in his study has shown that between 1960 and 1990, one-third of the states in the Third World experienced more than 20 years of military rule. Another one-third experienced lesser period of military rule, leaving only one-third of these nations with no experience of military government. While legislatures in the Third World are sometimes abolished or suspended by authoritarian rulers, they tend in due course to be reinstated as a symbol of regime legitimacy. In essence, the governing systems in major Third World countries, at least in the last decades, have typically embodied predominantly authoritarian features, which include a weak legislature with an underdeveloped committee system (Shaw 1998: 237–243).

Some good works (Agor 1970; Kashyap 1979; Jain 1991; Rubinoff 1996, 1998; Shastri 1998; Mezey 1979, 1985; Lee and Shaw 1979; Lowenberg and Patterson 1979; Ahmed 2002) have been conducted on the parliaments and parliamentary committees in some democratic Third World countries (both continuous and intermittent) such as India, Chile, Kenya Philippines, Costa Rica and Mexico. The wide variety of arrangements in legislatures in the Third World are noted in Shaw (1998), with case studies illustrating weak committee systems in the traditional and authoritarian Third World and stronger systems in continuous and intermittent Third World democracies. The Westminster tradition is prominent in India and Kenya where committees appear weak vis-à-vis the executive while the other three are patterned along the lines of US Congress where committees seem stronger than the traditional Third World committees.

Until recently, the committees found in legislatures in the Third World typically accorded with a generalization about them by Blondel (1995: 261): "Outside Western countries, the committee system is usually not well developed. In many Third World countries, few committees exist and which do meet infrequently". It appears the situation is changing, keeping pace with the resurgence of the democracy in the Third World. The strength of a nation's legislature is correlated to the strength of that nation's commitment to democratic procedures (Olson and Mezey 1991). Hence, in fledging democracies such as Bangladesh, Nepal and countries in Latin America, the committees have the prospect to play some significant role in holding the government to account.

Factors determining the strength of parliamentary committees

Mainstream political science has increasingly focused on the issue of committee strength. One influential comparative survey determined the strength in different countries according to two criteria: their legislative activities and their ability to scrutinize government (Lee and Shaw 1979). Legislation making and oversight functions of the parliament are intertwined with policy-making and with power relations in and around committees. The strength of committees was interpreted in terms of several variables: party control, constitutional framework and developmental factors.

Another major comparative research project has focused on the strength of committees (Mattson and Strøm 1995). In this study, committee procedures (including committee assignments, chair selection and allocation, openness and the possibility of minority reports) and committee reports (including the power to initiate legislation, scrutinize bills, collect information and propose amendments) were identified to explain committee strength. This approach is rewarding because it offered a relatively straightforward means of comparing committees in different political systems.

A strong committee in a legislature is one that has a significant independent impact on public affairs (Shaw 1998: 235). Of nine attributes of parliaments, most closely related to the ability of parliaments to function independently in the public policy process, five referred to characteristics of the committee system (Døering 1995; Mattson and Strøm 1995). Autonomy of committees from the government was a component of the policy-making capability of the legislature. These findings confirmed the observation of Lees and Shaw (1979) that committee autonomy from government and party control is the key element in an active and influential legislative committee system.

Parliamentary committees are Janus-like in that they have two distinct, but intersecting attributes: they are repositories of expertise and knowledge and are also the means for the expression of political power. They can develop knowledge in a sector of public policy as they parallel the structure of government ministries and as they become permanent and build a core of experienced members. To the extent, however, that they build power in a legislature as a function of their expertise, executives and political parties attempt to control committees through both the allocation of members and the exercise of party discipline (Olson and Crowther 1998).

For Mezey (1979: 64) legislatures with strong policy-making power have highly developed committee systems. Legislative committees have appeared as a vital component of the policy-making process, sometimes as structures of encouraging policy expertise in the legislature through a division of labor, sometimes as instruments for allowing the legislature to supervise the policy implementation activities of the bureaucracy and sometimes in both capacities (Olson and Mezey 1991: 14). Key factors determining committee strength can be organized into two broad headings. These are as follows:

- Contextual political institutional factors
  - constitutional arrangement;
  - bicameralism/unicameralism;
  - political party.
- Intra-institutional factors
  - functional arrangement;
  - structural arrangement;
  - procedural arrangement.

Contextual political institutional factors

CONSTITUTIONAL ARRANGEMENT

The major constitutional variation relevant to our analysis is that between parliamentary and presidential form of government. Parliamentary systems are based on the presumption that the executive will arise from the legislature – a fusion of powers – and take the lead. The separation of powers in presidential systems creates a legislature that is independent of and is usually designed to serve a check and balance on the executive branch. Parliamentary systems are therefore associated with weaker committees than presidential systems, which possess stronger committees (Hazan 2001: 83–84).

In separation-of-powers systems, the creation of strong and assertive parliamentary committees is the natural result of efforts by legislatures to strengthen their hands in competing with executives. Assertive committees in parliamentary systems potentially threaten the primacy of governments, executives and, not least, legislative and partisan leaders in the chamber itself – all antithetical to the principle of unified political leadership and responsibility central to classical parliamentary government. Thus active parliamentary committees are inherently at odds with the classical model of parliamentary government (Longley and Davidson 1998: 2).

Legislative committees in parliamentary systems are much weaker because they are controlled by the majority members of the majority party, which in turn is controlled by the cabinet. The cabinet manages the legislative process and does not let desired bills die along the way. Committees act as forums for debate that sometimes produce minor or technical amendments but rarely substantial changes (Dickerson and Flanagan 1998: 288).

The more the executives seek to control the content of legislation, the more they must control the work of committees. The more the executive or parties dominate the policy content of legislative work, the less important and active committees tend to be. The intention of executives or ruling parties to maintain their legislative control will lead them to keep major legislative activity and decision-making on the floor where members are more visible and more easily controlled through party discipline. For these reasons, prime ministers in both Britain and Canada, irrespective of party, have in the past opposed proposals to increase the capacities of committees within parliamentary system of each country (Longley and Olson 1991: 15).

One of the main limitations on the effectiveness of the committee has ironically been ministerial responsibility. Ministerial responsibility allows the executive to control the supply of witness and information to parliament. It also dictates the officials appear before committees with the consent of the minister (Flinders 2001). The experience of select committees has demonstrated their essential powerlessness in the face of executive recalcitrance (Judge 1993: 79).

It is ministers who control both the membership and resources of the parliamentary committees charged with holding them to account. Selective membership reinforced by party discipline ensures that the power relationship is not threatened (Cremin 1993). The crucial point for accountability is that the chair has the power to nullify the committee-protecting witnesses avoiding issues and employing their casting vote to protect the government (Flinders 2001: 114).

Committees in parliamentary bodies have been less attractive to their members for two reasons:

1 the ability of the members to obtain cabinet posts which dilutes their interest in forming strong committees;
2 the fear of the leadership that strong committees would only further fragment what is already a multiparty system (Francis 1989: 4).

Within the Westminster model, with the ever-present struggle between the executive and the legislative arms of the government, the executive usually takes measures to prevent public embarrassment in committee. To accomplish this, the executive feels obliged to control the activities of the committee with its majority, thus reducing the non-partisan mode of debate and deliberation within the committee. Executive are often compelled to restrict the scope of enquiry of a committee and to influence the outcome of the committee investigation.

Any member caught in the limelight due to criticism of his/her own government will likely never be chosen for leadership roles in the government. Members are encouraged within the Westminster model to vent dissent within caucus but not publicly. This ultimately circumscribes the members' role in committee and in the house lending credence to the popular belief that private members are there merely to vote along party lines without speaking out on issues that they enunciated during the last election (Barnhart 1999: 8–10).

The importance of legislative committees is limited especially in those systems adhering to the Westminster model. In Great Britain, party leaders consistently resisted the formation of committees because of their potential for establishing a source of policy expertise outside the party that ultimately might jeopardize party discipline (Mezey 1994: 433). In Britain, it took more than 600 years for a comprehensive, specialized, permanent group of departmental committees to emerge in the House of Commons in 1979 (Shaw 1998: 790).

The organization and working of parliamentary committee systems are of considerable importance especially if the committees are endowed with strong powers in the legislative process (Damgaard 1995: 312). This is evident by a bifurcation of standing committees (for legislative scrutiny) and select committees (for particular enquiries) in British parliament which helps limit parliamentary effect. Government control of a parliamentary majority has also been manipulated to extend structures that facilitate the passage of government measures and to circumscribe those that may enhance parliamentary scrutiny and influence (Norton 1990b: 15). Thus under the Westminster system, the committees' scope of operation is limited to making reports and recommendations to the house and the reports have only persuasive value.

The select committees in the House of Commons, whose purpose is to oversee administration, are not authorized to use their oversight powers in an attempt to influence policy. In the British system, the cabinet and the parliamentary majority determine policy and guarded their prerogatives jealously against the encroachment of parliamentary oversight committees. As the leadership of administration consists of the leadership of the majority party in parliament, it is not surprising that parliament is limited to administrative oversight and is precluded from supervision and control over administration which in the US grows out of the separation of powers (Loewenberg and Patterson 1979: 274).

In separation-of-powers systems, active parliamentary committees come naturally as a result of efforts by legislative bodies to develop legislative tools and resources to strengthen their grip in competing with executives (Longley and Davidson 1998: 2). Congressional committees, unlike the cabinet in the parliamentary systems, are powerful organizations for managing the legislative process. The committees in the US Congress monopolize the legislative procedures: bills begin in committee, are discussed and examined there and can be killed in committees without the inconvenience of a vote on the floor of the House (Ball and Peters 2000: 186).

The foundation of committee power in the US consists of gate-keeping, information advantage and proposal power. If a majority of the committee does not prefer a bill to become law, the committee can refuse to report it (although the provision of discharge petition remains there). This prevents the floor from considering it, which effectively gives the committee a veto (Groseclose and King 2001: 208). Approximately 87 percent of all bills that were referred to committees in the 102nd Congress did not reach the floor (Oleszek 1996: 3).

Committees as agenda-setters in their respective jurisdictions are able to enforce many of their policy wishes not only because they originate bills but also because they get a second chance after their chamber has worked its will. This occurs at the conference stage in which two chambers of a bicameral legislature resolve differences between versions of a bill. Thus the explanation of committee power resides in the rules governing the sequence of proposing, amending and especially of vetoing in the legislative process (Shepsle and Weingast 1987: 87).

BICAMERALISM/UNICAMERALISM

One of the strengths of upper House committees can be that they may not be controlled by government. This gives them a different perspective than from lower House committees. Upper Houses without government majorities may embark on investigations in committee, which provide genuine and demanding scrutiny of policy. Second chambers have more time and are better suited for the work of investigations and scrutiny of bills and can make a major impact on government policy. The relatively lower media profile of upper Houses can enable committee to work undisturbed, further encouraging the culture of consensus that is the strength of committee work (Russel 2000: 176–177).

The Bicameral Rivalry Theory can explain regularity between the constitutional structure of a country and the power of committee within the country's legislature (Groseclose and King 2001: 196). Unicameral parliamentary systems usually do not have committees strong enough to veto legislation (Shugart and Carey 1992; Shaw 1979). The chief executive is most likely to exercise decisive control over the legislative process in regimes whose national legislature is unicameral or if bicameral – in which one chamber is dominant over the other and legislative committees are attenuated. By contrast, multichamber and separation-of-power systems usually have strong committees. Legislatures with two active chambers and assertive committee systems are more likely to act independently of the chief executive on policy issues (Longley and Olson 1991: 17).

Bicameral legislatures (as in the US) in which committees are not the central actors in resolving differences between the chambers will not possess strong committees, *ceteris paribus*. It is in this regard that the British parliament is of some interest. The institutions of cabinet government reduce the need for representatives of two chambers to meet in conference to resolve differences. The centralized leadership of cabinet confers agenda power in both chambers on the same single group of ministers. They possess proposal power and they control (either explicitly or through bargaining) the amendment process. There is no need for ex post reconciliation since the cabinet may choose the policies that survive both chambers ex ante (Shepsle and Weingast 1987: 102).

POLITICAL PARTY

As with the connection between parliamentary party autonomy and legislative policy-making role, the connection between the strength of committee system and the strength of the legislature's policy-making role has been well documented. Weak committee systems are almost always associated with weak legislature (Shaw 1979).

As a factor that conditions committee behavior, party is probably more important than any other single influence that can be isolated. Shaw (1979) observed in his comparative in-depth study of eight legislatures that in six out of eight countries, the pull of party affiliation is clearly stronger than the pull of committee affiliation.

In fact it would not seem much of an exaggeration to say that committees in legislatures are as they are largely because the party systems are as they are. Indeed, there is a wide utilized arrangement in legislatures that might be said to constitute official recognition of party influence: namely the assignment of members to committees in portion to party strength in chamber. This is required by constitution in Italy; elsewhere it is required by standing orders or usage. The intension is to ensure each committee replicates party divisions in the chamber and to give the majority party or coalition a majority in each committee (Shaw 1998: 787).

In a parliamentary system, it is the parties that form the governments and appear to direct parliamentary works. Parties typically aim for government office, policy influence and party unity. The parties, particularly their leadership, can largely influence/dictate the functioning of parliamentary committees by monopolizing its de facto power in the appointment of MPs to parliamentary committees, and sanctioning or rewarding the members according to their performance in the light of party aims. The reward is more tempting and bears more potential in attempts to control the behavior of committee members (Damgaard 1995: 309–323). Unlike the separation-of-power system in the US, party preferences take precedence over the policy expertise and constituency interests of committee members.

Factors that inhibit committee integration or autonomy can be identified. Ministers are members of British standing committees and tend to dominate them; these committees are more cohesive than German committees where ministers are not members. The type of work committees are doing is also relevant. British select committees are entrusted with executive oversight, and they tend to be less cohesive than British standing committees, which deal with legislation. Turning to another factor when committees deal with issues about which the parties feel strongly, there tends to be more committee cohesion than when dealing with technical and other issues about which the parties do not feel strongly (Ornstein 1981). Thus the strength of a legislative committee system varies inversely with the strength of the party system in a legislature (Walkland 1983).

Even in the separation-of-power system as in the US presidential system, where party domination is inherently weak, if the same party constituted a majority in several elected bodies (presidency, House or Senate), the check and balance between the different bodies can become less effective. This is evident in the 104th Congress when the Republican held a majority in both Houses of Congress. Newt Gingrich, the Speaker of the House emerged like a prime minister leading a majority party within a parliamentary system and asserted central leadership control over the functioning of committees, the heart of US Congress. In an attempt to establish massive party control over the members, the Speaker formed task forces instead of committees to deal legislations. He reduced the number of sub-committees and committee staffers and budget (the number of committee staff positions fell from 1854 positions in the 103rd Congress to 1233 in the 104th – a fall of 33 percent. Committee budgets fell from US$222.3 million to US$156.3 million). He ignored the prevailing principle of seniority in the appointment of committee chairs and limited the tenure of committee chair to six years, which is opposed to specialization, a cardinal feature in the US committee system. He circumscribed the power of the chair and controlled the agenda setting of committees. Of the bills which reached the floor in the first three months 78 percent did not pass through. In essence, the Speaker established party control over the members and undermined the committee system (Unekis and Frank 1997; Groseclose and King 2001; Campbell and Davidson 1999).

When parties exert only a weak control over legislative committees, the committees are free to develop a life of their own and make a strong contribution to the outputs of the legislatures. Lack of party control can result either from noncohesion or multipartism. Therefore, the lack of party discipline in the US Congress explains the strength of American committees and the multipartism of the Chamber of Deputies explains the relative strength of Italian committees (Shaw 1979: 395). Where, on the other hand, committees are weak, one tends to find a high level of control over them by a single cohesive party whose members are in the majority on the committee. Single party dominance appears to shift the scene of political action from the legislative committees to other venues, either on the floor, or to the executive branch. The reform in Britain in 1979 strengthened the select committees but the committee system is still a rather weak one. The result was rightly predicted by Wheare (1955: 157) decades earlier when he wrote

> There can be no doubt whatever that if a system of specialized standing committees were set up in Britain and were composed in proportion to the party strength in the House, the government would control the committees just as it controls the House.

Internal structure and organizational differentiation of the parliamentary parties affect how party deputies on committees can interact with fellow party members and leaders. Some Western European parties have an internal system of working groups, which parallel the structure of parliamentary committees. The members of the party working groups are the party's delegation on the parliamentary committee, and they, in effect, become the party's experts on the jurisdiction of the committee. If parties wish to define a party position on a committee topic, it may be the party's own members on the committee who shape the party position (Schuettemeyer 1994: 38).

By creating a party infrastructure with regular meetings and leadership positions, parliamentary party groups enhance their capacity to affect the deliberations of leaders and their own members in formal committees. Moreover, party committee meetings provide the backbenchers with the opportunity to vent their views and grievances in an environment that is free of publicity and political opponents. (Norton 1998a: 199–200). In the British House of Commons, specialized party committees predate considerably specialized parliamentary committees and have provided an important conduit for backbench influence (Norton 1979, 1994a). In India it appears that the most important committees in parliament are the committees of the ruling party. Likewise, the influence of party committees in German parliament is enormous (Shaw 1998: 788).

Intra-institutional factors

FUNCTIONAL ARRANGEMENT

Contemporary legislature can no longer function without committees than a cabinet could operate without department (Shaw 1979: 419). The two most significant functions of parliamentary committees in the larger political system are making decisions with regard to legislation and authorization and oversight of administrative actions. Committees provide their parent legislature with the structures that are essential to fulfill its role and to control itself in the process. Therefore, democratic accountability between elections is exercised not only by the representatives in the chamber but also by the committees at work (Hazan 2001: 5).

It is unwise to think of oversight as something different from legislation. While an assembly and its committees' oversight function and its legislative function may be separable analytically, they are so complementary as to be inseparable in practice. Legislation requires oversight that identifies the need for remedial legislation, which in turn becomes the subject of renewed oversight and then additional legislation, and so on. From this perspective, institutional changes that enhance an assembly and its committees' role in making legislative decisions are very likely, sooner or later, to be reflected as well in the assembly's capacity and commitment to conduct oversight. In fact, the best oversight often takes place during committees' legislative hearings (Bach 2000: 42).

The investigatory function is an extreme case of oversight, usually triggered by the discovery of official malpractice. Reviewing and investigating the conduct of administrative agencies is the type of legislative activities that even an authoritarian regime is likely to permit. Even without raising questions about the propriety of a given policy or ideological rationale, it is possible to ask if the policy is carried out efficiently and effectively by the relevant committee members and thus keep surveillance over the activities of the executive (Blondel 1973: 93–102).

A major function of parliament and parliamentary committees concern financial matters, which consist of ex ante appropriation and budget allocation to government ministries and agencies and ex post financial oversight to evaluate efficiency, effectiveness and economy of resources. Budget is treated as the lifeblood of an organization. The committee which can play a significant role in budget allocation of a public organization appears to be stronger than those committees which periodically review the use of money after post budget allocation.

In UK, as well as most other Commonwealth parliamentary regimes, after introduction of budget to the House and general debate, it is scrutinized by committees (some in Committee of Whole House, most in standing committees); then, it is returned to the House for final consideration. The scope of committee operation in budget allocation is logically limited. Under parliamentary government, the prime minister and cabinet submit an annual budget that the parliament usually debates but typically approves without substantial change. For the parliament to disapprove the budget would almost certainly be judged tantamount to a vote of no confidence that requires the government to resign (Bach 2000: 12). Of course the Public Accounts Committee and the departmental select committees exercise considerable ex post financial scrutiny of public organizations.

In Congress, by contrast, the president's budget submission early each year only begins a protracted process of detailed review, amendment, argument and negotiation that usually continues until October 1 (when the new fiscal year begins) and often beyond. During this process, every figure in the budget is subject to challenge and change, either at the recommendation of one of the appropriations committees or by an amendment that an individual member offers during a plenary debate.

The implications of this process are profound, not only for budget control but also for the general character of the relations between Congress and the executive branch of the federal government. Each cabinet secretary knows that his or her budget request first must be approved by (actually, negotiated with) the president and his budget advisors. But the secretary also knows that it is ultimately Congress, more often than not accepting the recommendations of its appropriations committees, that decides how much money he or she actually will receive to continue the activities of the department. Herein lies the answer to a question sometimes asked by MPs from democratizing regimes who are visiting Washington for the first time: "When Congress asks government officials for information, why should they provide it?". The reason, of course, is that a recalcitrant cabinet secretary risks paying a price in the form of punitive budget cuts. Or to put it more generously, it is very much in the interest of all cabinet secretaries to win the support and confidence of the appropriations sub-committees that largely control the annual budgets for their departments (Bach 2000). Moreover, the House Appropriation Committee, the Government Reform Committee and the Budget Committee exercise rigorous ex post financial oversight of the executive.

Committee reports submitted to the parliament are the empirical evidence of the activities of different committees. Reports also illustrate different stages of committee involvement in carrying out its task. Formally, there is no compulsion for the production and presentation of committee reports in some legislature, like the UK House of Commons.

In the British parliament, committees usually report to the House after an enquiry or assignment is over. When the committee publishes the reports, they have no formal means of ensuring that their recommendations are acted upon. They have to rely on the force of argument, on publicity and on unanimity. But by putting a lot of materials in the form of report to the public record, the committees contribute greatly to the transparency of the operations of government departments (Judge 1993). The government is committed to responding to each report usually within two months, the responses are sometimes positive, frequently neutral and on occasion dismissive (Drewry 1985). Currently debates over committee reports are held on three days known as estimates days. They have been supplemented by three Wednesday morning sittings given over for debating reports. In US Congress, committee report is obligatory for the committee to submit it to the House immediately once it is ready and the recommendations of committee reports are binding.

STRUCTURAL ARRANGEMENT

Although it is customary to refer to legislative committees as if they were well-defined phenomenon, in reality, they appear in diversified varieties. Committees vary in functions, size, composition and degree of institutionalization and along many other dimensions (Strøm 1998: 29). The structural features of committees will be discussed under the following sub-heads:

1 types and tenure;
2 jurisdictions;
3 numbers;
4 size;
5 multiple memberships;
6 sub-committees.

Types and tenure In general, committees can be divided into two distinct categories: permanent (sometimes called standing committees) and ad hoc or special committees. Permanent committees are, as a general rule, specialized. In permanent committees, the jurisdiction of the committee is defined by the subject matter which tends to parallel the structure of the administrative or cabinet agencies such as health, defense, education, finance, etc. and is entrusted with the study of all bills or other matters relating to that particular field. There are types of permanent committees including financial committees that have specific oversight and auditing functions. Usually they are appointed for entire lifespan of the parliament. The long and guaranteed term of the office of a committee equips its members an opportunity to acquire real knowledge and specialization on their assigned fields (IPU 1986: 625–626).

Permanence is important in that it ensures a continuous mechanism for enquiry and encourages a corporate spirit to branch out. A corporate spirit may help offset the influence of party to excel committee influence. This is demonstrated most notably not by a comparison of committees in different legislatures but by comparison of two sets of committees in a single legislature: the standing and select committees in the British parliament (Norton 1994: 23). The proceeding of standing committees which is ad hoc and deals with legislative scrutiny are adversarial, with party clashes being essentially an extension of what takes place in the chamber. Select committees, which are permanent and parallel to government departments, have developed a more bipartisan approach with reports frequently being agreed on a unanimous or cross-party basis. Though other variables contribute to the political influence of select committees, permanence appears an independent variable in reducing party hegemony (Drewry 1985; Norton 1993).

The US Congress is organized into permanent subject-matter committees that determine the major decision shaping a draft bill before the full chamber considers it. Committees have broad authority to adopt amendments and redraft bills and it is the committee's version of a bill that is considered by the full chamber. In addition to reviewing and reporting draft bills, these committees also perform the oversight function. In the British parliament, the departmental select committees, which are permanent in nature and parallel government ministries, perform oversight (to examine the expenditure, administration and policy in the principal government departments) function (Benda 1997: 19–21). Permanent committees in major European parliaments are performing the dual function of legislation and oversight.

Ad hoc committees, which are transient in nature, are established to deal with a particular matter (e.g. a bill) and cease to exist after the completion of their designated task followed usually by the submission of a report to the house. Ad hoc or special committees are found alongside permanent committees in most countries. The British parliament relies on ad hoc committees to review draft bills.

Jurisdictions Exclusive jurisdiction enhances the power of a committee. On the contrary, lack of exclusive jurisdiction restricts the range of committee influence (Norton 1994: 25). Committee systems vary in the extent to which their structures parallel that of government ministries. When committee systems are organized in such a way that each ministry has a specific committee that legislates and oversees its policy area, committees are more likely to become a repository of expertise for the legislature and the operations of ministries are likely to be subjected to more careful scrutiny. But when committee structures bear no relationship to the structure of the administrative agencies, policy expertise and administrative oversight tend to wane and it follows that the capacity of the legislature to constrain/influence the government is likely to be less (Olson and Mezey 1991: 15). The US Congress as well as the parliaments of continental Western Europe illustrate the former category while the British bill committees illustrate the latter.

In the British House of Commons, standing committees have exclusive jurisdiction over bills but not over particular sectors of government responsibility. Finance bills will go to standing committee while economic policy will be discussed by a select committee. Moreover, unlike the select committees, standing committees only have jurisdictions when bills are referred to them (Norton 1994: 25).

A system of permanent committees with a defined jurisdiction and with durable membership provides legislators with the essential resources of time and experience to become familiar with the substantive issues within the jurisdiction of committee and help develop expertise in specific policy areas. They also become familiar with the executive agencies and the interest groups involved on their policy matters. If the party system allows the re-election of incumbents, a legislature with permanent committees may become a more experienced body on policy questions than is the cabinet with its constant rounds of ministerial changes (Olson and Mezey 1991: 14–15; Olsen 1994: 141).

Numbers Committee systems also vary with respect to the committee established. The greater the number of committees, the stronger is the committee. As Smith (1980: 167) notes, "the greater the number of small groups, the less amenable to government control they are than a single large one". The establishment of a Liaison Committee/Committee on Committees becomes inevitable to coordinate among different committees to let the committee system work as an integrated whole. The French national assembly has only six committees fixed by the French constitution to consider all bills and legislative proposals in their respective jurisdictions. In the French Assembly, which has got one of the weakest committee systems in Europe, this has been made deliberately to circumscribe the power of committees vis-à-vis the executive. In other countries, the parliaments are free to organize their own set's of committees which can lead to numerical fluctuations depending on the requirement of the time (Mattson and Strøm 1998: 267). In West Germany, for instance, the number of committees dropped from 39 in the first Bundestag to 36 in the second Bundestag due to decline in the number of parliamentary parties (Meny 1993: 204).

Committee size Size can influence the working of legislative committees. As small groups, committees may develop a consensus that breaks down political division. Small committees may take on a life of their own, achieving a large measure of integration (Shaw 1998a: 788). Small committees enhance the chance of specialization and expertise (Strøm 1998: 35). A system with too many committees and too many members overextend legislators and/or create duplication of their work and may be unwieldy. A 1994 study of defense committees in 30 legislatures concluded that "the size of a committee is crucial to their effectiveness" and "the majority of committees are efficient and workable with between 13 and 25 members" (George and Graham 1994: 12–13, 22).

Reasonable continuity of membership is required if small-group norms are to prevail. In some countries, as with British committees on legislation, there is marked discontinuity which runs against the flourishment of committee identity, solidarity and differentiation from the external environment. Moreover, legislators' loyalties and preoccupations external to committees (parties) can stand in the way of integration which is supposed to occur in small groups (Mezey 1998).

The larger the committee, the more it replicates the problems associated with the legislature in plenary sessions. Each member has a voice and vote less likely to affect deliberations and outcomes. The smaller the committee, the greater is the opportunity for detailed and in-depth deliberation (Norton 1994: 23). The French parliament which is generally termed as weak is an exemplar of a legislature with excessively large committees (the largest one with 145 members). Most of the Western European legislatures have small committees.

Parliamentary parties, particularly those in the government, may be expected to try to obtain a majority of committee seats to control both policy products and the allocation of internal power. While we lack comprehensive data from Western European parliaments on committee memberships, the example of Sweden may be instructive: the total number of committee seats is less than is the full membership of the parliament. The smaller the committees, and the fewer the number of committees, the greater the difficulty in arranging a proportional distribution of seats among the parties (Mattson and Strøm 1995: 269).

Multiple membership restriction Restrictions on multiple memberships facilitate specialization and expertise. It is not considered desirable to disperse the specialized knowledge and ability of a member over too many legislative fields. Moreover, if committee meetings are frequently held simultaneously, it can be physically troublesome and pressing for a member to turn up in more than one or two committee meetings (IPU 1986: 629). Specialization and expertise will be reinforced if the committee members concentrate their work on one and only one committee (Mattson and Strøm 1995: 271). In the UK, US, India and Bangladesh members may belong to more than one committee. Norway is the only country with a specialized committee system in which each legislator serves on one, and only one, committee of 12 permanent committees (Strøm 1998: 37). Likewise, few legislators serve on more than one or two specialized committees in Western Europe, though there are few formal restrictions (Damgaard 1995: 311).

Sub-committees Sub-committees may decrease internal decision-making costs while they may cause more conflict in full committee if they bias interest representation. It can exceed the capacity to consider many issues simultaneously (Strøm 1998: 38).

Sub-committees exist in a majority of European parliaments. While obviously sub-committees play a very significant role in Congress, not least since the 1970s, their role in Western European parliaments appears to be more limited. In the US Congress committees specialize in a particular field such as foreign affairs, finance, defense, etc. Committees can also constitute a number of sub-committees that can facilitate further specialization.

The size and diversity of committees' jurisdictions influences the number of sub-committees established in US Congress. The democratization of committee procedures in the 1970s made the sub-committee assignment process a matter of self-selection. On the one hand, the growth of what sometimes was called "sub-committee government" was criticized as fragmenting Congress and complicating the legislative process. On the other hand, the same development created many more forums of activity, each with a more narrow, specialized focus than the standing committees and, in principle at least, each able to look more intensively at a smaller slice of governmental activity (Deering and Smith 1997)

PROCEDURAL ARRANGEMENT

A factor that conditions the working of legislative committees concerns procedure. Committee procedures tell us a lot about the organizational principles of a parliament. Typically standing order/rules of procedure predetermine the ways in which committee conduct their business. These procedures reflect patterns of majority rules and minority rights within parliaments and generate opportunities for legislative outputs. A number of committee procedures will be interpreted in this regard:

1 agenda-setting;
2 committee assignments;
3 chair selection and allocation;
4 committee resources;

5 committee openness;
6 hearings and documents;
7 minority reports;
8 committee stage in deliberation.

Agenda setting The ability to set the legislative agenda is a crucial source of committee power. To be autonomous decision-making bodies, committees must stand free from governmental involvement in their internal affairs (Strøm 1998: 47–48). Agenda-setting power can further be dealt under the following four sub-heads:

1 the committees' right to initiate legislation;
2 their authority to rewrite bills;
3 the control of the committee timetable;
4 their methods of obtaining information: specifically the rights to summon witness and documents.

These formal powers are likely to have an important impact on committees' ability to constrain/influence government independently of such external actors as party leadership, chamber majorities and the government (Feno 1973: xiii).

In the British House of Commons, there is some limited agenda-setting capacity. The departmental select committees can determine their own agenda but they have no responsibility of legislative scrutiny. Standing committees have no such agenda-setting capacity and their deliberations can be, and variously are, limited by guillotine motions. The bills and amendments tabled by the House before the committee become the agenda of the committee. On the floor of the House, except for certain Fridays devoted to private members' bills (accounting for less than 5 percent of the time of the House), the legislative timetable is controlled by the government (Norton 1994: 28). On the other hand, in the US Congress and Italian parliament, two chambers control their own timetable and agenda and can amend government proposal almost without restriction (Strøm 1998: 48).

This agenda-setting capacity combined with specialization through committees, further facilitates the viscosity of legislatures through inducing greater input from outside groups. Olson and Mezey (1991) place particular emphasis on the role of interests groups hypothesizing that parliamentary policy activity will increase as groups themselves become more specialized as they grow in number and if they disagree among themselves. The greater the input from interest groups, the more informed members are and the greater potential to pit alternative knowledge against that of the executive (Norton 1994: 29).

Committee assignments Composition of committee is crucial in securing executive accountability. Usually the opposition members are more inclined than the treasury bench MPs to dig out the irregularities by the government. The chair position of the committee is very significant. He can call all the meetings, influence agenda-setting and vote in the case of a tie on any issue. If all the committee chairmen and majority members (including the ministers) are from the ruling party, it becomes difficult to secure executive accountability against the will of the ruling party. This structural arrangement can enable the government to impose its preference on the opposition members in the committee.

Committee memberships in Western Europe are usually proportional to party size in the parent chamber (Mattson and Strøm 1995: 276), reflecting a consensual rather than majoritarian approach to this potentially contentious issue. Since most democracies in both Western and Central Europe are multiparty, and since governments are usually coalitions, power sharing among the parties has become the typical practice.

In the US, committee members are elected by the House proportional to party strength while the committee members in UK are nominated by the committee of selection supposedly free of influence from the Whip. The membership does not include ministers and members of the opposition front bench (Norton 1998: 699).

In fact as long as ministers sit on committees as members and do not appear before them as witnesses, they will have a natural advantage over backbench members. This will enable ministers to influence the setting of agenda and manipulate the working of committees. As senior party leaders, ministers have the ability to help many government backbenchers achieve their career aspirations. Alternatively they can block them. This may be seen as a deterrent against backbenchers taking a critical view of the working of a particular ministry (Ahmed 1998: 84).

Committees which have small and informed memberships are likely to have a stronger capacity to constrain government than large committees composed of amateur members. Committee members may constitute informed members by virtue of their pre-legislative background or because of a degree of knowledge built up over time through specialization within legislature or through ministerial office. An informed membership is better able than a non-specialist membership to subject bills and government proposals to sustained scrutiny; members with some degree of expertise are more likely to know what to look for and what questions to enquire than members lacking that expertise (Norton 1998: 10). Personal characteristics of the individual members can also affect how committees function. In Central Europe's new parliaments, the gap between members' skills and committee jurisdiction can lead to either lack of attendance or willingness to follow party preferences. Sufficient attendance to meet quorum requirements for committee meetings is a problem (Agh 1998).

It is important in this regard to enquire whether committee members are chosen for their knowledge and interest in the policy arena covered by the committee or not. Though the committee on selection in the British House of Commons is required to have deference to the qualification of members in nominating members of standing committees, service on the committee is seen as a chore and most are nominated to make up members rather than because of an interest in or specialist knowledge of the subject covered by the bill. At other end of the scale, the US Congress stands as the prime example where members seek membership of committees because of a particular interest in the sector usually a constituency-related or group-related interest (Norton 1994: 25). In Western Europe, Denmark serves as a good example of a legislature where there is a relationship between committee responsibilities and the interests (general or group-specific) and background of members (Damgaard 1992: 39–40).

Chair selection and allocation Committee chairs are usually allocated proportionally among the parties, resulting from inter-party negotiations in advance of the formal procedures of officer election. Little, however, is known of these negotiations (Mattson and Strøm 1995: 277–278). With closely balanced coalition-opposition party ratios in Sweden, the coalition parties chair major committees, while the opposition parties are allocated vice-chair positions. In India, committee chairmen are appointed by the presiding officer. He is also ex officio chairman of some committees. Chairs are distributed proportionally among the parties based on their strength in the House. Conventionally the PAC is headed by an opposition MP. In UK, the provision is quite similar to that of India.

In the US, membership on committees and sub-committees varies according to numerical strength of party in the house, with the major party occupying the committee chairmanship and constituting the larger membership (Deering and Smith, cited in Ball and Peters 2000: 188). Chairs are elected by each committee.

Committee resources Clearly the professional committee staffs are eyes and ears for the committee leadership in their relations with the executive (Rosen 1998). The quality and quantity of committee staff tend to reflect the relative significance of the committee system to the legislative institution. For instance where the committees are of central importance (as in the US Congress), the committees are replete with qualified professionals who hold substantial authority and expertise. On the other hand, in legislatures where committees are less consequential, there are few staff who, not surprisingly, perform largely administrative functions (Benda 1997: 25). It is very easy for a government to make parliamentary committees impotent by not allowing them to have sufficient (and qualified) staff for research and support (Martin 1982: 237).

In the UK, committees are supported by staff of the Department of the Clerk of the British Commons. The staff of each select committee is led by the committee clerk. The task of committee staffs is confined to administrative and clerical services. The number of other staff varies. The average departmental select committee has three or four other staff.

Each of the 19 committees in the House of Representatives is authorized by law to hire 18 professional assistants and 12 clerical aides. The minority party in the House controls more than one-third of congressional staffers. In the Senate, committee staff is allocated to the minority party in proportion to the minority members on each committee. Most professional staff aides to committees are well educated. Apart from arranging meetings and hearings and managing the paperwork associated with legislating, committee staffs influence the agenda-setting decisions of investigations, negotiate on behalf of committees and their chairs and work to build coalitions in the committee, on the floor and in conference. Committee staffs also serve an important function of helping Congress "to compete with the expertise of the executive branch and to scrutinize the claims of special interests" (Deering and Smith 1997: 149–152). It can also be presumed that the more extensive the committee documentation, the more active and important is the committee system, on the grounds that legislators are provided with materials which they find useful.

Committee openness Some committee meetings are open, meaning that citizen and press can attend. The US belongs to the category of legislatures that usually open their committee meetings to the public. Committees in the US hold public hearings to gather information on legislation or controversial policy issues or to exercise oversight of the executive branch. Some legislatures including Sweden, Finland and Norway close committee meetings. Others hold a mix of public and private meetings. The UK falls in this category where committee meetings are private during deliberation but public when evidence is taken and committees are in legislative mode (Benda 1997: 23; Strøm 1998). The choice between the public or private nature of committee meetings affects the committee members' informational advantages (Strøm 1998: 42). Open committee meetings allow party leaders to monitor the performance of committee members and to enforce strict party discipline. Open committees enable citizens to follow debate closely on matters of public interest. These meetings become advertising fora for committee members. On the downside, the public and media scrutiny of open meetings may inhibit committee members from speaking as freely or reaching consensus as easily as they might have in closed meetings (Benda 1997: 23).

Hearings and documents Hearings constitute a significant oversight mechanism. Hearings are sessions in which committees or sub-committees receive testimony from witnesses, administration officials, interest group representatives, independent experts, civil society and constituents. Hearings often assist committees in gathering information about policy problems and solutions but they can also serve as platforms to publicize a cause. Thus while hearings have less direct impact on the content of legislation, they can be important tools in building majority coalitions for or against legislation (Smith and Deerings 1997: 158). In parliaments with a long tradition of conducting public hearings this reflects a desire for fuller information and enhanced administrative accountability (Shaw 1998).

Committee hearings may be conducted privately or be open to the public. The choice carries major implications for oversight. Private (closed) hearings have the potential to increase intra-party and inter-party cooperation and minimize government embarrassment. Hearings held out public view may foster substantive policy changes over political competition. However, closed hearings reduce transparency and deprive the media and the public of an important opportunity to engage in the process of policy development and implementation (Hamilton 1999). Open hearings by contrast may increase political incentive for executive oversight. From the US perspective, "at least with oversight hearings open to public view, members could envision the possibility of reaping some favorable publicity in recompense for their efforts" (Bach 2000: 8).

In fact, probably the most intensive and regular oversight takes place during the course of the hearings on the President's annual budget proposals that the House and Senate Appropriations Committees and their sub-committees in the US conduct each year. The purpose of these hearings is to inquire whether the President's budget requests for specific departments, agencies, programs and activities are justified, or whether Congress should provide larger or smaller sums instead. Congressional committees and sub-committees have the authority to issue subpoenas requiring those officials to appear at committee hearings and to bring with them documents the committee wishes to examine. In the most extreme cases, officials can be charged with contempt of Congress if they fail to comply with congressional subpoenas (Bach 2000: 12).

Information about and from the government is basic to both the autonomy and expertise of committees. Parliaments can only play a distinctive and deliberative role if they can independently obtain information and expertise from the government. An alternative method of gathering information is by calling for documents from private or public institutions or citizens. The right is circumscribed when a committee lacks authority to demand documents and/or lacks the means to punish the violators. It is also restricted when the set of persons and institutions obliged to disclose documents is limited (Mattson and Strøm 1995: 293–295).

Minority reports The ability of a committee minority to submit its own statement on proposed public policy varies among Western parliaments, but is associated with the measures of committee autonomy. Minority reports can serve as effective vehicles of information to the floor. Where minority reports are allowed, the floor may gain either several policy options or an assurance that the report presents a cross-partisan consensus (Mattson and Strøm 1995: 283, 301; Agh 1998). Among the major European countries, parliaments that do not permit minorities to submit reports include Denmark, France, Ireland and the UK. In these parliaments the majority party thus has important prerogatives regarding agenda control and legislative initiatives (Döring 1995; Mattson 1995). In legislative committees in Bangladesh, India and the US, minority dissent is included in a single committee report. The plenary considers committee recommendations with the original bill.

Committee stage in deliberation The possibilities that committees can exercise independent policy judgement is increased if committees act on legislation prior to substantive floor consideration. Continental European parliaments, contrasted with the Westminster model, usually provide for committee consideration prior to floor debate (Mattson and Strøm 1995: 284; Döring 1995: 233–235). This trait is associated with committee initiation and amendment powers (Mattson and Strøm 1995: 301).

In countries such as India, Bangladesh and the UK where a bill is first debated by the House before it is referred to a committee, the debate serves the purpose of making clear the general principles of the bill. Here the task of committee is to relieve the house of all question of detail by minute scrutiny of both the form and substances of every clause of the bill. Although they can amend a bill, its scope is limited by the fact that no amendment conflicting with the main purpose and principles of the bill set out earlier by the house is likely to be admissible. Hence, committees have relatively restricted power (IPU 1986: 961–962).

There is a clear relationship between the timing of committee consideration of legislation and the strength of committees. Strong committees are associated with plenary consideration of bills. Of the ten legislatures in the work of Malcolm Shaw (1979), those which referred bills to committee prior to floor debate were usually those which appeared to have strong committees and those which had floor debates before committee deliberation were those ranked further down the scale in terms of committee effect. The reasons for the relationship are simply put by Shaw:

> If a committee can consider a bill before it is taken up to the floor, the chances of the committees influencing or determining the outcomes tends to be greater than when the lines of battle have been predetermined in plenary meetings.
>
> (Shaw 1979: 417)

Conclusion

The earlier discussion convinces us that strong parliaments are a prerequisite to strong committees. The capability of parliaments and parliamentary committees to constrain government is largely determined by broader politico-institutional, socio-economic and cultural variables. However, to focus exclusively on those variables results in a flawed portrait of parliamentary strength and discounts their capacity to have some independent impact on outcome. That impact may be modest but it exists and varies from parliament to parliament (Norton 1998a: 205).

The politico-constitutional arrangement of a polity goes a long way to determine the degree of parliament and parliamentary committee strength. In a Westminster model, in terms of legislative–executive relations, the separation of powers is absent, the tendency being for political executives to operate within legislature and to lead it. The typical consequence has been strong executives and weak legislatures and legislative committees (Shaw 1979). On the contrary, the separation of power in presidential systems, as in the US, creates a legislature that is independent and usually designed to serve as a check and balance on the executive branch. Presidential systems therefore possess stronger legislatures and legislative committees. Even parliaments in a parliamentary system have got the potentials of being strong parliaments and parliamentary committee system if the configuration of governments is coalition/minority by nature. Here lack of party control over the legislatures stems from multipartism. This is exampled by a good number of continental European legislatures. Even in the separation of power system as in the US presidential system, where party domination is inherently weak, if the same party constituted a majority in several elected bodies (presidency, Congress or Senate), the checks and balances between the different bodies can become less effective and function like a legislature in a parliamentary system.

In a parliamentary system of Westminster type combined with single-party control of committees, the committees tend to be weak whether they are predominantly permanent, specialized type and rich resourced as in Canada and Japan, or whether they consist of a mixture of ad hoc and permanent committees with ad hoc committees playing a major role as in Britain and India (Shaw 1979: 398–399).

Structural and procedural committee attributes cannot override the particular type of political environment within which the committees operate. Various indicators lead one to expect a strong committee system in the Japanese Diet. Japanese committees are permanent whose jurisdiction parallel the executive departments, specialized, generously staffed and organized along the lines of the US Congressional committee system. However, Congress is recognized as having the most powerful committee system in the world, whereas the Diet has one of the weakest. Most committee work in the Diet appears to be futile. Baerwald (1979) accounts for it by enumerating the pre-legislative stages in policy formulation in Japan. A proposed bill is usually drafted by the appropriate ministry and then considered by the party groups, the party leaders, the government and the cabinet. Only after this process is the bill thoroughly debated in the Diet and redrafted to suit all the divergent forces and factions making up the executive and only then it is referred to committee. By the time the bill reaches a standing committee it has been subjected to so many accommodations that it is unthinkable for the committee where the government has a disciplined majority to alter it (Shaw 1998; Hazan 2001). Hence, agenda-setting (committee stage of deliberation is a part of agenda-setting) power of the parliament and parliamentary committees is a crucial internal factor which strives to determine the strength of committees to constrain the executive.

Based on the preceding analysis the concluding remarks of this chapter can be encapsulated by Shaw (1979: 417) who has developed a multivariant factor-dependent structure, which can help assessing the relative strength and weakness of a committee system.

1 Presidential system + absence of party control + committee before floor = strong committee.
2 Parliamentary system (Continental) + absence of party control + committee before floor = strong committee.

3 Parliamentary system (Westminster) + single-party control + committee after floor = weak committee.

In essence, after taking the politico-social environment of parliamentary committees into account the specific structural and procedural attributes of committees themselves can be considered to weigh the capability of parliamentary committees to call the government into account. It is only at this point that the size, membership, permanence, secrecy, finance, staff, etc. of committees should receive attention.

This does not imply that the internal features of committee strength are insignificant and superfluous. Given a congenial socio-political context, permanent small-size specialized committees paralleling the government ministries having considerable agenda-setting power and broader jurisdiction of both legislation and oversight can play a complementary role to make a legislature strong enough to hold the government to account. In fact, a strong legislature is a prerequisite to a strong committee system and vice versa.

The following three chapters which are more applied (Chapters 5–7) thoroughly investigate the role of parliament and parliamentary committees in

Table: 4.1 Intra-institutional Features of Committee Strength (Continuum)

Features	*Strong committees*	*Weak committees*
Number	Flexible and contingent	Rigid and fixed by constitution/statute
Agenda setting	Legislature/committee sets its own agenda	Government set agenda
Size	Small	Larger
Tenure	Permanent	Ad hoc
Jurisdiction	Committees parallel to government departments	Committees don't replicate government departments
Scope of function	Broad (perform both law-making and oversight functions)	Narrow, confine either to law-making or oversight function
Evidence-taking (hearings)	Yes	No
Chair	Proportional	Majoritarian
Ministers as member of committees	No	Yes
Committee stage in deliberation	Before plenary	After plenary
Resources	Rich	Poor
Right to summon witness	Yes	No
Right to request documents from the government	Yes	No
Minority report	Allowed	No
Consideration of budget and committee involvement	Yes	No

Source: Prepared by the author.

Bangladesh, India and Sri Lanka respectively in holding the government accountable in the light of the of the theoretical lens developed in the previous chapters backed by primary and secondary data. All the three case studies have common features in terms of chapter organization. Each chapter is organized into three major sections: the parliament in its political context, historical development of parliamentary committees and formal institutional arrangements of committee system and its real-world ability to hold the government to account.

5 Parliamentary control and government accountability in Bangladesh

The role of parliamentary committees

This chapter is organized into four major sections. With a view to assessing the extent to which the external environment has been congenial for the parliament to thrive, the first delineates the broader context of the Bangladesh parliament within which it works. The second section reviews the historical accounts of the development of parliamentary committee system in Bangladesh from its inception to date. This is essential in order to determine the trajectory of committees' development and performance with regard to holding the government accountable for its performance and checking the government on the right track, which might have consequences for the functioning of the present committees. The evolution of committees has been depicted systematically in tune with the tenure of different (*Jatiya Sangsad* – Bengali name of the parliament in Bangladesh) JSs (first JS, second JS and so on). This section is followed by a brief sketch of the institutional arrangements of the committee system in Bangladesh to review whether the prevailing rules of the committees are in conformity with the features of a strong committee system or not. The fourth section analyzes the extent to which the formal arrangements of the committee system in Bangladesh have been able to ensure government accountability based on the empirical data generated from numerous sources.

Bangladesh parliament in its political context

Bangladesh is a South Asian nation which underwent approximately 200 years (1757–1947) of prolonged colonial rule by the British and later 24 years (1947–1971) of "internal colonial" rule by Pakistan. The history of politics in Pakistan was the history of military and bureaucratic domination where democracy never got a fair chance to thrive due mainly to the failure of the political leadership.

Bangladesh has a chequered history of politics too. Immediately after the independence in 1971, Bangladesh started well with a parliamentary system of government but could not last long in the wake of authoritarian rule and military intervention in politics. The parliament in Bangladesh did not have a natural growth for a long time; it in fact, remained suspended and or abolished for a substantial period of time largely due to military intervention in politics.

Between 1975 and 1990, the country remained under absolute military rule for eight years.

The stability of the parliament had been marred from the beginning. None but the seventh JS in the post-independent Bangladesh, including the fifth one, which was constituted after a free and fair election, completed its full duration (see Appendix, Table A2.1 for details) due to military intervention, political turbulence and confrontational politics between the party in power and the opposition.

Bangladesh is a multiparty parliamentary democracy. It is a unitary state. There is a unicameral parliament in Bangladesh which is composed of 300 members directly elected for five-year terms from single-member constituencies on the basis of adult franchise and additional 30 female members appointed by the assembly itself (the constitutional amendment reserving 30 seats for women over and above the 300 regular parliament seats expired in May 2001. However, the fourteenth amendment to the constitution passed in the eighth parliament on May 16, 2004 provided for 45 reserved seats for women to be elected by the 300 members of the parliament and their distribution among the political parties proportionally based on their representation in the House for the next ten years). Cabinet is selected by the prime minister and appointed by the president. The government remains in office as long as it enjoys the confidence of the parliament. The JS selects, for five-year term, a president to serve as ceremonial head of state. But with the thirteenth amendment to the constitution, the president's role becomes significant at times when parliament is dissolved and a caretaker government is installed to supervise the elections. The chief adviser and his/her colleagues remain responsible to the president during their interim period of stay in power. Generally speaking, the president plays into the hands of the ruling regime. Refusing to do that means they leave the presidency. The unceremonial exit of former president Badoruzzoha Chowdhury (in 2002) responding to a call by the BNP parliamentary party is a glaring example of the captivity of the presidency to the incumbent government in Bangladesh.

Most of the survey respondents (for questionnaire survey result through this chapter, see Appendix, Table A1.1) disagreed (90 percent) with the statement that institutionally committees are much weaker in parliamentary systems than in presidential systems. The mean score is 0.5 only. The respondents opined that notwithstanding the parliamentary system reintroduced in Bangladesh in 1991, parliament could not contribute significantly to the emergence of a strong parliament and parliamentary committee system. However, they were not in favor of switching the political system from parliamentary system to the presidential one. Within the existing parliamentary system, committees could be made stronger and more effective, if the confrontational political culture mainly revolving around the two top leaders of the two major political parties in Bangladesh could be transformed to a consensus one by bringing some institutional changes that leave some space for the opposition political parties to act, they stressed.

On the question of the introduction of an upper chamber and the utility of Upper House committees in Bangladesh parliament in a bid to make the executive accountable, only 20 percent of the respondents answered in the positive. The majority of respondents opposed the proposal and warned of its devastating consequences. Given the confrontational political culture in Bangladesh, they maintained that the introduction of a second chamber will make things further complicated and deteriorated. The instrument of checks and balances will ultimately result in stalemate and political instability. Those who support the statement had their own argument. They think that power and authority in Bangladesh are highly centralized and checks and balances between different branches of government are inadequate. The introduction of a second chamber can moderate the political race between the two major parties in Bangladesh and create some political space for the opposition parties. If one party has majority in one chamber and another chamber is dominated by another party, political parties must have to compromise in order to avoid political deadlock and instability. This will take time to get institutionalized but over time political parties will learn to compromise and share power with rival parties.

Bangladesh has a written constitution. Any proposal to amend any major article of the constitution in Bangladesh requires not only the vote of two-thirds majority of members in the parliament but must also be vetted in a national referendum. The plurality electoral system has in fact helped most of the governments in Bangladesh to form governments based on manufactured majority. The first-past-the-post (FPTP) electoral system permitted the BNP (Bangladesh Nationalist Party) in 1991 with 31 percent of the popular vote, BAL (Bangladesh Awami League) and its alliance in 1996 with 38 percent and BNP and its alliance with 57 percent (BNP alone 41 percent) of the popular vote to form government. The prevailing electoral system has made the political game extremely competitive and undermined the representation of the electorates to the parliament. Of note, the Bangladesh Election Commission, which is a constitutional body, conducts the national parliamentary elections under the supervision of Caretaker Government. There are no rules to regulate party funding for elections. Complaints of irregular fund-raising and expenditure are reported frequently in the local media.

The constitution in Bangladesh provides for judicial review of legislative actions, thereby imposing some checks on the arbitrary actions of the legislature and or the government that are inconsistent with the provision of the constitution. The Supreme Court has shown an increasing readiness to issue orders requiring the government to come before it and justify its actions. However, the Supreme Court is barred to review money bills.

Constitutionally, the position of prime minister is an extremely powerful one in Bangladesh. After 1990, the levels and degrees of control enjoyed by the president were simply transferred without significant tuning to the prime minister. In a parliamentary form of government, ministers have a direct collective responsibility to parliament. This is absent in Bangladesh, instead ministers merely serve to aid and advise the prime minister and their continuity as ministers is dependent upon the good will of the prime minister. Moreover, the centralization of power is further accentuated by the placement of numerous vital portfolios and agencies such as Defense, Establishment, Energy and Mineral Resources, Armed Force Division and so on directly under the prime minister (World Bank 1996: 51, 105).

In fact the prime minister in Bangladesh has become too powerful to be called to account by any formal political institution but the people in the next election. The prime minister's office remains immune from oversight by any parliamentary committee. He/she never attends any meeting of standing committees on vital ministries where she is an ex officio member. In fact, it is the prime minister who approves the final list of committee members and chairmen before it is presented to the House.

Prime ministers had been seen interfering in the operations of the Standing Committee on several occasions. For instance, the *Daily Star* reported (January 5, 2001) that the original committee report prepared in 1997 on the Magurchara gas field blowout was not submitted to the Parliamentary Committee on Energy at the suggestion of the former Prime Minister Sheikh Hasina. She was in charge of the energy portfolio. The officials of the US oil company Unocal (previously Occidental) responsible for the blowout, incurring huge financial and environmental loss for the country, did not appear before the committee, which was backed by the former prime minister. Moreover, the immediate past Prime Minister Khaleda Zia had been seen holding talks with chairmen of different committees and instructing them not to criticize the minister and deliberate corruption-related issues in the committee meetings, which could damage the images of the government. For instance, a three-member sub-committee was formed in January 2004 to probe the allegations of corruption in import and distribution of CNG (Concentrated Natural Gas) auto-rickshaws against Communications Minister Barrister Nazmul Huda and was asked to submit its report in 30 days (*Prathom Alo*, January 8, 2004). The report never came out public and this was largely believed to be at the intervention of the prime minister.

Under the current constitution, strong ties of party loyalty make it unlikely that parliament will become an effective instrument of holding the executive to account. Article 70 of the constitution restricts floor crossing and prescribes a delegate role for the MP. For instance, an MP who is elected as a nominee of a particular party cannot vote against his/her own party in the parliament nor can he/she abstain from voting defying party directives. Those who fail to comply with party decisions risk losing membership of the parliament (GOPRB 1996: 54–55). This provision undoubtedly circumscribes the autonomy and free spirit of the individual members.

Committee members were asked about the anti-defection law and its impact on the behavior of MPs attending committee sessions. 51 percent of the respondents completely agree that the existing floor crossing article in its current shape circumscribes the individual freedom of MPs and it certainly has an impact on the functioning of committee too. On the issue of floor crossing, the mean score of the respondents is 2.5 which indicates that majority of the respondents are against the prevailing constitutional provision of floor crossing. Major opposition political parties in Bangladesh in the 1990s had boycotted the parliament for a long time. A considerable proportion of the opposition MPs, due to this article, could neither ventilate their discontent with the leadership of their parties nor could they attend the plenary sessions by taking risk of losing the membership. Moreover, many treasury bench MPs would like to criticize the wrongdoings of government in the parliament if the article were not there. However, the majority of the respondents were of the view that the floor crossing article should be there and apply exclusively to the vote of no-confidence which can ensure their individual autonomy and sustain political stability simultaneously.

An analysis of the view of respondents concerning the relationship between the control of their parties over them and the level of committee strength, 80 percent hold that there is a strong correlation between these two variables. However, most of the respondents belonging to treasury bench think that in Bangladesh, the influence of party over the committee member is not substantial and they are free to work in committee on their personal capacities without fear or favor. The respondents from the opposition party observe that although committee sessions are more informal and cordial, committee members get sharply divided on major policy issues and corruption cases. They feel that the presence of the minister concerned as a committee member has an adverse impact on the behavior of government backbenchers in the committee. The government backbenchers who constitute the majority membership of parliamentary committees in Bangladesh may find it risky for their future career development to call a minister who is senior to him in party hierarchy to account.

Constitutionally the parliament is required to meet within 60 days from the previous session. This provision attests that the parliament has ample scope to meet more frequently and turn itself into a forum for debate and deliberation. But three major obstacles to running the plenary session smoothly are: constant boycott of the parliamentary proceedings by the main opposition, lack of quorum and the partisan role of the Speaker.

The political ritual of boycotting parliamentary sessions has gained momentum since 1991. All the major parties boycotted parliament while they were in the opposition sometimes for months, claiming that they had hardly any opportunity to engage in real debate on legislative and national issues. Parliament thus becomes a rubber stamp agency in the absence of the main opposition to approve government proposals without any obstacle. Furthermore, whenever they were present in the plenary sessions, they conceded to frequent walkouts sometimes on silly and mundane issues.

Quorum crisis is a recurrent phenomenon in the Bangladesh parliament which inflicts a huge financial wastage on the exchequer. In its 322 workdays so far (up to February 28, 2006), the eighth JS has only once witnessed the presence of 60 legislators – the minimum number required to begin a sitting on schedule. Parliament Watch, the database of Transparency International Bangladesh (TIB 2003, 2004, 2005) reveals such delays in 240 workdays (only one began on time in 14 sessions – first through fourteenth) has cost the nation about BDT 144.8 million (US$2.07 million) wasting 9554 minutes. Each minute of session requires an estimated spending of BDT 15,000 (US$214).

The Speakers of the parliaments have proved themselves as party agents rather than neutral guardians of the House. Formally, the Speaker is not required to resign from the party which nominates him once he assumes the office of Speaker. The Speaker of the House can be removed by a motion of simple majority, which has made the Speaker extremely vulnerable to the ruling party. This has compelled the Speaker to shake off his neutrality and play in favor of the ruling regime. The prime ministers in the 1990s have been seen many times to dictate and run the House after their will.

A strong but disciplined opposition is a prerequisite for the effective functioning of a parliamentary democracy. Most of the parliaments except the fifth and the seventh (see Appendix, Table A2.1 for detail) in the post-independence Bangladesh have been monopolized by a single party which in fact have encouraged and enabled the ruling regimes to use the parliament as a party agency rather than a forum for public deliberation and giving accounts for their actions. However, more competitive parliaments like the fifth and seventh in terms of partisan composition did not also make them more significant policy contributors. This paradox requires further clarification.

The competition for power between the two major parties has been too stiff to keep the parliament running and complete its full term let alone be a policy contributor. In the political arena, the two major parties have hardly been seen to compromise on significant national issues. The relationship between the ruling party and the opposition is characterized by a high degree of animosity and conflict. The major two parties abhor and demonize each other and the chiefs of these parties have not even been on speaking terms with each other since the restoration of democratic governance in Bangladesh in 1991. Perhaps Evans (2001: 86) is right when he states "the acrimonious relationship between the two ladies – Prime minister Khaleda Zia and the BAL leader Sheikh Hasina continues to pose the most acute danger to the political stability in Bangladesh". Some respondents attribute this troubled relationship between the two to the hereditary democracy in Bangladesh. The opposition are seldom allowed to ventilate their grievances and opinion in the plenary sessions, which in turn provoke them to stage frequent walkouts or boycott the JS, and organize street protests (Ahmed 1997b: 90).

Due to the lack of compromise between the two contending parties in Bangladesh, within two years (1995–1996) 173 days *hartal* (strike) was observed by the opposition party causing perpetual trauma to the economy and daily life of Bangladesh. Moreover, from 1996 to 2003, more than 100 days *hartal* was observed by the main opposition party in Bangladesh. According to a press statement given by a former finance minister, each day's *hartal* incurs an estimated loss of BDT 386 crores (US$67 million) (*Daily Star*, September 29, 2003). A UNDP (2005: 2) study finds that the average cost of *hartals* to the economy during the 1990s is 3 to 4 percent of GDP (roughly estimated). A glaring and recent instance of the warring relationships between the government and the opposition in Bangladesh parliament is the latter's boycott of the 48th Commonwealth Parliamentary Association (CPA) conference held in Dhaka (October 4–11, 2003) which is unprecedented in 91 years history of CPA.

When asked about the role of opposition in holding the government accountable, an overwhelming 100 percent of respondents maintained that a strong but disciplined opposition was at the heart of parliament and parliamentary committees. They believe that it is the opposition in the parliament who has a natural tendency to keep a watchful eye on the functioning of the government and criticize the government whenever it gets a chance to do so and keeps it on its toes. Committee sessions become lively with the presence of the opposition members. There was very strong opposition (see Appendix, Table A2.1 for details) in the last three parliaments (fifth, seventh and eighth). They opined that there must be some sort of agreement and consensus between the government and the opposition on nationally significant matters such as resolving the ethnic conflicts in Chittagong Hill Tracks (CHT), banning student politics at educational institutions, tackling the rise of militant religious extremism and so on. The governing party/coalitions must be accommodative and should have the willingness to provide political space for the opposition to run its activities.

Parliament is the formal supreme law-making institution in Bangladesh. Nevertheless, government monopolizes the legislative process from initiation to approval in Bangladesh. Prior to the present time the government sponsored bills in the parliament, all the bills/ordinances are approved by the cabinet. All bills passed by the JS since the early 1990s have been initiated by the government (see Appendix, Table A2.2 for details). According to the Rules, government business shall take precedence everyday except Thursday when private members' business shall have priority. In Bangladesh, out of over 300 bills submitted to the JS by private members, only 6 private members' (all from treasury bench MPs) bills have been passed since independence in 1971 (see Appendix, Table A2.2 for details).There exists no provision in the Rules for opposition day as one can find in many established democracies. Most of the amendments on bills moved by the opposition in JSs were also rejected along party lines (Ahmed 2003: 65).

Moreover, the executive government in Bangladesh has established and continued its dominance over the legislative process by promulgating ordinances. Governments frequently (see Appendix, Table A2.4 for details) resorted to this emergency law-making i.e. advising the president to promulgate ordinances (when the JS is not in session or when it stands dissolved) to deal with politically sensitive and controversial bills. The role of the JS thus remained limited to validating them in the actual sense. Nearly 35 percent of the laws passed by the fifth JS were originally introduced as ordinances. Comparatively speaking, the first JS passed the maximum number of ordinance-turned bills (53.3 percent), while the second JS enacted less ordinance-turned bills than the other JSs with the single exception of the seventh JS which mostly followed a routine process of law-making. Out of a total of 190 bills passed by the seventh JS, only five (2.6 percent) owed their origin as ordinances (Ahmed 2003). By promulgating ordinances the ruling government likes to get the bills passed in a hurried manner without giving enough time to the opposition to criticize. This mode of law-making also signals to the government backbenchers to toe the party line.

One of the important ways parliaments can hope to influence legislation is by having bills thoroughly scrutinized in committees. In Bangladesh, although the Rules empower the standing committees on ministries (SCMs) to scrutinize bills and other resolutions moved in the House, rarely did any bill have a committee-stage hearing (see Appendix, Table A2.2 for details). Of the total laws enacted by the fifth JS, only eight were scrutinized by committees. However the seventh JS was exceptional case in this respect. All bills passed by the seventh JS have had a committee stage hearing. However, in the eighth JS, the majority of bills have been passed without any committee-level scrutiny chiefly because of the belated (20 months) formation of committees on ministries.

It can be observed from the preceding analysis that the parliament in Bangladesh is not a law-making/policy-making rather than a bill-approving body. In sum, formally and practically, the parliament of Bangladesh is weak and it does in no way dominate over the executive. This can further be supported by a comparative study conducted by Pennings (2003) on the constitutional control of the executive in 45 parliamentary democracies including Bangladesh, India and Sri Lanka.

All the respondents (100 percent, with a mean score 4) were of the view that a strong parliament is a prerequisite for a strong committee system and vice versa. They admit that within the prevailing political context, parliament is very weak vis-à-vis the executive and so is the parliamentary committee system. The current parliament is characterized by a strong government (which has a two-third majority in the parliament) and a weak opposition. Over time since 1991, the parliament has lost its reputation as a prime political institution. It has become an institution of regime maintenance and failed to hold the executive accountable. The respondents reported that the committees started well in the fifth JS and committees were formed immediately after the inauguration of the new parliament and the opposition continued to attend committee sessions despite boycotting the House. They apparently played some role in making the government behave. From the seventh JS onward, due to failure of the two

Table 5.1 Constitutional strength of parliament vis-à-vis government in three selected South Asian democracies

Country	*Constitutional control*	*Consensus democracy*	*Presidentialism*	*New democracy*	*Rigid constitution*
Bangladesh	0.33	0.17	0.17	1	0.67
India	0.33	0.33	0.5	0.5	0.5
Sri Lanka	0.17	0.33	1	0.5	0.67

Source: Pennings (2003: 552–553).

Notes
Constitutional control: the higher the score, the more constraints are put on governments. Consensus democracy: the higher the score, the higher the level of consensus democracy. Presidentialism: the higher the score, the more power are assigned to the president. New democracy: the higher the score, the newer a democracy. Rigid constitution: the higher the score, the more rigid a constitution. Highest score – 1, lowest score – 0

major political parties to reach a consensus to bring about some institutional changes to the committee system to make it more functional, committees lost their earlier charms and became a lackluster institution. Thus the parliamentary committee system fails to contribute significantly to transform the parliament as a strong institution to check the power of the executive.

Development of parliamentary committees in Bangladesh

Although the Rules of Procedures framed by the first JS provided for the setting up of an elaborate network of committees including the standing committees on Ministries (SCMs), these were mostly honored in the breach (Ahmed 2003: 131). In the first JS, there were only 14 standing committees (permanent) including a PAC and only a few committees on non-important bills. Only one report on the rules of procedures was submitted and accepted during the fifth session of the first JS during Mujib regime (Choudhury 1994: 122). Though PAC was formed, it was chaired by a treasury bench member. In the first parliament PAC met only three times between 1973 and 1975 and did not produce any report. What was even worse, not only did the public officials outnumber the MPs in attendance but they also played a dominant role in the deliberations of the PAC while members used to remain silent (Huq 1989: 40). Again, unlike other democratic countries Comptroller and Auditor General (CAG)[1] had been made responsible to the president instead of parliament. The rules of procedure provided the provision that the minister relating to a particular committee would be ex officio chairman of the ministerial committees and the scope of operations was formally confined to the examination of bills and legislative affairs (Halim 1998: 412–414).

In the second JS, the initiative was taken to advance and activate the committee system. The House established seven standing committees, a few select committees on non-important bills and 36 ministerial committees (which was formed in March 1980, a few months after the British House of Commons pioneered the departmentally-related select committees) which, were to be chaired by the ministers concerned, including the technocrat ministers. The chair was not under any obligations to regularly convene meetings of committees. The Rules were amended in June 1981 requiring each SCM to meet at least once a month. The second JS made another important modification in the Rules specifying that technocrat ministers be not allowed to head different SCMs. Many DPCs set by the second JS scrutinized a large number of bills. But, none of these committees submitted their report to the House. Two crucial factors have been identified by Ahmed (2002: 133) influencing the creation of an elaborate network of committees by the second JS (and also the fifth). One was the presence of a sizable number of opposition MPs in it (one-quarter of the total MPs belonged to the opposition). Second, and perhaps more importantly, committees provided an important institutional means for accommodating a large number of government backbenchers who could not be accommodated in the cabinet despite enlarging its size.

The second JS set up the PAC on the April 30, 1979. However, for nearly one year, it remained virtually inactive; it held only one meeting deliberating over procedural matters. The PAC was initially chaired by a treasury bench member, who was later replaced by an opposition senior member. Within a year the PAC held a total of nine meetings. An Estimate Committee was also formed for the first time with a treasury member as the chairman.

The third JS only had standing committees and no ministerial committees. During the martial law regime of Ershad an ad hoc PAC prepared three reports. The fourth JS set up an impressive committee system. At the first session, eight standing committees, a few select committees and 32 ministerial committees with similar procedures as under Zia's system were formed. Interestingly the so-called fourth parliament produced as many as five reports – two on PAC, one each on Committee on Estimates, Committee on Public Undertakings and Committee on Governmental Assurance (Aminuzzaman 1993: 58). The fourth parliamentary elections were boycotted by all major political parties amid widespread rigging and low voter turnout (10–15 percent). The military ruler's party got an absolute majority of 252 seats. To give the parliament some sort of legitimacy as well as keeping a large number of government backbenchers busy, the committee system was activated. The PAC seemed to be active during the fourth JS. It was formed with an opposition (so called) MP as it chairman. The first report prepared by the PAC included 635 objections out of which 277 were resolved and the committee demanded reports from the relevant department about the rest of the objections. Two reports sent by the House were discussed and submitted during the fourth parliament (Chouhury 1994: 142).

The initial lead in broadening the scope of activities of the ministerial and financial committees was taken by the members of the fifth parliament. The fifth JS was more legitimate and representative than the earlier JSs because it was elected through a free and fair election and was represented by a strong opposition (see Appendix, Table A2.1). Hence, the opposition, the government backbenchers and the civil society pressed the government hard to form the parliamentary committees as early as possible and demanded the strengthening and rationalization of the committee system to make government accountable.

Until, the changes made in the Rules of Procedure in February 1992, the main functions of the ministerial committees were confined to examining bills and other matters referred to by the parliament. Following the amendment of the Rules of Procedure, it could review the works relating to a ministry, which fall within its jurisdiction, enquire into any activity, irregularity or serious complaints in respect of the ministry and make recommendations. Besides, parliamentary committees are required to meet at least once in a month, failing which the Speaker can direct the secretary to convene a meeting of the defaulting committee. Like the oversight committees, the two main financial committees – the Public Accounts Committee (PAC) the Committee on Public Undertakings (COPU) have also been granted more permissive powers. They are empowered to report to parliament on the remedy of the irregularities and lapses of public bodies (Ahmed 1998a: 77). This could be seen an important departure from the past which might set the Bangladesh parliament apart from other legislatures in the region. All committees were headed by the treasury bench MPs and ministers. However, several opposition MPs in the fifth JS held chair positions of a number of sub-committees.

The government made inordinate delays and actually formed committees unilaterally after lapse of two years' time of the seventh JS. The ruling party never consulted BNP, the biggest opposition party in the parliament prior to forming the standing committees. The PAC was still chaired by a government backbencher; CAG was still in the amputated position.[2] Following the revision of Rules of Procedure in June 1997, each ministerial committee was headed by a government backbencher. However a minister was still an ex officio member of the relevant ministerial committee. Out of the 35 chairmen of ministerial committees in the seventh JS, 34 belonged to the ruling party and one to its coalition partner. Like its counterpart in the fifth JS, the PAC of the seventh JS also appeared to be very active. It devised some different, albeit important, ways of working. For example, unlike its predecessors that mostly examined the CAG reports that were more than a decade old, the PAC of the seventh JS examined both current and old reports. Moreover, following the recommendations in the PAC's third report, the office of CAG has created performance audit cell and introduced "value for money" audit on a selective basis. Some public organizations have already adopted this new type of auditing. This can be seen as a significant improvement over the past.

The committees in the eighth JS were also constituted in a unilateral manner after consensus dialogue between the treasury bench and the opposition over the composition of the committees failed. The whole process of unilateral formation of standing committees by the government came to an end in more than 20 months after the newly elected parliament kicked off leaving the main opposition (BAL) slots blank in a hurried manner. None from the opposition bench was appointed chair of any committees. The BAL decided not to send their nominees for inclusion in the committees formed since May 2003 onward to protest the denial of its demand for allocation of committee chairs according to proportional representation in the House by the government. External pressures (UNDP, Donor Consortium, visiting foreign parliamentary groups) were substantial behind the formation of these committees. At one stage, the UNDP warned the government to withdraw its funding from the ongoing project titled "Strengthening Parliamentary Democracy". Most of the committees started working without the participation of the opposition members. Since the formation of committees in July 2003, over 100 standing committee meetings had been held without the participation of the main opposition MPs (*Daily Star*, October 27, 2003). This is unprecedented in a functioning democracy. Later, the main opposition MPs have been included in the committees and they have been participating in different committee meetings since November 2004, 16 months after the formation of the committees without the main opposition.

Institutional arrangements of committee system in Bangladesh and its real-world implications

Parliamentary committees in Bangladesh derive their origin to and gain legitimacy from the constitution. Article 76 of the constitution provides the basis of the parliamentary committee system in Bangladesh for such enforcement. The constitution makes it mandatory for the parliament to set up a Public Accounts Committee (PAC) and a Privileges Committee (PC) and empowers it to constitute as many standing committees as it considers necessary (GPROB 1996: 62–63). Rules of Procedure of the parliament are the other major source of institutional rules to keep the vehicle of committee in motion. Appointment, term of office, functions and the main lines of procedure for conducting business of the committee are regulated under the Rules of Procedure and the directions by the Speaker issued under those rules (BJS 1997).

Typology of committees (tenure, number and size)

There are two major types of committee in the Bangladesh parliament.

Standing committees

These committees are usually appointed by the House/the Speaker for the full term of the parliament. Currently, the Bangladesh parliament has 50 standing committees (39 ministerial committees, three financial committees, eight other committees). Committee members range from eight to 15. Each ministerial committee (39) consists of ten members. The Public Accounts Committee (PAC), Committee on Public Undertakings (COPU), Business Advisory Committee are composed of 15 members while Committee on Government Assurance is composed of eight members and House Committee on Rules of Procedure has 12 members.

Select committees/special committees

They are ad hoc bodies and cease to exist as soon their job is done. These committees meet the demand of the emergency situation. For instance, due to the delay in the formation of different ministerial committees until November 16, 1997, in the seventh JS, a special committee was constituted temporarily. All the bills introduced in the House were sent to this special committee appointed by the House for the purpose. The only one special committee ceased in the seventh parliament after the establishment of ministerial committees.

Out of a large number of parliamentary standing committees in Bangladesh our focus is on the following committees, which are said to keep a watchful eye over the government and hold it accountable for its actions. The oversight role in general, confines to Public Accounts Committee, Committee on Estimates, Committee on Public Undertakings, and the individual ministerial committees.

PUBLIC ACCOUNTS COMMITTEE (PAC)

This is a 15-member committee that acts as the watchdog of public accounts. It examines the report of the Comptroller and Auditor General. PAC ensures that the public expenditure conforms to the authority, which governs it, and every appropriation has been made in accordance with the provision. The PAC selects important paragraphs and comments from the audit reports of the Comptroller and Auditor General (CAG) for in-depth scrutiny in committee meeting where permanent secretaries (called secretary in Bangladesh) as the principal accounting officers are to answer and clarify for the financial management of public organizations and take remedial actions to correct the deficiencies stated in audit reports. The PAC can also fortify the principal accounting officers against the temptation of financial irregularities.

The committee publishes its own report, which is in turn placed before the whole House of the parliament. These PAC reports on the auditor general's report include the responses of the ministries and executive agencies along with the recommendations of the committee. By tradition as well as by administrative practice (not formally), these recommendations are binding on the executive agencies. Subsequently, the committee monitors the progress of implementation of its recommendations through its follow-up meetings (CAG 1998: 14).

COMMITTEE ON ESTIMATES (COE)

This committee examines the estimates (annual detailed statements of public expenditure proposed to be undertaken by the government in a financial year) presented before the parliament as to whether they are prepared with maximum possible efficiency and economy, suggests alternative policies and evaluates whether the money is well laid within limits of policy implied in the estimates. The Committee on Estimates appears to be the one that has been formally entrusted with the responsibility of formulating alternative policy consideration for the government.

COMMITTEE ON PUBLIC UNDERTAKINGS (COPU)

This committee is also composed of ten members. It assesses the performance of public undertakings and suggests for their functional improvements. It also examines the reports of the CAG on public undertakings.

Standing committee on ministries (SCMs)

Every standing committee on the ministries shall consist of not more than ten members including the chairman who shall be appointed by the House provided that a Minister shall not be the chairman of the committee. Each standing committee shall meet at least once a month and the functions of a committee is to examine any bill or other matter referred to it by the parliament, to review the works relating to a ministry which fall within its remit, to inquire into any activity or irregularity and serious complaint in respect of the ministry and to examine if it deems fit any such other matter as may fall within its scope and to make recommendation.

There are no standing committees in JS to oversee some very crucial executive offices of the government such as the Prime Minister's Office, the President's secretariat and the Parliament secretariat where spending from public exchequer and public functions are involved. Likewise, Bangladesh parliament does not have any separate committee on subordinate/delegated legislations, nor are these dealt/supervised by any other committee.

Committee structure

According to Rule 246 of the Rules of Procedure, the standing committees on each ministry shall be formed as earliest as possible from the inauguration of any new JS. Delay in forming the committees divests the parliament of its right to perform its key function of oversight of the executive in a competent manner. In this regard the date of first sitting of the House and that of the formation of committees are crucial to understanding the extent to which the parliament is willing to hold the government accountable from the very beginning of a new parliament. In the fifth JS, all but two committees were formed within six months of its inauguration. In the seventh JS, the government formed ministerial committees, after a lapse of two years from its start. The eighth JS also took 20 months to complete the formation of committees unilaterally.

On the question of the formation of all committees in the inaugural session of a new parliament, 95 percent of the respondents were in favor of such idea. The respondents think that the formation of committees immediately after the inauguration of a new parliament provides committee members an opportunity to keep a watchful eye on the business of government from the start. In the eighth JS, a proposal to form standing committees by third session of a newly elected parliament has been adopted by the Committee on Rules of Procedures.

As 20 months were lapsed on mere formation of ministerial committees in the eighth JS, the entire administrative apparatus of government had been immune from any legislative oversight during this time. The government was a free rider and virtually accountable to none. During this 20 months, the nation came across a number of important issues such as the excesses done by the police in a female students' dormitory at the University of Dhaka, the wheat scandal in Bogra involving five ruling party MPs, biggest ever arm hauls recovery in Bogra, leakage of question papers of public service examinations conducted by the Public Service Commission six times in two years, deployment of armed forces to restore law and order and making indemnity laws to immune them from civil laws for whatever they had done during this operations. Task forces/committees were formed by the government to investigate these incidents. Government bureaucrats and former judges rather than MPs were appointed as members/chairmen of these committees. If parliamentary committees were formed in time, they could have addressed these issues and called the government to account.

In Bangladesh, most of the committees are permanent and committee members/chairs are in general appointed for the full term of a parliament. Usually chairmanships/memberships committees remain the same for the life of parliament. In Bangladesh, average turn over of committee members is around 10 percent due mainly to death, shuffling/reshuffling of committee composition.

Most of the respondents (87 percent, mean score is 3.7) think that the terms of committees should be coterminous with life span of the parliament to give members enough time to develop expertise and expand their horizon of knowledge on different aspects of governmental activities. Most respondents believe that this is a good feature of the committee system of Bangladesh which can help committee members to develop specialized knowledge and expertise to make committees more effective.

Respondents were sharply divided on issue of ministerial committees' correspondence to government ministries. Sixty percent (all from the ruling coalitions) of the respondents agreed completely that ministerial committees should parallel the structure of government structure. However, almost all the respondents from the opposition feel that in Bangladesh there are too many ministries (57 cabinet ministers, state ministers and deputy ministers) to have control and run efficiently. Large-size cabinet incurs huge amount of money from public exchequer and weakens the numerical strength of parliament. They favored the reduction of the number of ministries from 37 to 20 or so. A good (20 percent) number of respondents disagreed with the proposal and suggested that given the situation that number of reduction of ministries is impossible in Bangladesh, it is better to group several ministerial committees into one like the system in India based on the nature of functional operations for effective functioning of the committees. For instance, the Ministry of Agriculture, Water Resources and Food can be grouped under one committee which will help to reduce the number of standing committees on ministries. The treasury bench MPs were completely against the proposal to group several ministries under one standing committee. The opposition MPs explained why the treasury bench MPs were reluctant reduce the number of committees. If the ministerial committees are grouped functionally, the number of ministerial committees will sharply fall down from 37 to 20 or so and thus the chairmanships. This means a good number of MPs will no longer enjoy the status of chairmanship which gives them prestige and privilege. Currently there are too many committees (over 50) to be provided with secretariat supports.

Eighty percent of the respondents completely agree that small committees (consisting of 15–20 members or so) enhances committee specialization and bridge party division. The size of most of committees in Bangladesh ranges between eight and 15. But due to poor attendance of committee members, most committee sessions become even smaller. They think that in a small session, committee members get to know each other intimately and have more time and scope to talk and express their views on specific matters. This is how sometimes, political division is overcome and committee members regardless of party affiliation can decide on consensus.

On the question of selection of members based on their own interest, experience and expertise rather than the government or the political parties, 64 percent of the respondents completely agreed. This is beneficial for committee specialization. In general, the interest and preferences of members are usually obtained before they are appointed into a committee by their own political parties. Sometimes, seniority prevails over academic background and expertise in committee membership/chairmanship selection. In doing so, it is ensured that the interest of the individual MP does not conflict with that of the political parties. Some opposition MPs reported that the incumbent government made minor shuffling in the list of members submitted by the opposition for committee composition against the will of the party and MPs. An opposition MP who was seen to be assertive in defense committee in the seventh JS was dropped from the defense committee in the eighth JS and placed in a relatively less significant committee.

In Bangladesh, committee chairmen are elected by the committee unless nominated by the parliament. The Speaker and deputy Speaker act as ex officio chairperson of the Business Advisory Committee and Library Committee respectively. The Speaker also nominates the chairpersons and members of House Committee and Committee on Petitions. A minister cannot be a chairman of any parliamentary committee. There is no specific rule in the distribution of committee chairs. Usually it is the ruling party, which occupies all the chairs of committees. In the fifth and the seventh parliament, the ruling party sustained its domination by allocating 56 percent and 60 percent of the memberships among the ruing party respectively although its party strength in the House was 51 percent and 53 percent respectively (see Table 5.2).

All the committee chairs were occupied by the government and alliance MPs in the fifth, seventh and eighth JSs. Even the committee chair[3] of the strong PAC committee was also occupied by a treasury bench member. Ruling party's inclination to staying in safe side is evident from this deviation. Thus the structural arrangement of the committee system in Bangladesh has enabled the government to impose its preference on the opposition members in the committee. Whenever the opposition members in committees did attempt to unearth financial irregularities or corruption (such as the purchase of MIG-29 fighter plane and Korean frigate cases in the seventh JS), voting drew the final result in favor of the incumbent government.

Fifty percent (mean score is 2.1) of the respondents completely agreed that the composition of the committee (including the chairmanship) should be based on proportional strength of the parties in the House. Members were politically divided on the question of proportion distribution of chairmanships among the parties. However, all respondents irrespective of party affiliations were of the view that committee memberships must be made proportionally. 30 percent of the respondents (majority from the government) who disagree with the statement of proportional distribution of chairs think that given the immature and confrontational political culture in Bangladesh, chairmanships (except PAC and

Table 5.2 Party distribution of total committee chairs and members in percentage (proportional and actual)

JS	*Fifth parliament (1991–1996)*				*Seventh parliament (1996–2001)*			
Position	*Chairs*		*Members*		*Chairs*		*Members*	
Party	Proportional	Actual	Proportional	Actual	Proportional	Actual	Proportional	Actual
Treasury bench	51%	100%	51%	56%	53%	98%	53%	60%
Opposition	49%	nil	49%	42%	47%	nil	47%	40%

Source: *Sangsad Bulletin*, 1991 on first, second, third and 17th session; *Sangsad Bulletin*, 1996 on first, second and eighth session, Bangladesh Parliament Secretariat.

COPU) of committees should remain with the ruling party or coalitions unless and until a healthy political culture develops. Those who agreed completely with the statement had their own arguments. They argued that a committee was a mini-parliament and in term of chair selection attention must be given to uphold the representative character of the House.

In response to a question eliciting their opinion on the exclusion of ministers as members from committees, the majority of the respondents answered in the negative. They argued if the minister would chair the committee (being the political head of the ministry) it was easier for him to implement committee recommendations. A small group of respondents (25 percent) agreed that in order to maintain the separation of power, ministers who were from the executive branch should be excluded even as members from committees. They think that the government backbenchers who constitute the majority membership of parliamentary committees in Bangladesh may find it risky for their future career development to call ministers who are senior to them in party hierarchy to account. The minister is treated as a father figure and to interrogate the minister vigorously in committee sessions may be taken by the minister as overt disrespect. The prevailing cultural values of showing deference towards a superior and reluctance to make a superior accountable is also substantiated by our questionnaire survey. The mean score of responses on the issue of exclusion of ministers from committee membership for securing better political and administrative accountability is 1.8, which attests to the majority of respondents' sharp disapproval of the proposed statement.

The rank and status of a minister in the social hierarchy in Bangladesh is quite high. He/she belongs to the elite strata of the society usually with a reputed and affluent family background, long experience in politics and a highly developed network. The proposal of disallowing a minister to continue as a member of a parliamentary committee, which oversees the activities of public organizations under the ministry where he/she is the chief executive, is unacceptable and contrary to the prevailing cultural values in Bangladesh.

The mean score of the respondents' understanding of the statement of allocating the chairs of the financial committees exclusively to the opposition members with relevant background for securing better government accountability is 3.2. This is a high response in favor of the proposal. None of the respondents, irrespective of the party affiliation, ruled out the inevitability of allocating the chairs exclusively to the opposition members.

The mean score of respondents' answers on the question of introduction of a Liaison Committee made up of the chairpersons of various committees under the leadership of the Speaker in order to coordinate the activities of different committees, avoid overlapping of work and reconcile ideas and suggestion for better activating the committee and establish keen surveillance over the executive is 3.0. This manifests major respondents' support for constitution of a liaison committee in Bangladesh. 55 percent of the respondents completely agreed with the statement. The respondents think that in the liaison committee meeting the Speaker and other committee members can discuss the activities and problems faced by various committees. Through the liaison committee, the Speaker can also keep track of the recommendations made by different committees and expedite the pace of implementation of recommendations and thereby make the committees more effective.

Three meetings of a provincial committee composed of all the chairmen of parliamentary committees were held in the seventh parliament. Committee meetings were presided over by the prime minister. In these meetings, the committee chairmen demanded clarifying their status and increasing logistic support including committee staff and computer facilities. Every time she skipped the issue of the status of the chairman. They also sought the prime minister's cooperation in implementing the recommendations of the committees on various ministries. They alleged that the ministries often did not cooperate with parliamentary bodies to scrutinize the performance of the ministries. This kind of periodic meeting could have been presided over and coordinated by the Speaker instead of the prime minister who was the chief executive. A tendency to control the operations of committees was evident from the prime minister's initiative. The current prime minister has been seen to do the same.

Committee procedures

When asked about the agenda setting capability of parliament 60 percent of the respondents agreed that committee's ability to set its own agenda was a crucial power to constrain government. They report that in Bangladesh committees are allowed to set their own agenda with regard to all issues except legislation. Committees deal with bills referred to them by the House where the decision of the majority party usually prevails. In Bangladesh, before a bill is referred to a committee, it is first debated by the House. Although the committee members can bring amendments to a bill, its acceptance or rejection is solely contingent upon the House where the ruling party is the majority.

Before 1996, bills were seldom sent to the committee after its first reading in the House. Since the seventh JS, most of the bills had been sent to the committee for consideration but no major change was brought, tolerated or accepted. In the Bangladesh parliament, there is no provision for pre-plenary discussion or deliberation on budget, financial bill or appropriation bill in the committees, which attests that the committees have no significant role let alone control in budget allocation of government agencies. In fact, the preparation of budget by the assistance of the bureaucrats rests exclusively with the province of the House in which the ruling party imposes its decision bolstered by majority votes on opposition members. This is a notable procedural limitation of the committee system in Bangladesh in holding the executive accountable. Only the post budget expenditures are scrutinized and audited by the PAC and COPU and COE. Moreover, in Bangladesh, there are at least two significant extra-budgetary funds:

1 The Prime Minster's Relief Fund (PMRF);
2 the Private Fund of the Regiment (PFR).

The accountability requirement on each of these funds is that it produces a certificate at the end of the year as to the amount spent.

That committee stage of bill consideration should precede floor consideration was agreed completely by 32 percent of the respondents. Most of the respondents who disagree with the proposal think that this is an extreme mode of legislative reform proposal considering the role of committees in law-making in Bangladesh. They feel that in a parliamentary democracy the House should have a final say regarding law-making. Committees can deliberate the bills once they are tabled in the House and referred to committees.

The sittings of the committee are held in camera in Bangladesh. The deliberation of the meeting is, as per the Rules, confined exclusively to committee members and officers of parliamentary secretariat. However, in the meetings of ministerial and financial committees, officials including the secretary of concerned ministries and relevant public bodies remain present to clarify, explain and account for specific matter. Evidence, oral or written report or proceedings of the committee is confidential. On the question of the nature of committee session (open or closed) 91 percent of the respondents completely agreed that it should be closed which would help foster inter-party consensus and relax party discipline. Most of the respondents believe that considering the socio-political culture in Bangladesh, committee sessions must be closed. Sharp party division within the committee sessions is not seen very often. That will disappear once committee sessions are open to the media. MPs would like to play the same as they do in the House and consensus which is common in committee sessions will swing to confrontation.

They observe that, notwithstanding committee meetings that are held in private, the whole text of the committee deliberations is available in the print media on the following day. Over time, it has been a convention that the chair of committee briefs up the media after the meeting is over. Moreover, opposition committee members have been seen frequently disclosing the whole text of discussion to media particularly when it is about government corruption or irregularities.

The proposal of public hearings on legislative bills and other oversight matters was completely agreed by 90 percent of the respondents. They feel that hearings on bills, nationally significant policy issues and graft cases by the committee can be open to the mass media and concerned people. Over time, people's awareness of, and interest in, committees has been heightened. They can help committees perform better by providing useful information, new ideas and insights. The respondents reported that public hearings on bills or any other matter in committees had hardly been held in Bangladesh.

In Bangladesh, committees do have the right to send for papers and persons and usually the request of committees are complied with. But the government holds the right to decline to provide papers to the committees on the ground that its disclosure would be prejudicial to the safety or interest of state. Some 60 percent of respondents agreed completely with question of the committee's right to send for paper and persons and punish those who fail to comply with its demand. Some respondents felt that ministers should be excluded from summoning to the committees. It is the House where he should better be asked questions regarding the performance of his ministry.

There are specific laws and rules which explicitly make it a criminal offense for civil servants to disclose various kinds of information without authorization. For instance the Official Secrets Act of 1923 and the Government Servants Conduct Rules of 1979 bind the civil servant to an oath of secrecy even forbidding them to pass some official information to other government departments unless empowered by the government (World Bank 1996: 65). This is a major deterrent to ensuring transparency of administration and compelling the civil servants (and the minister) to furnish the committees with necessary information, papers or documents on demand. Government's right of refusal to produce a document on the grounds of state security has placed the government in an advantage position. The ruling political elite together with the senior bureaucrats determine which papers or documents will be made available to the committees relying on their discretion, convenience and caprice.[4]

Committee functions

Sixty percent of the respondents (the mean is 2.3 out of maximum 4) completely agreed that committees should have exclusive jurisdiction over legislation and oversight of the executive. They think that committees should play a significant role at various stages of law-making – from review of bill to review of act. They report that in Bangladesh, the parliamentary committees play no major role in law-making. Legislative bills are generally refereed to committees for scrutiny. Due to belated formation of committees a large number of bills did not have any committee stage scrutiny in the current JS. They think that committees should have major role in the oversight of administration too. Committees in Bangladesh have no role in budget allocation, which remains a prerogative of the House. PAC and COPU are empowered to examine the financial propriety of the money granted to government department and public corporations. However, if anything goes wrong and is exposed by the media in between budget allocation to the review of financial statements by PAC and COPU, Standing Committees on Ministries can pick up the issue for examination.

In Bangladesh, in the absence of any precise provisions in the Rules, a committee is not obliged to report to the House on matters other than referred to it by the House. According to Rules of Procedure, if the House does not fix any specific time limit for the presentation of the report by the committee, the committee is supposed to present the same within one month on which reference to the committee was made. Of course, the House can extend the time range of submission of the report by bringing a motion. Consequently, submission of reports to the House has been sporadic.

Regarding the submission of committee reports to the parliament, the available data elicits a dissuading scenario of committee performance. In the fifth JS, the highest number (29) of committee reports had been submitted. In the seventh

JS, 12 ministerial committee reports and five PAC reports had been submitted. No report was produced by other important financial committees like COPU and COE. This indicates poor performance of the committee system in Bangladesh at the implementation stage.

Let's take a look on the production of departmental committee reports in the British House of Commons. The departmental committees (16) of the British House of Commons issued a total of 193 substantive reports in the 1979–1983 parliament; 306 reports in the 1983–1987 parliament; 403 in the longer five-session parliament of 1987–1992. In total, in 12 years, the departmental committees have issued over 900 substantive reports. (Norton 1993: 100).

There remains no compulsion or convention for deliberating reports after their submission to the House too. Ironically, no deliberation ever took place on those very small numbers of committee reports submitted to House. Asked whether committee reports should be presented to the House regularly and debated as well, 70 percent of the respondents answered in the affirmative. The respondents think that deliberation on committee reports enables all members of a parliament to be apprised of the activities of various committees and provides an opportunity to accommodate constructive suggestions from members. Deliberation on the major recommendations in the reports also helps expose the malfeasance and maladministration of public organizations and exert moral pressure on the relevant bodies to implement the recommendations. It also keeps the civil society abreast of the functioning of committees and heightens positive image of committee members. Hence, it does have a publicity effect.

The minority are not allowed to present their own report in case of dissention in a committee session. A single report contains the "note of dissent" recorded by the minority. Respondents were sharply divided on a question about the presentation of the minority report in case of dissention in the committee meeting. 40 percent of the respondents (the mean score of the answer is 1.9) agreed completely that the minority should be allowed to present their own reports which would reflect that the committees were not dominated by the government. They report that in Bangladesh, decisions in committee sessions are mostly made on consensus basis. However, the cordial and non-political atmosphere in committee sessions has deteriorated over time. Those who opposed the proposal argued that if necessary, the same report could contain the dissent of the minority and serve the same purpose.

In Bangladesh, committee recommendations are advisory in nature. Several committee chairmen in a seminar expressed their frustrations about the execution of committee recommendations and complained that ministers simply overlooked recommendations (*Daily Star*, April 5, 2004). Respondents were asked about the issue of enforcement of committee recommendations. 45 percent of the respondents majority of whom were from the opposition completely agreed that committee recommendations should be made mandatory for the government. Implementation of recommendations of committees regardless of the contents would have a salutary impact on the improvement of the performance of the government bodies, they believed. But those who opposed (30 percent disagreed completely) the proposal thought that recommendations should be advisory, as is case in most of the countries. The executive has been mandated by the people to rule the country and the implementation of the recommendations of committees should be left to the executive.

A proposal was presented before the respondents that in order to follow up and monitor the state of implementation of the committee recommendations, an action-taken sub-committee should be formed and in case of failure to comply with, the government offices should submit an explanatory note. 78 percent of the respondents completely agreed with the proposal. Many of the respondents recalled that in the fifth (1991–1996) Bangladesh parliament, action-taken sub-committees functioned well and made some contributions towards implementing committee recommendations. They believed, in the absence of any institutional mechanism to monitor and follow up the recommendations, this might be a good mechanism to reintroduce.

Committee resources

Table 5.3 depicts a comparative account of the background characteristics of the MPs in the first, fifth, seventh and eighth JSs which are further analyzed in terms of educational qualification, occupation and parliamentary experience. The seventh JS, as it appears from the following table had more graduates and experienced members than the fifth JS. 45 percent of the total MPs in the seventh JS were graduates while 15 percent were undergraduates. The fifth as well as the seventh JS were populated more by MPs having general educational background than MPs having specialized background in law, politics and administration (Rashid 1997). It appears from Table 5.3 that MPs with business as the occupational background constitute the largest single elite group in the fifth and seventh JSs (59 percent in fifth JS and 48 percent in seventh JS). A major (68 percent in the fifth JS and 40 percent in the seventh JS) segment of the MPs who entered parliament in the 1990s was newcomers and lacked the basic operational experience of the parliament let alone the specialized assignments in committees. Moreover, they were not provided with any specialized training on legislative and administrative affairs which might help improve their capability and competency to perform their tasks.

Now in order to compare the competency strength of MPs with bureaucrats, let us have a look inside the bureaucracy. Almost all the permanent secretaries in charge of different ministries are highly educated. Most of them held Masters degrees from reputed universities in Bangladesh. Some of them received PhD/training from overseas universities too. Moreover, they had undergone intensive probationary and in-service training after their entrance to the civil service. They had gained vast experience (32 years or more) in running administration under diversified civil and military regimes.

The preceding analysis supports that in Bangladesh, the senior bureaucrats who are chief executives of different government ministries are in a relatively advantageous position than the MPs in terms of educational background,

Table 5.3 Background Characteristics of MPs in the first, second, seventh and eighth JSs (%)

Background	*Fifth JS (1991–1996) N=330 (%)*	*Seventh JS (1996–2001) N=318 (%)*	*Eighth JS (2001–) N=300 (%)*
Education			
Postgraduate	28.8	40.3	45.6
Graduate	43.3	45.3	43.7
Undergraduate	27.9	13.5	8.4
Others	–	0.9	2.3
Occupation			
Businessmen	59.4	47.8	45.7
Lawyers	18.8	14.8	11.7
Professionals	15.5	8.5	10.6
Landholders	3.9	6.9	2.3
Politicians (full-time)	2.0	3.1	2.3
Others	0.4	18.9	27.4
Parliamentary experience			
Newcomer	58.8	39.9	25.33
Experience of one JS	21.8	26.7	25.67
Experience of more than one JS	13.9	33.4	46.67
Not available	5.5	–	2.33

Source: Calculated and compiled by the author from Maniruzzaman (1992), Rashid (1997), Ahmed (2002), TIB (2004).

expertise and experience, numerical strength, information acquisition and material resources accumulation. Moreover, in Bangladesh, the bureaucracy is better institutionalized than the parliament as an institution (Rahman 2000). Hence the MPs are lagging behind the bureaucrats in terms of major competency components, which deter the committee members to establish command over bureaucracy and thereby hold them accountable for their decisions and actions. This situation is further aggravated by the bureaucrats' passive attitude towards politicians in Bangladesh (Jamil 1998: 122).

A considerable percentage (approximately 9 percent) of the total number of MPs in the seventh JS belonged to the top bank-loan defaulter-coterie of the country. MPs with business as the occupational background constituted the largest elite group in the fifth and seventh parliaments (59 percent in the fifth JS and 48 percent in the seventh JS and 45.7 percent in the eighth JS) (Maniruzzaman 1992; Rashid 1997; TIB 2004). 29 members of seventh JS had been loan-defaulters to the tune of BDT 312 million, US$6 million) (*Financial Express*, August 22, 1996). Many of the top bank-loan defaulting MPs were in different committees in the seventh JS and were entrusted with ensuring financial propriety and keeping watchful eyes on the executive. For example, 29 defaulting MPs held a total of 46 committee positions (9.4 percent) out of 472 positions available in the seventh JS. Among the loan defaulting committee position holders, nine were former cabinet ministers, six (13 percent) were committee chairmen in the seventh JS.

Total number of telephone bill defaulting MPs in eight parliaments in Bangladesh since her independence till May 30, 2003 (*Daily Prothom Alo*, March 14, 2004) is 619 and the total amount of defaulted money is BDT 8,37,42,000 (US$ 1.4 million). Among the telephone bill defaulting MPs are Speaker, deputy Speaker, whips and present and former ministers too. According to Members' of Parliament Remuneration and Allowance (amended) Act, 1992, the MPs pay the telephone bills by themselves. According to this law, the MPs receive BDT 4000/6000 per month as telephone expenditure from the government exchequer. All MPs had withdrawn that allowance for phone bills but surprisingly many of them had not paid their telephone bill. This evidence is disgraceful for MPs as people's representatives and makes them no different from the top bank loan defaulting businessmen. For the bureaucracy, this is a substantial proof of MPs' misdeeds and abuse of power and privileges which constrain the moral right and conscience of MPs to voice against the malfeasance done by the bureaucracy.

Ninety percent of the respondents agreed completely that full-time professional and experienced legislators coupled with low turnover of committee membership can help active and powerful committees to emerge. Respondents opined that an MP's experience in government and committee work really matters for his performance in committee. Most of the respondents expressed their discontent with the salary and benefits they get from the parliament which they believed prevented them from becoming full-time politicians. Data from minutes of six selected committees in the seventh parliament manifests that the average turnover of committee membership is 10 percent that is not helpful for a stable committee to emerge. However, chairmanships of committees are stable.

The parliamentary committee staff in Bangladesh has no separate entity. The parliament secretariat is headed by a secretary who is assisted by one joint secretary, one deputy secretary and one assistant secretary. These senior officials are on deputation from various government departments and depend on them for career advancement. They are thus likely to owe their loyalty more to the government than to the parliament (Kashyap 1979; Ahmed 2002). The staff of committees are organized into seven sections under the parliament secretariat. Each committee section consists of an assistant secretary, one/two committee officers and two office assistants. Committee staffers are over stretched and ill-equipped with facilities. One senior staff is associated with as many as ten committees at a time, not to speak of numerous sub-committees (Khalequzzaman 1999: 15). Only four committee rooms are available for all 50 committees and a large number of sub-committees for holding meetings. Few rapporteurs are available for writing the verbatim of the committee meetings and typing machines are used to prepare committee proceedings which slow down the production of committee reports. Computer supports are yet to be provided.

Each chairman has a personal secretary who has been recruited from outside the secretariat. In addition, there are 88 temporary staff (recruited on political consideration) in the chairmen's offices of different committees in the eighth JS. All the personal secretaries are drawn from different cadres of Bangladesh Civil Service (BCS) such as BCS (Administration), BCS (Education), BCS (Health), BCS (Engineering) and so on. An interesting point to note is that personal secretaries of chairmen are allowed to attend committee meetings which is a stark breach of the Rules of Procedure. Only MPs and parliamentary secretariat officials who are concerned with committee works can attend committee meetings. All the personal secretaries are drawn from the executive branch of government (different government ministries) who are supposed to come before the committees when they are summoned to do so.

Interviews with some personal secretaries of chairmen reveals a very dangerous trend of mixing up the legislative branch with the executive. Personal secretaries may leak important information/messages to other government officials belonging to their own cadre who are summoned to appear before the committee and give their account to the MPs. This can help the errant officials to know what is happening inside the committee beforehand and enable them to find ways and means to escape from tough interrogation by the committee members. In a seminar organized by the parliamentary secretariat, a good number of committee chairmen expressed their preferences for having personal secretaries from BCS (administration) cadre.

This can jeopardize the main goals of the committee operations. There are allegations that personal secretaries of some chairmen of standing committees on ministries are using vehicles of ministries and other logistics such as computers, fax machines, telephones etc. have been brought from the concerned ministries which are overseen by committees. Their penchant for having personal secretaries from BCS (administration) cadre is obvious. The officials of this privileged cadre have a major role in policy formulation, policy implementation, information regulation and resources distribution and has an integrated network from the secretariat to field-level offices spreading all over the country. Thus having a personal secretary from this cadre will better facilitate a chairman's access to state resources and will serve his personal and constituency interests. This has certainly added a new dimension of fusion of power to an already highly fused political system.

The academic background of committee staff is general in nature and most of them lack the specialized knowledge required for committee operations. In the fifth parliament, a separate secretariat for the parliament was established. Since 1992, only one batch of committee officials had been recruited through open competitive examination conducted by the PSC (Public Service Commission). They were not imparted with relevant training to perform their specialized tasks. Furthermore, no individual committee member is provided with staff support to carry out his/her responsibility in a competent manner. Consequently, the logistic supports available for committees in Bangladesh are insignificant and inadequate. In the absence of availability of staff and other resources, most committees remain virtually handicapped.

In response to a question about the necessity of a separate committee secretariat supported with a healthy budget, sufficient numbers of specialized/competent staffers and adequate logistic support, 77 percent of the respondents answered in the affirmative. About 20 percent of the respondents expressed their reservations about the first part of the question but favored the second one. They felt that the committee branch could be strengthened within one parliamentary secretariat and that the establishment of a separate committee secretariat was unnecessary. However, all the respondents unanimously expressed their discontent with the existing logistic support system of committees and strongly urged the government to extend and upgrade it.

In Bangladesh, committees can seek advices from experts in their respective fields if required. Earlier, committees have been benefited from the hearings of external experts on several occasions. However, experts can render their advice only, the final decision regarding the matter consulted rests exclusively with the committee. All respondents (100 percent, with mean score 4) were of the view that committees should benefit from the expertise and knowledge of external experts who are relatively independent of the executive and political influence. Experts should be invited and more frequently consulted with, they observed.

The real-world working of selected committees in Bangladesh

The proper functioning of the committee system relies to a large extent on the formation of committee, operations of the committee and committee competency. Members' attendance, frequency of committee meeting, average time spent for each meeting and agenda of deliberation have been used as benchmarks for evaluating the committee performance. Committee members must show up in the committee meeting to participate in deliberation on different issues. Of note, the presence of a considerable number of opposition members is a prerequisite for making committee session more dynamic and robust in securing government accountability. If the committee does not meet regularly, the possibility of issues related to executive accountability will not be deliberated. If the committee remains inactive for long, the insurance of executive accountability simply disappears. Moreover, adequate time is also essential for the agenda of executive accountability to be deliberated in detail and concrete decisions made on it.

Agenda of deliberation tells us about the nature of issues (corruption, routine discussion on public organizations, personnel administration, irregularities or inefficiency of public bodies, etc.) the committees deliberate as well as the practical involvement of committee (initiation, recommendation and implementation) in ensuring executive accountability.

Financial committees

Public Accounts Committee (PAC)

From the available data on the PAC in the seventh JS (see Table 5.4), it is obvious that on average about 53 percent of the total members did not attend the committee meeting. A quorum is one-third (five) of the total number of members of the committee. Two out of an average of seven members attending the committee meeting were from the opposition. So the treasury bench members got a free hand to make the decision according to their preferences. The committee met twice a month regularly. It spent an average of two and a half hours per meeting. The PAC also submitted five committee reports in the seventh JS. We can take the instance of departmental committees in the UK which meet each week while the House is in session with meetings lasting between 60 and 90 minutes (Norton 1999: 93). Considering this instance, the average frequency of meetings and average time spent for each committee meeting of the PAC in the seventh JS are satisfactory.

AGENDA OF DELIBERATION

The PAC discussed audit objections of different public organizations under different ministries regarding financial irregularities in different financial years involving billions of BDT. Various types of audit objections are follows:

- Impropriety – cases of violation of rules and regulations or budgetary stipulations.
- Loss, damage and wastage – occurrences that are caused by the negligence of duties or inefficiency of the management.
- Theft, embezzlement, fraud and misappropriation – cases of loss due to willful malpractice by public functionaries (CAG 1998: 29).

Table 5.4 Nature of financial committee activism

Nature of activism	*Committee*	*JS*					
		First	*Second*	*Third*	*Fourth*	*Fifth*	*Seventh*
Number of meetings held	PAC	3	9	–	6	52	105
	COE	9	7	–	21	26	25
	COPU	–	84	–	36	48	26
Number of sub-committees formed	PAC	–	3	–	4	4	1
	COE	–	–	–	1	–	7
	COPU	–	–	–	3	4	3
Number of reports prepared	PAC	–	1	–	2	4	5
	COE	–	–	–	1	–	–
	COPU	–	1	–	3	2	–

Source: Ahmed, 2001c: 91; 2002: 150 and BJS Secretariat, Committee section-2.

Table 5.5 Operation of three financial committees in the seventh JS

Name of committees	*Number of meetings held*	*Average attendance (%)*	*Total number of committee members*	*Average duration of meeting*	*Average frequency of meetings*
PAC	103 (65)	47	15	2.5 hours	15 days
COPU	26	80	10	3 hours	70 days
COE	25	63	10	2.75 hours	70 days

Source: Compiled and calculated by the author from first, second and third, fourth and fifth (1996–2001) reports of Public Accounts Committee in the seventh JS, July 2001, the proceedings (first to tenth meeting) of Committee on Public Undertakings, (BJS, 1997–1999), The proceedings (1st to 21st meeting) of Committee on Estimates (BJS, 1997–1999a), in the seventh JS and *Daily Star*, September 29, October 23, November 29, 1999; April 4 and 11, 2000.

According to the Chairman of PAC of the eighth JS, very few of the hundreds recommendations made by the PAC on the audit observations over the years have been implemented by the government agencies. This can be attributed mainly to the absence of any effective mechanisms to enforce implementation of the PAC recommendations (Rashid 2003). However, the PAC in the seventh JS made some important recommendations to resolve the objections raised by the CAG. Data regarding the implementation status of the recommendations are partially available from the agenda of deliberation of some sample meetings in the seventh JS. Audit objections on Bangladesh Railway involving BDT 17,450 million (US$336 million)[5] was discussed. Of it, BDT 2040 million (approx. US$39 million) had already been realized; departmental steps had been taken on the objections involving BDT 4590 million (US$88 million) and objections on BDT ten million (US$0.19 million) had been written off.

But the state of implementation of committee's recommendations can be available in more detail from the PAC's fifth report in the seventh JS (see Figure 5.1 below). In pursuance of the decisions taken by the committee in the first 65 meetings in seventh JS, BDT 2270 million (approx. US$39.14 million) had been recovered; BDT 9290 million (approx. US$160.17 million) had been adjusted. In the case of objections and comments relating to BDT 10,430 million (approx. US$180 million), the ministries had been asked to take departmental actions and inform the committee. The committee had decided to re-discuss audit objections and comments relating to BDT 1630 million (approx. US$28 million) at an appropriate time.

The problems of ensuring executive accountability by the PAC can be broadly categorized into two: problems at the initiation level and problems at the implementation level. Problems at the initiation level can be further grouped into two: problems accruing from the limitations of office of the CAG and problems of the PAC itself. Of note, the PAC made recommendations regularly.

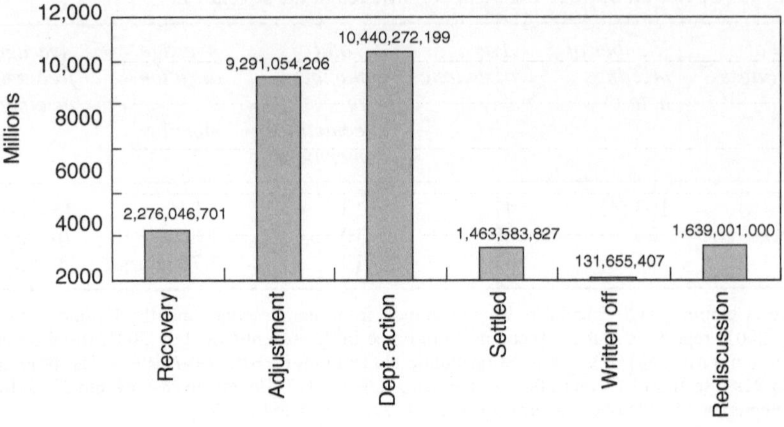

Figure 5.1 Action taken up to the 65th meeting of PAC in the seventh JS (up to 2000).

PROBLEMS AT THE INITIATION LEVEL

Since the Public Accounts Committee (PAC) bases its actions entirely on the reports of the CAG, its shortcomings have a baneful effect on the performance of the PAC. The CAG is the first line oversight agency, empowered to examining all public accounts while others like the committees and Bureau of Anti-Corruption are selective investigatory agencies. The CAG cannot perform satisfactorily for a number of reasons explained below.

The autonomy of the CAG, which is a constitutional body, is severely curtailed by placing it as a subordinate office under the Ministry of Finance. The CAG has to depend on the Ministry of Finance and the Ministry of Establishment for budget and recruitment of its staff (CAG 1998: 3). The CAG is appointed by the president of the republic on the advice of the prime minister without consultation with the parliament or PAC. The CAG's tenure is protected in the same way as that of a Judge of the Supreme Court. He cannot be dismissed at political will. However the constitution requires the CAG to retire at the age of 60. Since a CAG is usually appointed at the age of 57, this leaves a short three-year term for him to realize his dream. More stability in this office is needed (World Bank 2002c: 61).

The selection of organizations for audit by the CAG is done based on random sampling among public organizations (CAG 1998: 29). Hence the turn of audit for a particular ministry, department or undertaking comes only after several years and there are some whose turn does not commence at all. (Ashraf 1999: 10). In fact the CAG examines only 17–25 percent of all auditable units each year (World Bank 2002).

The CAG carries out conventional audits whose focus is more on verification of transactions rather than performance. The CAG does not have a professional staff even single chartered accountant (World Bank 1996: 53). Audit is carried out by the civil servants (mostly with general educational background) belonging to the audit and accounts cadre of the BCS.

The CAG has been suffering from backlog of its audit functions. When the relevant report is issued years later (delays of five to eight years are not uncommon), it is assiduous to take action in cases of financial impropriety or administrative negligence particularly given the frequent transfer, infrequent retirement and occasional demise of civil servants. It is to mention in this regard that the audit and accounts report of the year 1996–1997 have already been placed before the parliament which reflects some kind of progress in reducing the backlog.

When implementing agencies deviate from audit rules, they are not subject to prompt and effective sanction. Also the existing practice of allowing an implementing agency to respond to the preliminary audit observations within 45 days is rarely enforced. A delay of more than 16 years (see Figure 5.2) in taking effective preliminary steps in response to audit objections testifies to this assertion (BJS 2001).

The PAC itself is also suffering from the same malaise of backlogging. Of the 799 audit reports submitted by the Comptroller and Auditor General's (CAG) Office to eight parliaments since the independence of Bangladesh, the PAC disposed of only 146 (18 percent) cases involving BDT 4000 crore (US$702 million only). A backlog of 653 audit reports submitted by the CAG involving BDT 24,000 crore (US$4.2 billion) had been stranded in the PAC for further deliberation in the committee meeting (*Daily Star*, August 1, 2003). The CAG Office's attempt to clear its own backlog has resulted in further sharp increase in the total number of the reports at the end of PAC. This load is

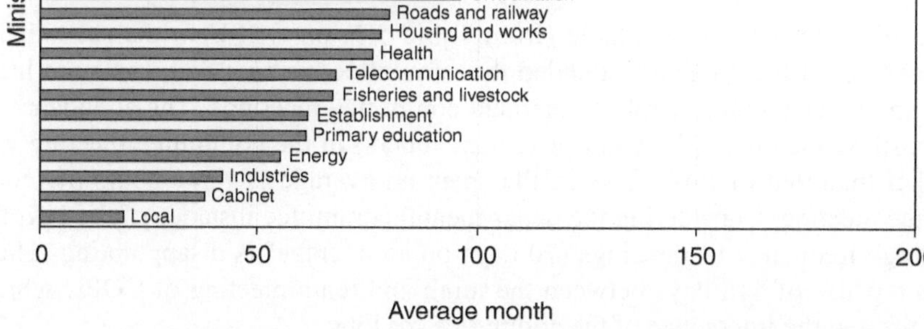

Figure 5.2 Delay of the ministries in taking effective preliminary steps in relation to audit objection.

gradually mounting as the CAG Office is improving its own performance (Rashid 2003). If one meeting of PAC takes place everyday (which is practically impossible, usually the committee meets twice a month) and discusses over one audit report, it will take at least 653 days to end discussing on the already submitted audit reports.

PROBLEMS AT THE IMPLEMENTATION STAGE

Very few of the hundreds of recommendations proposed by the PAC have been implemented by the concerned government agencies (CAG 1998: 6). A major hindrance in getting effective results and impact from the recommendations of the PAC is the absence of any institutional arrangement to follow up action on the recommendations or to monitor the implementation of its decisions. The PAC has no research or monitoring unit to perform this task. Unlike the fifth JS, there was no "action taken" sub-committee in the seventh JS, which might exclusively follow up and oversee the status of the implementation of its recommendations. Legally, the recommendations of the PAC are not binding on the executive. Consequently, the departments are not usually forfeited either for disregarding the recommendations of PAC or rendering any reasonable explanation of ignoring the PAC.

After the formation of the PAC in the second session of the seventh JS, it started functioning. Despite the low attendance of the members in the committee meeting the PAC met regularly and discussed financial irregularities of different public organizations. The concerned civil servants attended these meetings and explained audit objections against their organizations. The committee members unanimously made some useful recommendations to resolve these objections and irregularities. Hence, the PAC in the seventh JS had played a commendable role in ensuring financial accountability of the executive at the initiation and recommendation levels despite shortcomings. But the impact of PAC operations at the implementation stage – the most important stage of committee involvement in ensuring executive accountability was marginal.

Committee on public undertakings (COPU)

According to the data available (from Table 5.5) on COPU in the seventh JS, 80 percent of the members attended the committee meeting that was quite high. On an average, eight members attended committee meetings. The attendance of opposition members (three out of four members) in the committee meeting was higher than that of PAC. The COPU spent an average of three hours per committee meeting. Considering the departmental committee instance of the UK, the average frequency of meetings (70 days on an average) is disappointing. There was a pause of 418 days between the ninth and tenth meeting of COPU which, manifested the impotence of the committee for long.

AGENDA OF DELIBERATION

The committee examined the working of different public corporations and made useful recommendations in resolving problems. Five of ten committee meetings deliberated issues having policy and financial significance like irregularities on the tender process of the National Curriculum and Text Book Board (NCTBB), alleged involvement of officials in system loss and irregularities in DESA (Dhaka Electricity Supply Authority), investigation on the irregularities committed by an employee in the Bangladesh Tea Board, disciplinary measures of delinquent officials of the Power Development Board (PDB) and audit objections raised by the CAG. One meeting reviewed the status of implementation of the earlier recommendations. In the remaining committee meetings, deliberations were confined to the routine discussion on the operations and problems of different public bodies. The committee made a number of recommendations to resolve the deliberated problems in all the committee meetings. Most of the recommendations were not implemented. For instance, a three-member subcommittee was formed to prove into the alleged irregularities in paper purchase for NCTTB, and was advised to present a report. However, the committee did not ultimately produce any report.

Recommendations on PDB and Petrobangla were partially implemented. According to the PDB chairman, systems loss had been reduced by 10 percent to 32 percent in one year. As regards to bill collection, a marked progress was observed as PDB collected BDT 880 million (US$17 million) in January 2000 as against BDT 580 million (US$11 million) in January 1999. Out of audit objections amounting to BDT 22,000 million (US$423 million), PetroBangla resolved audit objections amounting BDT 13,000 million (US$250 million) in six months. Likewise, in the fifth JS, the first and second committee reports produced by the COPU were more critical in their observations. These revealed a vivid description of corruption, irregularity and mismanagement of public corporations in Bangladesh. The committee even identified the organizations and persons responsible for these irregularities in running public enterprises and made specific recommendations to rectify them. However, no corrective action had taken place on the basis of these reports (Ahmed 1998: 81).

The COPU started well after its constitution in the second session in the seventh parliament. But it did not meet regularly although the attendance (80 percent) of members was higher compared to PAC. At one stage the committee had been inactive for over a year. This reveals that from the initiation stage the prospect of the COPU to play an assertive role to hold the executive accountable was at stake. The committee also deliberated a number of issues related to bureaucratic accountability. The committee made useful recommendations in all its ten committee meetings. Only recommendations on PDB and Petrobangla were partially implemented. In short, the implication of COPU in ensuring executive accountability at the initiation and the recommendation level is moderate and minimal at the implementation stage.

Committee on Estimates (COE)

From the available data from Table 5.5 on COE, it is evident that 63 percent of the total members attended the committee meeting. On an average seven members attended the meeting. The COE spent an average of 2.75 hours for each committee meeting. The average frequency of committee meeting (70 days) is disappointing.

AGENDA OF DELIBERATION

The committee deliberated routine matters like sector-wise budget allocation and development planning of different ministries and the implementation status of projects under some corporations in six meetings out of nine reviewed. In the remaining three meetings, the committee deliberated on accountability matters such as investigation of corruption and fraud in DCC's (Dhaka City Corporation)s' Environment Development Project and various irregularities involving embezzlement of approximately BDT 200 million (US$3.8 million) in procurement of paper by National Curriculum and Text Book Board (NCTBB) for printing primary school textbooks.

In six meetings, the committee did not make any significant recommendations. In three meetings, the committee made some recommendations to resolve various issues including the constitution of a five-member sub-committee in order to submit a report on the progress of the project within a month and for further investigation into the alleged corruption in DCC's Environment Development Project and suggestion of exemplary penalty against the officials responsible for the alleged irregularities in NCTBB. No major recommendation was implemented. The committee failed to submit the report on the allegation of corruption and misappropriation in DCC's BDT 1460 million (US$28 million) Environment Development Projects within the fixed time limit.

The COE started well after its constitution in the second session in seventh JS. It met far less regularly than other financial committees. At one stage, the committee had been inactive for over a year. In the meantime a new chairman took over the leadership of the committee. The committee deliberated few issues related to government accountability. The committee made recommendations in three committee meetings only which evidenced its poor performance at recommendation stage. None of these few recommendations was implemented. In sum, the implication of COE in ensuring executive accountability at the initiation and the recommendation stage is marginal and non-existent at the implementation stage.

Selected standing committees on ministries

Standing Committee on Ministry of Establishment

Based on data available from Table 5.6 on the Standing Committee on Ministry of Establishment, it is obvious that on average 66 percent of the members

Table 5.6 Operations of standing committees on three selected ministries in the seventh JS

Name of committee	*Number of meetings held*	*Average attendance (%)*	*Total number of committee members*	*Average duration of meeting*	*Average frequency of meetings*	*Number of reports submitted*
SCOMOE	31	66	10	3.25 hours	26 days	0
SCOMOA	29	70	10	3 hours	36 days	0
SCOMOD	34	70	10	2.75 hours	39 days	1

Source: Compiled and calculated by the author from the minutes of (first to 14th meeting) of Standing Committee on Ministry of Establishment, (BJS, 1997–1999b), the minutes (first to 13th meeting) of Standing Committee on Ministry of Agriculture (BJS, 1997–1999c), and the first report of Standing Committee on Defense (2001), in the seventh JS (BJS 2001b, Bangladesh Parliament Secretariat).

Notes
SCOMOE – Standing Committee on Ministry of Establishment.
SCOMOA – Standing Committee on Ministry of Agriculture.
SCOMOD – Standing Committee on Ministry of Defense.

attended the committee meeting. The committee spent an average of 3.25 hours for each committee meeting. The average time interlude between two consecutive meetings of the committee is 26 days which was at par with committee's formal requirement to meet once in a month. However, there was an unusual pause of 51 days between the ninth and tenth meeting of Committee on Ministry of Establishment.

AGENDA OF DELIBERATION

Most of the committee discussions revolved around the promotion policy and resolving inter-cadre conflicts in the civil service. The committee received hearings from different cadre associations regarding their demands. The committee deliberated cases of irregularities and lapses such as the allegation regarding the misappropriation of money by Dr. M. Shahjahan and corruption charges against the Thana Nirbahi Officer (TNO) of Dawudkandi thana (name of a sub-district) in two meetings. Of 14 committee meetings reviewed, no recommendation was made in four meetings. The committees made some recommendations such as instruction to the Ministry of Establishment to present a report on the alleged corruption charges against the TNO of Dawudkandi sub-district and a report on the investigation of corruption case against Nitya Gopal and punishment under departmental disciplinary action. Most of the committee's recommendations were not implemented.

The committee was formed almost two years after the inauguration of the seventh JS. During this period, legislative surveillance over the operations of the ministry was non-existent. After the formation of the committee, it met at an average frequency of 26 days. Average attendance of members (66 percent) in the meeting was relatively high. The committee deliberated few issues related to executive accountability. The committee made recommendations in ten meetings out of 14 meetings reviewed, most of which were not implemented. In short, the impact of the Standing Committee on Ministry of Establishment in calling the government to account was limited due to its poor performance in initiation, recommendation and implementation levels.

Standing Committee on Ministry of Agriculture

Based on data available from Table 5.6 on the Standing Committee on Ministry of Agriculture, it is obvious that on average, 70 percent of the members attended the committee meeting. The committee spent an average of three hours for each committee sitting. The average time interlude between two consecutive meetings of the committee was 36 days which did not match with committee's formal requirement to meet once in a month. Unusual pauses between two consecutive meetings of the Standing Committee on Agriculture, for example, between the third and fourth meetings, tenth and eleventh meetings and eleventh and twelve meetings was 61, 75 and 143 days respectively (BJS 1997–1999). This manifests the committee's interrupted performance at the initiation stage.

It discussed numerous issues including routine discussion on the activities of different public agencies under the ministry. It also deliberated issues related to bureaucratic accountability like irregularities in Bangladesh Agriculture Research Council (BARC) and irregularities in the sugarcane sector. The committee started its work two years after the first session of the seventh parliament. After its formation, the committee met at an average frequency of 36 days. However, it had remained inactive periodically. Average attendance of members (70 percent) in committee meetings was relatively high. The committee deliberated few issues related to government accountability. The committee did not make any specific recommendations in seven meetings out of 14 meetings reviewed. No committee recommendation was implemented. This shows the committee's dismal performance at all levels.

The Standing Committee on Ministry of Defense

The committee started its operations almost two years after the first session of the seventh parliament. It held 34 meetings in the seventh JS. The average frequency of committee meetings was 39 days. Average attendance of members in the committee was 70 percent. It spent an average of 2.75 hours per meeting for deliberation. It also submitted a report to the House. It formed a sub-committee which also produced six interim sub-committee reports.

AGENDA OF DELIBERATION

The major agenda of deliberation of the Standing Committee on Ministry of Defense included alleged irregularities in the trial of the killers of the former president Ziaur Rahman in 1981, the controversial purchase of MIG-29 fighter jets at the expense of US$124 million for the Bangladesh Air Force and the purchase of a Korean frigate at the cost of US$100 million for the Bangladesh Navy. Most of the agenda was related to government accountability.

The air chief, the navy chief and the defense secretary attended several committee meetings and answered different queries on the mentioned issues by members. An attempt to unearth the alleged large-scale embezzlement of public money in the purchase of MIG-29 fighter planes and Korean frigate was foiled by the refusal of the government (with the support of treasury bench committee members) to supply the committee members with necessary document on the grounds of state security.[6] Thus the existing system of maintaining secrecy of information is a major deterrent to ensuring transparency of administration and compelling the civil servants to furnish the committees with necessary information, papers or documents.

Although the members deliberated on defense-related issues, the attempts yielded no substantial results. The committee made some important recommendations, which were not implemented. Of note, the committee did not make any recommendations in three out of ten meetings reviewed.

The role of the Standing Committee on Ministry of Defense in ensuring government accountability, therefore, was intermittent at the initiation stage, moderate at the recommendation stage and insignificant at the implementation stage. The committee's endeavor to ensure transparency and responsiveness of government were thwarted by the government's denial to provide necessary documents on state security ground.

From the preceding discussion on the operations of three ministerial committees, it is evident that these committees have not been successful in ensuring government accountability. Their endeavor is half-heartedly confined to initiation and recommendation stages. At the implementation stage their role to ensure government accountability is virtually in despair.

Very few cases can be cited when the recommendations made by the ministerial committees have been implemented. The recommendation of Standing Committee on Ministry of Establishment not to take further decision on inter-cadre promotion unless a comprehensive policy is formulated considering seniority, salary discrimination and promotional scope was partially implemented. Two other instances might be mentioned in this regard, which were not covered by the committees under my empirical research arena. But the Standing Committee on Ministry of Establishment played a significant role to implement the recommendations (these were related to personnel matters – suspension of civil servants) made by the other committees.

Dr. Emdadul Huq, Director General of the Livestock Research Institute was made OSD (Officer of Special Desk) on recommendations by parliamentary Standing Committee on Ministry of Fisheries and Livestock due to his involvement in various irregularities. However, he was reinstated later allegedly at the initiative of a minister (*Daily Star*, August 6, 2000). Several ministers have been seen forgiving errant officials defying the recommendations of committees. "We're neglected. The ministry doesn't recognize let alone execute our recommendations. Only the press has kept us visible to the public by reporting our activities", observed Abdul Mannan, Chairman of the parliamentary Standing Committee on the Ministry of Agriculture in the eighth JS at a seminar (*Daily Star*, April 5, 2004).

Moreover, the Health and Family Planning Ministry suspended three doctors of National Institute of Cardiovascular Disease (NICVD) on the alleged negligence of duties in the treatment of Bhutto, a Jatiya Party MP following the recommendation of the committee on the concerned ministry. Probably this was the first time when any committee took only ten days to recommend on any irregularity and the ministry took only four days to implement the recommendation. Of note, the late MP was a colleague of the committee members who investigated the alleged irregularities. These instances were of course exceptions and involved no political risk for the incumbent government.

Conclusion

The prevailing formal institutional structure of the political system in Bangladesh appears handicapped in checking the unbridled power and authority of government and ill-equipped in calling the government to account. All the major characteristics of a strong legislature are virtually absent in Bangladesh. State power is highly centralized rather than dispersed. The president is a titular head of state and he performs according to the advices of the prime minister and plays into the hand of the ruling regime. All the major political institutions including the Speaker of the parliament have been politicized and used against the major opposition parties in the country. Major local government institutions have been dysfunctional for over a decade. The parliament and parliamentary committees have been dominated and monopolized by the ruling government. No space has been left for the opposition political parties to participate and contribute to the governance system. The opposition is thus left out to the street. Thus the external environment of the parliament and parliamentary committees has largely determined the way parliament and committees have performed in Bangladesh.

Institutionally, the parliamentary committee system in Bangladesh is prominently modeled on the Westminster system. In fact, many of the key[7] features of the committee system within the Westminster tradition which at least bear the potentials of checking the monopoly of governmental power and calling the government to account are unfortunately missing in Bangladesh. Parliamentary committees in Bangladesh are permanent and correspond to governmental structure. Their jurisdictions are comprehensive ranging from legislation to oversight to investigation. Formally the committees can select their chairs and members. In practice, the final list of committee chairs and members must win the nod of the prime minister. The committees meet in camera and decide on the basis of majority. Committees can partially set their own agenda and have the power to send for papers, persons and documents with the exception that government may decline to produce a document on the ground that its disclosure would be prejudicial to the safety or interest of the state. They can consider legislative bills referred to them by the House and do not have any role in budget allocation and demands for grants. The institutional arrangement of the committee system in Bangladesh thus places the government (the major party) in an advantageous position to be the ultimate arbiter on any issue of governance. Moreover, the parliament secretariat is not in practice independent of the executive. The incumbent government has enormous influence/control on the working of this institution. A dangerous trend of recruiting personal secretaries of chairmen from different cadres is diverting and displacing the ultimate of goal of the committee system from legislative oversight to personal benefits of MPs and government officials. This has further weakened the existing committee system in Bangladesh parliament. In sum, institutionally Bangladesh has got a weak committee system with marginal scope in ensuring executive accountability.

In terms of ensuring government accountability, the role of the PAC is confined largely to the initiation and the recommendation stages with moderate implications at the implementation level by recovering a considerable amount of money from the delinquent civil servants. The implication of the COE in securing executive accountability at the initiation and the recommendation stage is insignificant and missing at the implementation stage. The role of the COPU in ensuring executive accountability at the initiation and recommendation stage is moderate and minimal at the implementation stage.

It is obvious from the operations of three selected ministerial committees that their endeavor to ensure executive accountability is half-heartedly confined to the initiation and the recommendation stages. At the implementation stage, their role to ensure executive accountability is virtually missing. The major thrust of all these committees was on regularity and financial propriety. The opposition MPs very often had exposed the issues of discussion and the deviated actions of public officials to the media disregarding the formal restrictions to do so and thus played a significant role in making the working of committees more visible.

Response from the government departments in implementing the recommendations of different committees is lukewarm. The decision of committee is not binding on the government agencies and no mechanisms and initiatives exist to keep track on the implementation of committee recommendations. No punitive measure is taken on account of non-compliance of committee recommendations. The implementation of the recommendations made by the committee is also contingent upon the willingness of the government of the day.

The domination of the ruling party is evident in the structural and functional arrangement of the committee system in Bangladesh. Structurally the committee is arranged in such a way that without the assent of the party in power no action can be taken to make the executive accountable. The stalwarts (including the party chief) of the ruling party have enormous influence from the formation of committees to the implementation of committee recommendations. The institutional domination of the ruling party has also been reflected in the real-world functioning of the committee in securing executive accountability in Bangladesh. Prime ministers in the 1990s have been seen interfering in the operations of committees.

Unlike earlier JSs, committees in the eighth JS have started working without the participation of the main opposition MPs. Lack of minimum understanding between the two major political parties on the term of references of committee operation accounts for this. In the absence of the main opposition MPs who are generally considered as the key players in making committees lively and vibrant, the effectiveness of these committees in ensuring executive accountability is in question. Even committees in the current JS do not meet regularly. A dozen committees have violated the JS Rules by not holding meetings within 30 days. Of them, four committees have failed even to hold a single meeting since their formation in July 2003 (*Daily Star*, October 26, 2003). Some committees including COPU could not hold committee meetings due to quorum crisis. Burning issues have been dropped several times from the agenda of committee deliberation at the directive of higher government authorities. A definite trend of degeneration of parliament and parliamentary committees is in sight in the eighth JS.

Questionnaire survey/interview of MPs reveals that MPs are discontented with the current performance of the committee system and lend their support in favor of a thorough overhauling of the existing committee system in the Bangladesh parliament. However, the respondents were found clearly divided on reform proposals which advocated of empowering the opposition and accommodating the same in the governance system.

6 Parliamentary control and government accountability in India

The role of parliamentary committees

This chapter aims at examining the working of parliamentary committee system in the Indian parliament in order to map the nature and extent of influence exerted by these committees in making the government accountable. For a systematic presentation and better understanding of the issue, this chapter is further organized into three parts i.e. the Indian parliament in its political context, the historical evolution of the parliamentary committee system in India, the formal arrangement of committee system and its real-world implications in constraining government and calling it to account.

The Indian parliament in its political context

India is the world's biggest democracy in term of population size. It has been a stable and vibrant democracy since its independence from the British in 1947 (except the brief authoritarian interlude of the 1975–1977 National Emergency under Indira Gandhi) and parliament has remained at the heart of its democratic advancement. The military had stayed away from politics and never hindered the democratic continuity. The Indian political system was patterned after the majoritarian and adversarial Westminster model. India inherited the plurality electoral system from the British. The balance of power in the Indian federal system was asymmetrical in favor of the central government from the outset. The founding fathers had given the central government the right to dismiss state governments and to replace them with direct rule from the center for the purpose of dealing with grave emergencies. The union government of India consists of 28 states and seven union territories. States with bicameral legislature are Karnataka, Maharashtra, Madhya Pradesh, Uttar Pradesh, Bihar, and Jammu and Kashmir (*Hindu*, December 3, 2001).

The key to the success of the Indian democratic system operating within an extremely heterogeneous society according to Lijphart (1996: 252–266) was due to Congress party's power sharing strategy. Even though India was not an avowed consociational system, yet all the features of that system could be found there such as government by grand coalition, cultural autonomy (constitutionally guaranteed minority rights), proportionality (distributing portfolios among different religious, regional, linguistic groups and to backward classes) and minority veto.

A fully-fledged parliamentary system of government with a modern institutional framework was established in India with the coming into force of the Republican constitution in 1950, the country became a republic. The Indian parliament came into being with the first national elections in independent India in 1952. Under the constitution, parliament consists of the president of India, the Council of States (*Rajya Sabha*) and the House of the People (*Lok Sabha*). The President is elected by the members of an electoral college consisting of the elected members of both Houses of Parliament and the elected members of state legislatures (only MLAs of Lower House in case of bicameral state legislature). The president holds office for a term of five years from the date on which he enters upon his office. Although the president of India who is the head of the state is a figurehead, he can exercise some discretion including the power to withhold assent even to money bills. He cannot however return a money bill for reconsideration to the House (Ahmed 2001: 24).

The Indian parliament is bicameral in which the *Lok Sabha*, (the lower House) enjoys more important power. The *Lok Sabha* has 545 members: 543 elected from single-member constituencies (79 seats are reserved for scheduled castes and 41 for scheduled tribes) and two representatives of Anglo-Indians appointed by the president (*The Economist*, September 5, 2003). Legislations can originate in either House and in order to become law, legislation must pass each House and have the assent of the president. In case of any disagreement between the two houses, it is resolved in a joint sitting of both Houses. As council of ministers is responsible only to *Lok Sabha* and money bills must originate in that chamber, the *Rajya Sabha* has failed to create a distinctive identity for itself (Rubinoff 1999: 17). The *Rajya Sabha* has the power neither to introduce money bills nor reject them. At most, it can delay money bills for two weeks since at the end of that period a money bill pending before the *Rajya Sabha* is considered to have passed (Kapoor and Mehta 2002: 8).

Membership of *Rajya Sabha*, as provided in the constitution, cannot be more than 250 – 238 members representing the States and Union territories and 12 members nominated by the president. The *Rajya Sabha* is led by the vice-president of India who is the upper chamber's ex officio chair. The representatives of the States are elected by the elected members of State Assemblies in accordance with the system of proportional representation by means of the single transferable vote. The representatives of the Union territories in *Rajya Sabha* are chosen in accordance with law enacted by parliament.

There are 12 members nominated by the president from amongst the persons having special knowledge or practical experience in such areas of life as literature, science, art and social service. Presently, the *Rajya Sabha* has 245 members. This membership has changed from time to time since its inception in 1952. It has gradually increased from 216 in 1952 to 245, its present membership. The *Rajya Sabha* is not subject to dissolution, but as nearly as possible one-third of the members retire on the expiration of every second year. The term of office of a member (both elected and nominated) is six years.

The *Rajya Sabha* plays a role secondary to that of the *Lok Sabha* in that it has no control over the executive branch. A key reason for the lesser importance of the *Rajya Sabha* is the extended dominance of the Congress in national and state level legislatures until 1977. Nevertheless, during emergencies, if the *Lok Sabha* is under suspension, the *Rajya Sabha* can become a forum for voicing of public concerns and thus serve a check on any exercise of arbitrary power by the executive (Baxter *et al.* 2002: 77). A key factor in India's bicameral parliamentary system where the role of the *Rajya Sabha* and the relationship between the upper and the lower Houses had assumed a new dimension, especially after the end of the single party dominance and the emergence of smaller parties in coalition governments at the Centre and in the States. The *Rajya Sabha*, dominated by the Congress and its allies during the 13th *Lok Sabha*, was not a secondary rubber stamp body. In matters of ordinary legislation it had equal powers with the *Lok Sabha*. The incumbent government had to compromise a lot with the main opposition in getting its policies through the two Houses. Nevertheless, the numerical superiority of *Lok Sabha* matters. In any joint sitting, the *Lok Sabha* outnumbers the *Rajya Sabha* by two to one.

At the heart of executive-legislative relations is the budgetary process. In India, the parliamentary budget process is allowed to last up to 75 days. After the general discussion on budget the parliament is adjourned for a fixed period (25 days on an average). During this recess, the budget/demand for grants of the ministries/departments is scrutinized by 17 departmentally-related standing committees (DRSCs). MPs in Indian *Lok Sabha* are allowed to reduce expenditure and vary taxation. Increases in expenditure require the recommendation of the president. Taxation is also dealt with slightly differently to expenditure in that changes take effect immediately but the House still has 75 days to approve. The reports of the committees are then considered by the House. The post-budget expenditures are scrutinized and audited by the Public Accounts Committee (PAC), Committee on Public Undertaking (CPU) and Committee on Estimates (COE).

In India, the parliament constitutionally assumes the sole responsibility for law-making. In practice, legislation has been a monopoly of the executive government. Of 3317 private members' bill (from 1952–2001) only 14 private members' bills – nine introduced in the *Lok Sabha* and five in the *Rajya Sabha* – have been enacted so far. Two of these 14 bills were from members other than the ruling parties (Malhotra 2001: 170). The rules of procedure allow the scrutiny of legislation by committees in Indian parliament. However, bills are usually referred to DRSCs/select committees by the Speaker/the House after they are introduced in the House.

Most of the survey respondents (see Appendix, Table A1.1 for detailed survey result) completely disagreed (85 percent) with the statement that institutionally committees are much weaker in parliamentary systems than in presidential systems. The mean score is 0.7 only. The respondents opined that the parliamentary system introduced by the British in India had been working well against all odds and contributed significantly to the continuation of democratic governance in India, the largest functioning constitutional democracy in the world in term of population size. India celebrated the 50th Anniversary of the Indian Parliament in May 2002. Over the years, various reform measures have been introduced to make the parliament effective and rationalize and strengthen the parliamentary committee system in India. Within a parliamentary system (whose main characteristic is the fusion of the government and governing party), the parliamentary committee system in India has played a crucial role in calling the government to account. Most of the respondents were not in favor of switching the political system from parliamentary system to the presidential one. They think that within the existing parliamentary system, more scope is left to make committees stronger and more effective.

On the question of the efficacy and the utility of upper House committees in Indian parliament in a bid to make the executive accountable, an overwhelming 100 percent of the respondents answered in the positive. The *Rajya Sabha* has been an instrument of checks and balances and has played a crucial role in making the government accountable, they maintain. They think that within a parliamentary framework, the *Rajya Sabha* has been a living instance of diffusion of government power and authority in India which has helped create some political space for the opposition parties to operate and moderate the political race among the contending political parties. If one party holds majority in one chamber and lacks the same in another chamber, participating political parties must have to compromise in order to avoid political deadlock and instability. That has been the case in India several times. Over time political parties have learnt and got accustomed to compromising and sharing power with rival parties which has enabled parliamentary democracy to get institutionalized in a multiethnic society like India and has contributed substantially to holding the government accountable.

All the respondents (100 percent, with mean score 4) were of the view that a strong parliament is a prerequisite for a strong committee system and vice versa. They admit that within the Westminster parliamentary system, parliament is inherently weak vis-à-vis the executive and so is the parliamentary committee system. Most of them believe that the parliament could not fare best due to sporadic quorum crisis (one-tenth of the total membership of each House makes a quorum) and frequent interruptions/adjournments due to disorderly scenes (26 percent of allocated time was lost in thirteenth *Lok Sabha* due to interruptions).[1] However, they invariably termed the parliament as functioning fairly. Presence of strong oppositions has been a key feature of the parliaments since 1989. Despite being predominantly an institution of regime maintenance, the Indian parliament has played significant role in holding the executive accountable too. The respondents felt that the committees had performed well and still been in the process of evolution.

India has a written constitution. A bill to amend the constitution must be passed in each House of the parliament by a majority of the total membership of that House and also by a majority of not less than two-thirds of the members of that House present and voting. However, the constitution provides for judicial review of legislative actions, thereby imposing some checks on the arbitrary exercise of power by it. The Supreme Court of India for instance, declared several legislations passed by the parliament *ultra vires* of the constitution (Bhardwaj 1998; Ahmed 2001).

With the adoption of the Constitution Act of 1985, a member of a House who belongs to a political party becomes disqualified from being a member if s/he voluntarily gives up membership of such political party, votes or abstains from voting against the direction of the party without prior permission. The thirteenth *Lok Sabha* passed the Constitution (52nd Amendment) Act to bring some key changes in the existing anti-defection law. The amendment does not recognize splits of one-third of any legislature party as being legal as was the case in the original act. Now, whoever defects, either individual or group, however large it may be, will lose his/her membership and cannot contest elections for at least six years. Nor can they hold any post of profit till they are eligible to contest polls again.

Committee members were asked about the anti-defection law and its impact on the behavior of an individual MP attending committee sessions. Only 35 percent of the respondents completely agree that the existing floor crossing article in its current form circumscribes individual freedom of an MP and it certainly has an impact on the functioning of committees too. On the issue of floor crossing, the mean score of the respondents is 1.9 which indicates that the majority of the respondents support the prevailing constitutional provision of floor crossing. They think that the anti-defection law in its current form has made party discipline much more stringent than before. Most of the respondents believe that this law has obvious limitations. However, this law will minimize floor crossing and horse-trading and prove its worth for the political stability of the country in due course.

An analysis of the view of respondents concerning the relationship between the control of their parties over them and the level of committee strength, 95 percent hold that there is a strong correlation between these two variables. However, almost all of the respondents, irrespective of party affiliation, are of the view that in India, the influence of party over the committee member is not that substantial and once they are in the committees, they are allowed to work in committees on their personal capacities without fear or favor. Committee sessions are more informal and cordial. Committees generally function in unity and with consensus. They observe that backbenchers from the treasury bench and the opposition are allowed to express their views on the deliberated subject. Sometimes harsh criticisms of government by the opposition members have been entertained in committee sessions.

When asked about the role of opposition in holding the government accountable, an overwhelming 100 percent of respondents maintain that a strong but disciplined opposition is at the heart of parliament and parliamentary committees. They believe that it is the opposition in the parliament who provides constructive criticisms to the policies and programs of the government and serves as a shadow government. Since 1989 to date all the six parliaments were "hung parliaments" and there was very strong opposition invariably in every parliament (48 percent of the total members in the thirteenth *Lok Sabha* and 44 percent in the fourteenth *Lok Sabha* were from the opposition). The relationship between the two top leaders of the two major parties in India has been a working one over the years. On issues like foreign policy, defense, liberalization of economy, upliftment of minority groups and so on, there has always been a national consensus though there might have been some differences. In India the content and character of the opposition has undergone drastic transformation in recent years which has cast a major responsibility on the opposition in ensuring the smooth functioning of legislative institutions. The late 1980s and the 1990s witnessed coalitions of parties forming governments with the major opposition party choosing to sit in the opposition.

Elections have been in general free and fair. The prevailing electoral system purposely made it more difficult for the disparate opposition to win a number of seats commensurate with the vote it obtained and perpetuated Congress rule in a one-party dominant system for 30 years (Kothari 1964). Eight times the electoral system paradoxically produced a majority government while the electorate was casting most of its votes for the opposition parties. From 1952 to 1971, the Congress won between 54 percent and 73 percent of seats with between 40.7 percent and 47.8 percent of the votes (Weiner 1980: 69). No party was ever able to muster absolute majority of votes in a national election; so it was partly through the plurality system that INC (Indian National Congress) manage to secure hegemonic position (Enskat *et al.* 2001: 560).

The party system and electoral process in India have evolved over the last five decades. The one-party dominance of the first two decades slowly gave way to fragmentation of mainstream parties, proliferation of regional parties, representation of multiple ideologies and emergence of coalition governance in the next three decades. What we see today is thus transformation of the political scene from the one dominant party period (1952–1977) to a period of multiparty governance (1977–) (Malhotra 2002: 102).

By facilitating a measure of the much-needed decentralization or devolution power away from New Delhi to the states, the various coalitional configurations have restored some validity to regional grassroots democratic institutions. Moreover, under coalition governments, politics remains highly pluralistic. Since the prime minister and cabinet are chosen by multiple political actors, their power is also constrained by multiple constituencies. Today the complexity and fragility of the coalition governments, their rapid turnover and their dependency on region and state-based parties have sapped the executive capacity of the governments (Sharma 2003: 79).

The fragmentation of party system has also enhanced the powers of India's president. Since the early 1990s, presidents have acted in ways that stress the autonomy of their office. Not only have the rises of "hung" parliaments since 1989 given presidents much discretion in the formation of governments (albeit, presidents normally ask the party with most seats in the *Lok Sabha* to form the government), the presidents today openly challenge perceived "unconstitutional" ruling by the governments. Most importantly, presidents have ably resisted political pressure to invoke Article 356, the "president's rule" clause as part of a plan to unseat a democratically elected state government for partisan advantage. For instance, in 1997, President K.R. Narayanan rejected the United Front government led by Inder K. Gujral proposal to dismiss the BJP government in Uttar Pradesh (Sharma 2003: 80). Likewise, in September 1998, he rejected the NDA government led by Vajpayee proposal to dismiss the Rabri Devi government in Bihar (*Hindu*, October 3, 1998).

The Speaker is elected by the House from among its members. Unlike the British parliament he does not usually resign from the party under whose ticket he is elected. Out of 13 Speakers of *Lok Sabha* till date, four have been elected unanimously. Dr. Neelam Sanjiva Reddy is the lone Speaker since independence who after assuming the office of the Speaker formally resigned from his political party. However, Speakers are said to have run their offices in neutral manners.

There are over 200,000 local self-governing institutions in India. These bodies direct and oversee the functioning of the executive at different levels and geographies. The latest significant political development in India is the constitutional status and stability provided to *Panchyati Raj* (governance by a village council of five people elected by all adult members of the village) institutions. It is unique in the history of democracy anywhere to have over three million elected representatives – with one-third representation to women and reservations for deprived sections of the society – to be active participants in the business of the country's governance (Kashyap 2000: 133). There was an ascending order of local government from the village through block or sub-district, district to the state capital (Silva 2000: 54). Democratic institutions emanated from the Indian society and thus democracy found it easy to get consolidated in India over time.

While the Indian system of government and more particularly the parliament is basically patterned on the Westminster model, such significant departures have been made in adapting the system to Indian conditions that it can no longer be called a parliamentary system of the British type. In fact, it has several features more akin to the US presidential system than to Westminster (Kashyap cited in Kashyap 1979: 289).

Evolution of the parliamentary committee system in India

The antecedent of legislative committees in India was contained in the Montagu-Chelmsford Reforms of 1919, which recommended the establishment of committees. Standing committees initially germinated in the provinces and had reached the center by 1922. These committees were formal, elected and powerful bodies (Maheshwari 1968: 46). Each committee consisted of five members for a term of one year, two from the council of states and three from the legislative assembly. They considered all bills, including major questions of policy and issued annual reports. However, under British rule, these were absolutely advisory bodies and their proceedings were strictly confidential (Suri 1979: 28–29).

Of all the parliamentary committees of *Lok Sabha*, the Public Accounts Committee (PAC) was the oldest. It was first constituted in 1921 and the finance member of the Governor General's Council was the ex-officio chairman of the committee. It then consisted of 12 members of whom eight were elected by the non-official members of the-then central legislative Assembly and three were nominated by the-then Governor General. The committee continued to function under the old arrangement even after 1947, with the finance minister functioning as its chairman. This naturally restricted the free expression of views and criticism of the executive. In 1950, the committee became a full-fledged parliamentary committee under the control of the Speaker with one MP elected as its chairman (Malhotra 2000; Mathur 2002: 422). Prior to 1954–1955, the PAC comprised of 15 members elected by *Lok Sabha* only. Since 1954–1955, seven members of *Rajya Sabha* have been accommodated in the committee, thus raising its strength to 22 (Shrivastava and Shrivastava 1999: 29).

The Estimates Committee (EC) was constituted in 1950. Before constituting the Committee on Public Undertakings (COPU), parliamentary accountability over public enterprises has been exercised by the EC. Initially the Estimates Committee consisted of 25 members elected by the *Lok Sabha* from amongst its members. In 1956, the membership of the committee was increased to 30. With the establishment of a large number of public enterprises in India and the inability of PAC and EC to oversee the operations of these bodies, Committee on Public Undertakings came into being in May 1964. Originally the CPU consisted of 15 members (ten from *Lok Sabha* and five from *Rajya Sabha*). Eventually in 1974, in order to keep up with the expanding work, the member strength was raised to 22 (15 from *Lok Sabha* and seven from *Rajya Sabha*)

No real change in the nature of committees initially took place after the transfer of power in 1947. Following the adoption of the constitution that made India a republic in 1950, employees of the parliamentary secretariat instead of ministry personnel served as legislative support staff. However, once the constituent assembly was replaced with a new parliament after the election of 1952, the activities of standing committees were curbed (Singhvi 1979: 3). Nevertheless, Article 105 of the constitution made provision for legislative committees. Under its authority, consultative committees were constituted in 1954 in order to bring MPs close to the parliament. These bodies which existed for each ministry were completely informal and could be described more educational than advisory in function (Khadilkar 1979: 13).

The creation of subject committees was first discussed by the presiding officers of legislative bodies in India way back in 1978 (Malhotra 1993: 169). Earlier subject committees were constituted in the states of Kerala in 1980 and in West Bengal in 1988. The first concrete steps towards introduction of the subject committees was taken in the ninth *Lok Sabha* when three subject committees on Agriculture, Science and Technology and Environment and Forests were constituted with effect from August 18, 1989 (Shekar 2003: 92). Comprehensive rules were made to run these three committees. However, the parliament took more than a decade and a half to create full-fledged DRSCs committees.

Two major factors are worth mentioning with regard to the creation of DRSCs. It was only when the government of Prime Minister P.V. Narasimha Rao took office in June 1991 that progress could be made on the committee front. In a minority position (having 225 of 537 seats in the *Lok Sabha*), the new prime minister needed to find a mechanism that would involve the opposition yet not impede the functioning of his government. The then *Lok Sabha* Speaker Shivraj Patil played the most crucial role in enhancing the role of parliament and institutionalizing the committee system. An important aspect of a parliament's power is the power of the purse i.e. control over finance. While the *Lok Sabha* has the right to discuss, debate and approve the financial proposal of the government, over the years, these discussions have not permitted a detailed scrutiny of the budgetary proposals of the government. In most cases, the *Lok Sabha* has passed the demand for grants of departments even without a discussion. Between 1985 and 1995 on most occasions, more than 85 percent of the demands were passed without any discussion (Shastri 1998: 184–185). It was on March 11, 1993 that a joint sitting of the rules committees of *Lok Sa*bha and *Rajya Sabha* was held to discuss and approve the proposal relating to the formation of departmentally-related committees. The departmentally-related standing committees are the latest innovation in the ever-evolving process of parliamentary surveillance over the executive to ensure its accountability.

Institutional arrangements of parliamentary committee system in India and its implications in holding the government accountable

The constitution of India does not contain any detailed provision about the role and functions of committees. However, parliamentary committees in India are (structure, functions and procedures for conducting business of the committees) governed by the Rules of Procedure and Conduct of Business of the House and they function under the general direction of the respective presiding officer of the House. There are three sets of rules relating to parliamentary committees. While general rules are applicable to all committees, specific rules make provisions for particular committees and internal rules regulate the internal procedure of each committee and are made by committees themselves with approval of the Speaker.

Typology of committees

Parliamentary committees in India are of two broad categories: ad hoc committees and the standing committees. Ad hoc committees are appointed for a specific purpose and they cease to exist once they finish their assignments and submit a report. The principal ad hoc committees are the Select and Joint Committees on Bill. Others like the Railway Convention Committee (RCC), the Committees on the Draft Five Year Plans and the Hindi Equivalents Committees were appointed for specific purposes. Apart from the ad hoc committees, each

House of Parliament has standing committees like the Business Advisory Committee, the Committee on Petitions, the Committee of Privileges and the Rules Committee etc. (To get a comprehensive understanding of the types and nature of the parliamentary committees in India see Appendix, Table A3.1). Out of 48 standing committees (24 joint committees, 24 single-House committees) in the Indian parliament our focus will be on all the three financial committees (PAC, COPU and EC) and three selected DRSCs that are charged with oversight of the government. Besides, there are a large number of consultative committees (30 or so) headed by ministers in the Indian parliament which are precluded from the purview of my research. These committees do not have any financial or legislative functions. They are meant for informal discussions between the government and MPs on policies and programs of government and the manner of implementation thereof.

Other committees

Of special importance is yet another class of committees which act as parliament's "Watchdogs" over the executive. These are the Committees on Subordinate Legislation, the Committee on Government Assurances, the Committee on Estimates, the Committee on Public Accounts and the Committee on Public Undertakings and Departmentally-Related Standing Committees (DRSCs). Three financial committees – Committee on Estimates, the Committee on Public Accounts and the Committee on Public Undertakings and DRSCs play an important role in exercising a check over governmental expenditure and policy formulation. While the Estimates Committees is a committee consisting of 30 members exclusively from the *Lok Sabha*, PAC and COPU are in the nature of joint committees of parliament in that each consists of members of both Houses of parliament, 15 from *Lok Sabha* and seven from *Rajya Sahha*.

Select and joint committees

When a bill comes up before a House for general discussion, it is open to that House to refer it to a select committee of the House or a joint committee of the two Houses. A motion has to be moved and adopted to this effect in the House in which the bill comes up for consideration. In case the motion adopted is for reference of the bill to a joint committee, the decision is conveyed to the other House requesting them to nominate members of the other House to serve on the committee.

The select or joint committee considers the bill clause by clause just as the two Houses do. Amendments can be moved to various clauses by members of the committee. The committees can also take evidence of associations, public bodies or experts who are interested in the bill. After the bill has thus been considered the committee submits its report to the House. Members who do not agree with the majority report may append their minutes of dissent to the report.

Departmentally-related standing committees (DRSCs)[2]

Of the 17 DRSCs, 11 belong to *Lok Sabha* and six to *Rajya Sabha*. Each of these standing committees shall consist of not more than 45 members, 30 to be nominated by the Speaker from amongst the members of *Lok Sabha* and 15 members to be nominated by the chairman of *Rajya Sabha* from amongst the members of *Rajya Sabha*. The term of the members of these committees shall not exceed one year. However, according to a convention observed by national political parties, their members are allowed to a two year term on the committee. The functions of these committees are to consider demands for grants of concerned ministries, examine the bills referred to them, consider annual reports of ministries and national policy documents and report to the House committees. Of note, matters of day-today administration of the ministries/departments are not considered by DRSCs.

Structure

On the question of the formation of all committees immediately after the commencement of a new parliament (preferably in the inaugural session), 85 percent of the respondents were in favor of such an idea. The respondents reported that most of the committees in the Indian parliament were in most cases formed immediately after the commencement of a new parliament. That has become a practice. However, the financial committees and departmentally-related committees were not formed in the inaugural session of the thirteenth and fourteenth *Lok Sabha*. Delay in forming the committees divests the parliament of its right to perform its key function of oversight of the executive in a competent manner. On an average, earlier *Lok Sabhas* took two months to form the committees and committees took an average 20 days to get their business started with. The respondents think that in the era of coalition governance in India, it takes some time to negotiate with different political parties about the composition of large numbers of committees in Indian parliament. An interesting point to note is that since the date of dissolution of parliament, it took an average 3.5 months to get started with a new parliament in India in the 1990s. Thus in the last 15 years, the executive of caretaker regimes had been immune from any parliamentary surveillance for 15 months. The *Rajya Sabha*, which is a permanent House, kept a watchful eye on the operation of governments during this time, the respondents argued.

Most of the respondents (90 percent) think that the terms of committees should be made coterminous with the lifespan of the parliament. They think that this will provide opportunity to the members to develop expertise and allow continuity and consistency in approach. In India, most of the committees have permanent flavor and committee members/chairs are elected annually. Although the chairman is appointed for one year, conventionally he/she is allowed to serve between two and five years. This enables the chairman to gain valuable experience and expertise which may help develop specialization. In the thirteenth *Lok Sabha*, PAC had high turnover of chairmanship i.e. three chairmen in four years. Each committee has tenure of one year. This means members have no opportunity of specializing in a particular subject or group of subjects unless they can persuade their whips to let them continue to serve on particular a committee. This ad hoc nature tells upon the quality of work done by committees whose reports suffer from absence of critical analysis of the work of ministries under supervision (GOI 2002). Problems still remain with the turnover of the membership. In India, average turnover of committee members is 33 percent due mainly to death, shuffling/reshuffling of committee composition. This deters committee members from developing specialized knowledge and expertise to make the committees more effective.

In India, parliamentary committees functionally correspond to ministerial structure. Several ministries are organized and included under the jurisdiction of one broad committee. This is how the division of committees is based on the parliament's own functional needs. Most of the respondents were very critical about the issue of DRSCs' exact correspondence to government ministries. Only 15 percent of the respondents agreed completely that DRSCs should parallel the structure of government. Currently there are 44 central government ministries in India. There are 29 cabinet ministers and 48 state ministers. The respondents reported that this proposal having significant merits was utterly impossible and impractical to implement in Indian context. Each DRSC is a joint committee which has 45 members, 30 from *Lok Sabha* and 15 from *Rajya Sabha*. If each committee parallels the government structure then there will be 44 DRSCs. If the size of each DRSC is 45, it will require 1980 MPs to fill the available positions. From the fourteenth *Lok Sabha*, the size of DRSC has been reduced from 45 to 30. Even if the size of each committee is 30, the total number available committee positions will be 1320 which is far lesser than the combined total number (770) of MPs in *Lok Sabha* and *Rajya Sabha*. However, those who supported the proposal had their own logics. DRSCs have 45 members and a short lifespan (one year). The large size of the DRSC makes effective functioning difficult. Jurisdiction of the committees extends to more than one ministry. Such bunching prevents more focused work and reduces the scope of acquiring expertise by the members in respect of any departments.

Seventy percent of the respondents completely agree that small committees (consisting of 15–20 members or so) enhance committee specialization and break down party division. The size of the most of committees in India ranges between 22 and 50. The size of DRSCs has already been reduced from 45 to 30. But due to poor attendance (45 percent or so) of committee members, most committee sessions become small one in a deviated way. Although a DRSC is comprised of 45 members, on an average 20–25 (Table 6.4) members attend the committee meeting. The size seems to be big in theory, but is medium and manageable in practice taking the actual attendance of members into account. The system of sub-committee makes it more specialized and small. Usually a subcommittee consists of between ten and 15 members and a great deal of committee work is transacted through sub-committees. Some respondents raised a very important issue related with the small size of committees i.e. the number of the committee. They think that currently there are too many committees in Indian parliament to run efficiently and effectively. They feel that select committees on bills and consultative committees on ministries are redundant. Their functions can easily be accommodated by DRSCs which deserve to be reorganized and reformed.

Some 70 percent of the respondents completely agreed with the statement that the selection of committee members be based on their own interest, experience and expertise rather than the government or the political parties. They think that this is required for committee specialization and has consequences for committee performance. In general, the interest and preferences of members are usually accommodated before they are nominated into a committee by their own political parties. Sometimes, seniority prevails over academic background and expertise in committee membership/chairmanship selection.

The members of parliamentary committees are appointed or elected by the House on a motion or are nominated by the Speaker/chair of each House. Members of all financial committees, the Committee on Welfare of Scheduled Castes and Scheduled Tribes and the Joint Committee on Offices of Profit are elected every year by members according to the system of proportional representation by means of single transferable votes. Members of other committees are nominated by the presiding officer of the House concerned. This system of election ensures the representation of almost all parties and group in the parliament.

The chairman of a committee who enjoys adequate power to guide and regulate the work of the committee is appointed by the Speaker from among the members of the committee with the exception that the if the Speaker/deputy Speaker is a member the committee he as a rule is appointed as chairman (Kashyap 1979: 303–304).The incumbent government decides in consultation with the opposition parties the mode of distribution of chairmanship of different DRSCs according to proportional representation of parties in the parliament. Usually strategically important DRSCs such as Standing Committee on Defense, Standing Committee on Foreign Affairs and so on are headed by the treasury bench/coalition MPs. However, in the fourteenth *Lok Sabha*, the opposition NDA (National Democratic Alliances) threatened not to involve itself in any committee activities until its demand of allocation of chairmanship of some prestigious committees was met. The government later agreed to let the NDA head the DRSCs on Finance, Home and External Affairs.

Some 90 percent (mean score is 3.1) of the respondents completely agreed that the composition of the committee (including the chairmanship) should be based on proportional strength of the parties in the House. The respondents reported that Indian parliament had been practicing this for a long time. They argued that a committee was a mini-parliament and in term of chair selection attention must be given to uphold the representative character of the House. They think that the distribution of chairmanships of committees based on the proportional representation of the parties in the House has helped the opposition feel that they are accommodated within the governance system and contributed to lessening the political bitterness and confrontation between the government and opposition parties.

Unlike the US and Western Europe the chairmen of the committees in India in many cases are senior members/former union cabinet members and in some cases the leaders of the parties. A.B. Vajpayee (former prime minister) was the chairman of the Committee on External Affairs during 1993–1997. Mulayam Singh Yadav was the chairman of Committee on Petroleum and Natural Gas since December 1999. Mamta Baneerjee was the chairman of Committee on Railways during 1999. These are few illustrative cases to show that largely leaders/seniors members take up the mantle of chairmanships of the committees (Ramacharyulu 2003: 137). Some respondents report that in India, committee chairs are stepping stones to cabinet membership/chief ministerships.

Ministers are debarred from becoming members of any parliamentary committee in India. It is thus ensured that these committees function relatively independently of the influence of the executive and bring to bear an objective, judicious and non-party approach to the matter under their scrutiny and arrive at their findings and recommendations unanimously (Nair 2003: 152). In response to a question eliciting their opinion on the exclusion of ministers as members from committees, an overwhelming 90 percent of the respondents answered in the affirmative. They argued that in order to maintain the separation of power, ministers who were from the executive branch must be excluded from any parliamentary committee.

Since 1967, Indian parliament has started the tradition of having a leader of opposition as the chair of PAC (Supakar 1973). An exception had been made in 1989 when an MP was appointed chairman who belonged to a party which was an ally of the ruling Congress (I). The chairpersons of committees are usually chosen keeping in view of their leadership qualities and position of pre-eminence and experience. Two of the former chairmen of the PAC, namely Shri P.V. Narshima Rao and Sri Atal Bihari Vajpayee, rose to become the prime minister of India. One former chair of PAC, Shri R. Venkataraman, went on to become the president of India (Malhotra 2000). In the thirteenth *Lok Sabha*, the chairman of PAC was a former union cabinet minister and senior leader of the main opposition Indian National Congress (INC). Since inception, the chairman of the committee on Public Undertakings has been a senior member from the ruling party except during the periods 1977–1978, 1978–1979, 1990–1991, 1996–1997 and 1997–1998 when chairman belonged to an ally party. The Chairman of the Estimates Committee has always been a senior member of a party supporting the government from outside (Nair 2003: 152).

The mean score of the respondents' understanding of the statement of allocating the chairs of the financial committees exclusively to the opposition members with relevant background for securing better government accountability is 1.8. This is a below average response in favor of the proposal. Most of the respondents think that India should continue with what it has been practicing for long. They think that the chairman of PAC must be from the opposition and the other two from the government or its coalition partners.

While India has significantly broadened committee involvement in various parliamentary businesses over the last decade, coordination mechanism is currently lacking. Committees operate in a fragmented manner, thereby hindering the potential for well-informed amendments. For instance, the departmental committees charged with scrutinizing individual demand for grants are prohibited by rule from considering matters of day-to-day administration of concerned ministries/departments. They therefore lack background knowledge pertaining to the implementation of budget during the financial year. Similarly, the Public Accounts Committee does not complement the scrutiny of departmental budgets by 17 standing committees (Krafchik and Wehner 1998). The functioning of various committees like the Estimates Committee, DRSC and RCC sometimes overlap. It is not uncommon that same department or ministry may be taken up for examination by more than one committee during a year. More effective coordination among these committees could avoid overlap and consequent overload of scrutiny.

The mean score of respondents' answers on the question of introduction of a liaison committee composed of the chairpersons of various committees under the leadership of the Speaker in order to coordinate the activities of different committees, avoid overlapping of work and reconcile ideas and suggestion for better activating the committee and establish keen surveillance over the executive is 3.8. This manifests major respondents' support for constitution of a liaison committee in India. Of the respondents, 90 percent completely agreed with the statement.

Procedures

When asked about the agenda-setting capability of parliament, 70 percent of the respondents agreed that committee's ability to set its own agenda was a crucial power to constraint government. They report that in India, committees are not allowed to set their own agenda. Committees usually deal with bills/issues referred to them by the House where the decision of the majority party usually persists. The single committee which enjoys some sort of freedom to choose its own agenda is the PAC.

Bills are usually referred to DRSCs after they are introduced in both the Houses of parliament. We have seen in the theoretical framework that in a parliament where bills are introduced in the House before committee consideration, the parliamentary committees have a restricted role in law-making. India is not an exception in this regard. However, in two cases: The Trade Union (Amendment) Bill, 1994 and The Public Sector Iron and Steel Companies (Restructuring) and Miscellaneous Provision (Amendment) Bill, 1993, bills were so referred due to opposition protest even before their introduction. The recommendations/observations made by the DRSC on different ministries in their various reports have evoked positive response from the government.

That committee stage of bill consideration should precede floor consideration was agreed completely by 20 percent of the respondents. Most of the respondents who disagreed with the proposal think that this was an extreme mode of legislative reform proposal. They feel that in a parliamentary democracy, law-making should be the prerogative of the House. Committees can consider the bills once they are tabled in the House.

The sittings of the committee are held in camera in India. The deliberation of the meeting is, as per the rules, confined exclusively to committee members and officers of parliamentary secretariat. Evidence, oral or written reports, or proceedings of the committee is confidential until its placement to the House. On the question of the nature of committee session (open or closed) 70 percent of the respondents completely agreed that it should be closed which would help foster inter-party compromise and relax party discipline. Most of the respondents believe that considering the socio-political culture in India, committee sessions must be closed. Division along party line, is hardly seen in committee sessions. That will disappear once committee sessions are open to the media, they maintain. MPs would like to play the same as they do in the House and consensus which is common in committee sessions will swing to confrontation. They observe that notwithstanding committee meetings are held in private, the whole text of the committee deliberations is available in the print media on the following day.

The proposal of public hearings on legislative bills and other oversight matters was completely agreed by 85 percent of the respondents. They inform that hearings on bills or other issues are open to the mass media and concerned people. Over time, people's awareness of and interest in committees have heightened. They can help committees perform better by providing useful information, new ideas and insights. They reported that public hearings on bills or any other matter in committees had been many times undertaken in India.

In India, committees can send for papers, persons and records to permit a more thorough analysis of the subject being examined except where production of a document is certified by the government to be prejudicial to the safety or interest of the state. Refusal to appear before the committee or produce any document demanded by them may tantamount to breach of privileges and contempt of the committees. 70 percent of respondents agreed completely with the question of committee's right to send for papers and persons and punish those who fail to comply with its demand. Some respondents felt that ministers should be excluded from summoning to the committees. It is the House where she/he should better be asked questions regarding the performance of his ministry. Government's right of refusal to produce a document on the ground of state security has placed the government in an advantage position. An attempt to unearth the alleged large-scale embezzlement of public money in the procurement of sleeping bags and aluminum coffins was foiled by refusal of the government to supply the committee members with necessary documents on the grounds of state security, which was unilaterally determined by the ruling government.

Functions

Fifty-five percent of the respondents (the mean is 2.2) completely agreed that committees should have exclusive jurisdiction over legislation and oversight of the executive. They think that committees should play a significant role at various stages of law-making – from review of bill to review of act. With regards to bills referred to committees, they are required to consider the general principles and clauses of the bills and submit a report. However, the committees do not consider the financial bills and the appropriation bills. In India, bills are usually referred to DRSCs after they are introduced. In the thirteenth *Lok Sabha* (up to August 2003, see Appendix, Table A3.2) of the 276 bills that were passed by the parliament, 73 (26 percent) were referred to DRSCs. This is a noticeable improvement over the early years of independence when 12 percent (Morris Jones 1957) of the total bills passed by the parliament were referred to select committees earlier.

The respondents think that committees should have a major role in the oversight of the administration too. Committees in India have some role in budget allocation. After the general discussion on the budget is over, the *Lok Sabha* shall adjourn for a fixed period (25 days on average) and the committees shall consider the demands for grants during this recess. While examining the demands for grants, the committees are not permitted to make suggestions which would be in the nature of cut motions (they can recommend to increase the demand only), as such motions can be moved only in the *Lok Sabha* and the committees include *Rajya Sabha* members too. The demands for grants shall thereafter be considered by the *lok sabha* in the light of the Reports of these Committees. The House might confine itself to discussing specific points/recommendations made by the committees and, thus, might be able to discuss the demands of larger number of ministries/departments before the same are voted.

However, if anything goes wrong and is exposed by media in between from budget allocation to review of financial statements by three financial committees, PAC in addition can pick up the issue for examination. Some respondents expressed their reservation about giving the committee exclusive jurisdiction over law-making and favored the existing practice.

There remains no compulsion or convention for deliberating reports after their submission to the House. Ironically, no deliberation ever took place on those large numbers of committee reports (see Appendix, Tables A3.3 and A3.4) submitted to House. Asked whether committee reports should be presented to the House regularly and debated as well, 80 percent of the respondents answered in the affirmative. They think that committee reports which contain the deliberation of major policy issues and are critical in nature should be debated in House on specific days. It also keeps the civil society informed of the functioning of committees and the media can take the deliberation further.

Minorities are not allowed to present their own report in case of dissention in India. A single report contains the "note of dissent" recorded by the minority. Some 30 percent of the respondents (the mean score of the answer is 1.6) agreed completely that the minority should be allowed to present their own reports which would reflect that the committees were not dominated by the government. Most of the respondents think that decisions in committee sessions are usually made on consensus basis and a single report can contain the dissent of the minority and serve the same purpose.

The Indian parliament has devised a comprehensive and well-organized system of making recommendations and follows thereof (see Appendix, Table A3.7 for details). Every subject of deliberation in committee session invariably ends with an original report containing thorough analysis of the deliberated issue and recommendations to deal with the issue. There exist committee mechanisms to follow up the recommendations. The government is expected to indicate the action taken on recommendations within six months after the submission of a report but generally it takes longer. Then the committee keeps a watchful eye on the matter discussed and usually presents an action-taken report based on the responses of the ministries/departments to keep it abreast of the latest status of its recommendation. Although formally, the recommendations of parliamentary committees are not binding, the government generally accepts most of them. For instance, an analysis of action taken by government on the recommendations made by 11 committees chaired and administered by the *Lok Sabha* in their earlier reports of which action-taken Reports were presented during the years 1993–2002 indicates that the rate of acceptance of recommendation (see Appendix, Tables A3.5 and A3.6 for details) is quite high – 72 percent (55 percent of which were accepted by the government and 17 percent which the committees did not pursue in view of government replies). Data on available on selected DRSCs (see Table 6.5 for details) also supports the high percentage of committee recommendations accepted by the government.

Very often, recommendations that are really important or of some consequences (as we will see in the case of Bofors scandal, coffin scam, sleeping bags scams) were not accepted. Ministries have rarely accepted the recommendations/observations of the committees when they relate to substantive issues like changing procedures, taking action against errant employees or disturbing the status quo (*Hindu Bangalore*, May 18, 1995). The recommendations that tend to be accepted are those which are minor and create no difficulties for anyone or those which are in line with the current thinking of the government or the ruling party or coalitions (Kashyap 1979: 311). So far as the administration is concerned, committee recommendations provide a corrective future action. Moreover, the mere existence of these committees works as deterrent against irresponsible actions.

Respondents were asked about the issue of enforcement of committee recommendations. Only 30 percent of the respondents completely agreed that recommendations should be made mandatory for the government. Implementation of recommendations of committees regardless of the contents would have a salutary impact on the improvement of the performance of the government bodies, they believed. But those who opposed (60 percent disagreed completely) the proposal thought that recommendations should be advisory as was case in most of the countries. They report that in India, the government usually complies with the recommendations as a convention. The executive has been mandated by the people to rule the country and the implementation of the recommendations of committees should be left to the executive, they maintained.

A proposal was presented before the respondents that in order to follow up and monitor the state of implementation of the committee recommendations, an action-taken sub-committee should be formed and in case of failure to comply with, the government offices should submit an explanatory note. 100 percent of the respondents completely agreed with the proposal. They inform that in India, most of the committees have action-taken sub-committees and the system has been there for a long time. However, it is important to note that mere acceptance of recommendations by the ministries/departments does not automatically result in implementation of the same. No record is kept of the percentage of recommendations actually implemented and no follow-up device is in place to chase further. Hence the committees' jobs are usually done once their recommendations are accepted by the government. When asked about this issue, most of the respondents expressed their contentment with the existing practice. Respondents irrespective of party affiliation are of the view that committees' work is to persuade, not to press the government, influence not to interfere the administration.

Resources

Table 6.1 depicts a comparative account of the background characteristics of the MPs in the tenth, eleventh, twelfth and thirteenth *Lok Sabhas* which are further analyzed in terms of educational qualification, occupation and parliamentary experience. One of the striking features of membership pattern has been upward moving with regard to educational profile of members in successive *Lok Sabhas*. Members belonging to graduates and above have registered consistent improvement and the thirteenth *Lok Sabha* has emerged as the "most educated House". Their combined representation which was just 58.08 percent in the first *Lok Sabha* in 1952 rose to very high percentages of 80 percent in the thirteenth *Lok Sabha* in 1999 (Malhotra 2002: 112).

MPs with agriculture as the occupational background constitute the largest single elite group in all *Lok Sabhas* in the 1990s. A major (an average of 41 percent in all four *Lok Sabhas* in 1990s) segment of the MPs who entered the parliaments in the 1990s were newcomers and lacked the basic operational experience of the parliament let alone the specialized assignments in committees. Moreover, they were not provided with any specialized training on legislative and administrative affairs which might help improve their capability and competency to perform their tasks.

It is estimated that altogether 656 sitting and former members of the *Rajya Sabha* and the *Lok Sabha* owe Rs111.8 million (US$2.5 million) to the Mahanagar Telephone Nigam Limited and Rs63.2 million (US$1.5 million) to the New Delhi Municipal Council for water and electricity (*The Telegraph*, March 3, 2004). Many of these MPs were in different committees in thirteenth *Lok Sabha*

Table 6.1 Background characteristics of MPs in the Tenth, 11th, 12th, 13th LSs

Background	*Tenth LS (1991–1996) (%)*	*11th LS (1996–1997) (%)*	*12th LS (1998–1999) (%)*	*13th LS (1999–2004) (%)*
Education				
Postgraduate	33	35	33	32
Graduate	44	43	45	48
Undergraduate	23	22	22	20
Occupation				
Agriculturists	32	39	49	43
Lawyers	16	12	10	12
Political and social workers	18	20	18	20
Others	34	29	23	25
Parliamentary experience				
Newcomer	37	55	40	33
Experience of one LS	28	17	27	27
Experience of more than one LS	35	28	33	40

Source: compiled by the author from Malhotra 2002: (101–133).

who were entrusted with ensuring financial propriety and keeping watchful eyes on the executive.

Of the respondents, 95 percent agreed completely that full-time professional and experienced legislators coupled with low turnover of committee membership can help active and strong committees to evolve. The respondents opined that an MP's experience in government and committee work really matter for his performance in committees. Most of the respondents were not satisfied with the salary and benefits they get from the parliament which they believed prevented them from becoming full-time politicians. Available data on selected committees in the thirteenth *Lok Sabha* manifests that the average turnover of committee membership is around 30 percent that is not conducive to the emergence of a stable committee system. Chairmanships of committees are not stable either.

The *Lok Sabha* secretariat is an independent institution which functions under the guidance and control of the Speaker. In the discharge of his responsibilities, the Speaker is assisted by the Secretary-General of *Lok Sabha*, (whose pay scale, position and status etc. is equivalent to that of the highest ranking official in the government of India i.e. cabinet secretary), functionaries of the level of the additional secretary, joint secretary and other officers and staff of the secretariat at various levels. Presently, there are ten services categorized on functional basis, which cater to the specific needs of the House and its secretariat. Committees receive services from two categories – The Legislative, Financial Committee, Executive and Administrative Service (LAFEAS) and The Library, Research, Reference, Documentation and Information Service (LARRDIS).

To provide secretarial assistance to various committees in the *Lok Sabha*, separate committee branches (such as Public Undertakings Committee branch,

Urban and Rural Development Committee branch and so on) have been created under LAFEAS category. Each branch caters services to a particular committee. Each committee branch usually comprises of an additional secretary, a joint secretary, a director, a deputy secretariat, an under-secretary, committee officers and reporting officers supported by other staff. In addition, each chairman has got a personal secretary too. *Lok Sabha* secretariat is an independent body. It has full autonomy in recruitment, selection, training and promotion of its own staff. Even the present Secretary-General of the *Lok Sabha* is a direct recruit of the *Lok Sabha* secretariat.

Individual members have access to the parliamentary library and associated research and references services. A substantial increase of references handled has been noted since the introduction of this service. In 1950, 150 requests were dealt with, increasing to 425 in 1960, 700 in 1970, 3627 in 1980 and 5167 in 1990 (Krafchik and Wehner 1998).

The academic background of committee staff in *Lok Sabha* is general in nature. However, most of them have got experience in parliamentary affairs in general while lacking specialized knowledge required for committee operations. Most of the officials working under committee branches have been imparted with training by the Bureau of Parliamentary Studies and Training (BPST). Furthermore, no individual committee is supported by research staff to let the committee members/chairman carry out his/her responsibility in a competent manner.

In response to a question about the necessity of a separate committee secretariat supported with a healthy budget, sufficient number of specialized/competent staff and adequate logistic support, 60 percent of the respondents answered in the affirmative. About 15 percent of the respondents expressed their reservations about the first part of the question but favored the second one. They felt that committee branch could be strengthened within one parliamentary secretariat and the establishment of a separate committee secretariat was unnecessary. However, all the respondents unanimously expressed their discontent with the existing logistic support system of committees and strongly urged the government to extend and upgrade it.

In India, committees are entitled to seek expert advice and elicit public opinion while examining the demand for grants or bills referred to them. Earlier, committees have benefited from the hearings of external experts on many occasions. However, experts can render their advice only, the final decision regarding the matter consulted rests exclusively with the committee. All respondents (100 percent, with mean score 4) were of the view that committees should be benefited from the expertise and knowledge of external experts who are relatively independent of the executive and political influence. Experts should be invited and more frequently consulted with, they observed.

The real-world working of selected committees in India

Financial committees

Public Accounts Committee (PAC)

From the available data on the PAC in the thirteenth JS (see Table 6.2), we can note that on an average about 50 percent of the total members did attend the committee meeting. A quorum is one-third (seven) of the total number of members of the committee. Four out of an average of 11 members attending the committee meeting were from the opposition. The PAC met regularly and the average frequency of committee meetings was 27 days. The PAC held 55 main committee meetings and five sub-committee meetings. It spent an average of one hour 36 minutes per meeting. The PAC also submitted 63 reports in the thirteenth JS of which 33 were original and 30 action taken reports. Out of 63 reports, 55 had been released to the internet for public consumption.

AGENDA OF DELIBERATION

Although audit reports of CAG mainly form the committee's basis of the agenda for deliberation, its activities are not confined to matters contained in audit reports. The committee oversees and investigates the current activities of the government and exposes irregularities and malpractices of the executive branch. Thus PAC compensates the limitations of DRSCs which are not allowed to oversee the day-to-day activities of administration.

The CAG's report points out where the government has failed to perform and for what reasons. The reports of the CAG contain objections and remarks over errors committed by government authorities while spending money during a given financial year. Non-spending, underspending, overspending and misspending of allocated funds are all pointed out in clear terms in the report.

The PAC discussed audit objections of different public organizations under different ministries regarding financial irregularities in different financial years involving billions of rupees. A major agenda of deliberation was excess over

Table 6.2 Nature of committee operations (financial committees) in the 13th *Lok Sabha*

Name of committee	*Number of meetings held*	*Total number of members*	*Yearly average member turnout*	*Average attendance*	*Average duration of meetings*	*Average frequency of meetings*	*Number of reports presented*
PAC	55	22	33%/3	11 (50.1%)	96 min	27 days	63
COPU	18	22	32%/1	9.4 (42.8%)	52 min	81 days	57
COE	29	30	22%/1	14 (46.1%)	87 min	50 days	19

Source: Compiled and calculated by the Author from Indian *Lok Sabha* (1999–2004) Resume of Work of 13th *Lok Sabha*), Indian *Lok Sabha* (2004d).

voted grants and charged appropriations conceded by different ministries and public organizations. Some of the major agenda of deliberations include design and development of pilotless target aircraft, design and development of main battle tank – *Arjun*, aircraft accident in Indian Air Force, acquisition of SU-30 aircraft, Ganga action plan, abnormal delay in repair/overhaul of tanks, purchase of residence of Consulate General of India at Frankfurt. Most of the matters were concerned with government accountability. The PAC also deliberated widely publicized defense issues such as the procurement of defective sleeping bags for troops, and procurement of aluminum caskets for operation Vijoy (Army). It is obvious from the review of the issues that most the issues are old and have been carried over from the earlier parliaments such as eleventh and twelfth *Lok Sabha*. Two defense issues need special consideration.

PAC in the thirteenth *Lok Sabha* at its sitting held on December 19, 2001 decided to examine the entire report of CAG on "Review of procurement for Operation Vijay" and in that context they asked the Defense Ministry to make available the Central Vigilance Commission (CVC) report on defense deals. The Ministry declined to submit the CVC report on the plea that it was based on secret documents of the Ministry and reports of IB (Intelligence Branch) and CBI (Central Intelligence Branch), and supplying the report would be "prejudicial" to the interest of the state (Indian *Lok Sabha* 2003c). The denial of ministry of defense to submit the CVC report to the PAC resulted in forced adjournments of both the Houses by the opposition for several times and ultimately led to an abortive "no confidence motion" brought by the Congress in *Lok Sabha* in September 2004.

The Public Accounts Committee (PAC) of parliament has unearthed a major scam involving supply of defective sleeping bags to troops positioned at the world's highest battlefield Siachen. Describing the role of the Ministry of Defense as "questionable" in the purchase of 8588 sub-standard sleeping bags from a French firm at a cost of 11.86 million French francs, the parliamentary Public Accounts Committee expressed its shock that even though the firm had gone bankrupt, the ministry went ahead to negotiate another deal with it. "The questionable role of the Ministry of Defense particularly the officers responsible for execution of the contract be entrusted to an independent agency for thorough investigation", the PAC said in its forty-sixth report tabled in both the Houses of Parliament. The committee said 8588 sleeping bags were received from the French firm Monclear in six lots between September 1992 and June 1993 and were found to be sub-standard and could not be used by the troops at Siachen (Indian *Lok Sabha* 2003b).

The infamous Bofors case against the former Prime Minister Rajib Gandhi was very much the outcome of the report of the PAC which raised question about the quality of guns and the procedures followed in its purchase which led to the setting of a joint parliamentary committee to enquire into the matter and ultimately the fall of the Rajib Gandhi government in 1989. The findings of the PAC have led to more than one judicial inquiry too (TI 2004a: 44).

The problems of ensuring executive accountability by the PAC can be broadly categorized into two – problems at the initiation level and problems at the implementation level. Problems at the initiation level can be further grouped into two – problems accruing from the limitations of office of the CAG and problems of the PAC itself. Of note, the PAC made recommendations regularly.

PROBLEMS AT THE INITIATION LEVEL

Since PAC bases its actions mainly on the reports of the CAG, its shortcomings have a baneful effect on the performance of the PAC. The CAG in India is a constitutional body independent of the executive control. He is appointed by the president for a period of six year on the advice of the prime minister. The CAG is the first line oversight agency, empowered to examining all public accounts while others like the committees and CVC are selective investigatory agencies. The CAG cannot perform satisfactorily for a number of reasons explained below.

Discussions of CAG's reports by PAC and finalization of its recommendations have been slow. The two parliamentary committees PAC and COPU are able to examine only a few paragraphs and reviews out of large number of audit reports submitted to them which defeats the very purpose of parliamentary financial control and accountability of the executive which the parliament is required to enforce. For example, during 1997–1998, out of 16 reports submitted to the parliament containing 1209 paragraphs/reviews, the number of paragraphs/reviews selected for examination was 76 out of which only 16 could be discussed by the PAC (GOI 2001: 571). Likewise, in 1998–1999 PAC selected 7 percent of the total 1197 paragraphs included in CAG's Reports on Central Government. Actual examination was confined to 2 percent of the paragraphs. Reports on Central Excise and Customs Receipts and on Autonomous Bodies and Scientific Department were not discussed. Large-scale exclusion of items from examination and discussions restricts effectiveness of parliament (Mukhopadhyay 2002: 7). The situation is no different in the States. Unlike Britain and some other leading Commonwealth countries, CAG is not an independent officer of parliament.

In India, there is considerable delay in submission of appropriation accounts even of the Union Government to the parliament. A study of for eight years from 1992–1993 to 1999–2000 shows that it takes an average of over 15 months from the close of financial year for the audited accounts and the report thereon to be placed in the parliament. It takes another year for the PAC to examine and the parliament to approve excess expenditure (Mathur 2002: 427).

Although various government officials commit many irregularities while spending public money the CAG does not have the power to summon them and seek explanations for their decisions. Similarly, the CAG does not have the power to make the erring official pay for the loss caused by misspending of funds or for committing fraud while handling funds. In countries like Germany, Japan, China, France and New Zealand auditing officers have powers to summon erring officials and make them pay from their own pockets for losses caused by them to the state. In some serious cases the erring official is imprisoned after instituting criminal proceedings against him in a court of law (NCRWC 1901). The PAC chairman in the thirteenth *Lok Sabha* admitted the weakness of CAG not to mention the names of erring officials in CAG's reports and underscored the necessity to amend CAG Act of India to make it more powerful.

The CAG is assisted by about 6000 employees. Of late, many positions under the CAG are being filled by officers belonging to Indian Administrative Services (IAS) who lack the expertise and experience required for conducting audit. Moreover, the CAG does not have the necessary expertise to audit accounts of scientific and technical departments such as the Department of Science and Technology, Atomic Energy, Space Application etc. or review the economic policies of government (NCRWC 2001: 9–10).

The PAC itself is also suffering from the same malaise of backlogging. PAC Chairman Buta Singh told the *Indian Express* (May 8, 2003):

> It is true for the last 7 to 8 years, the PAC has been lagging behind in taking up CAG's reports and sometimes dealing with reports that 5 to 7 years old. The PAC has become laidback and no serious debate on these reports takes place in parliaments.

PROBLEMS AT THE IMPLEMENTATION STAGE

The effectiveness of committees can be judged by the responses of the government to their recommendations. The following data for the 20 years from 1980 to 1999 which cover the seventh *Lok Sabha* to 12th *Lok Sabha* will give an idea. The PAC gave 6112 recommendations out of which the government accepted 3709 recommendations – thus the percentage of recommendations accepted was 61. Subsequently about 10 percent of recommendations were dropped at the action-taken stage on receipt of government's replies. Another 10 percent were reiterated by PAC out of which some were accepted by the government. Thus it can be said about three-quarters of the recommendations were accepted. However, numbers may not always give a correct picture (Malhotra 2000: 182). These data are based on the action taken notes on the recommendations of the committee in its earlier reports. In the thirteenth *Lok Sabha*, 65 percent of the total recommendations contained in earlier reports submitted to PAC were accepted by the government (see Table 6.3 for details).

Sometimes PAC took several years (between five and seven years commonly) to finish off a contentious issue without any concrete result. Furthermore, mere acceptance of recommendations does not result in implementation of the same. It is the incumbent government which will implement the recommendations. When recommendations are concerned with major policy issues (Bofors scandal, coffin scam, sleeping bag scam) and politically sensitive, the government usually chooses to ignore committee recommendations. Sometimes, government ministries simply decline to provide documents to the committee in the pretext of national security as we have seen in the case of the coffin scam.

Table 6.3 Statement showing analysis of action taken by government on the recommendations made by three financial committees on their earlier reports presented in the 13th *Lok Sabha* (2000–2003)

Status of recommendations	*Name of committees*		
	Public Accounts Committee	*Committee on Public Undertakings*	*Committee on Estimates*
Total number of recommendations accepted by the government(with Percentage)	205 (65%)	11 (24%)	209 (70%)
Total number of recommendations which the committee did not pursue in view of government replies	38 (12%)	14 (30%)	24 (8%)
Total number of recommendations in respect of which replies of government have not accepted by the committee.	51 (16%)	12 (26%)	25 (8%)
Total number of recommendations in respect of final replies of were awaited	23 (7%)	9 (20%)	40 (14%)
Total number of recommendations	317	46	298

Source: compiled and calculated by the author from PAC, COPU and COE reports in the 13th *Lok Sabha*, *Lok Sabha* Secretariat, 2000–2003.

Despite all limitations, the PAC by its close scrutiny of accounts has earned a reputation of impartiality, firmness and grasp for details. The good work done by the PAC has helped greatly in improving financial control by the administration and assisted in the detection of many irregularities and even dishonesties. By its constant vigil, the committee has introduced financial discipline not only in expenditure but also in revenue. There is no doubt that if the PAC was not in existence, the condition of public finance would have been simply chaotic. Serious administrative lapses are brought to light by committee reports and by the consequent criticism in the House and the press and this helps in toning up the administration. (Muttemwar 2002: 402–403). Hence, the PAC in the thirteenth *Lok Sabha* had played a commendable role in ensuring financial accountability of the executive at the initiation and recommendation levels despite obvious shortcomings. But the impact of PAC operations at the implementation stage – the most important stage of committee involvement in ensuring executive accountability was moderate. However, the working of PAC has a publishing impact. It is largely believed by people in India that due to Bofors scandal unearthed by PAC, Rajib Gandhi had to concede an electoral debacle in the election that followed. So is the case with the NDA in relation to coffin scam brought to the light by PAC. The NDA lost its power in the next election too.

Committee on Public Undertakings (COPU)

From the available data on the COPU in the thirteenth *Lok Sabha* (see Table 6.2), it is evident that on an average about 43 percent of the total members did attend the committee meeting. A quorum is one-third (seven) of the total number of members of the committee. Four out of an average of nine members attending the committee meeting were from the opposition. The COPU did not met regularly and the average frequency of committee meetings was 81 days. The COPU held only 18 meetings in the thirteenth *Lok Sabha*. It spent an average of 51 minutes per meeting. The COPU also submitted 12 original reports of which five are action-taken reports and 51 study-tour reports in the thirteenth *Lok Sabha*. All reports had been released to the internet for public consumption. In term of average member attendance, frequency of meeting, production of reports and duration of meeting, COPU had lagged far behind other two financial committees. The committee had apparently been inactive for a long time and did not hold any meetings during the fifth (for six months) session and tenth session (six months) in the thirteenth *Lok Sabha*. But, in fact, the committee made a large number of study tours during this time. During study tours, formally no committee meeting is held and having study tours done, only study-tour reports are submitted to parliament. There is widespread apprehension among the people that most of the study tours aim at popular tourist spots which incur millions of rupees every each.

AGENDA OF DELIBERATION

The committee made a thorough discussion on Air India Limited. A major agenda of deliberation was concentrated on reports on action taken by government on the recommendations contained in three earlier reports of COPU presented in the 12th *Lok Sabha* such as follow-up actions on the report of CAG (Commercial), senior level posts in public undertakings, Pyrites, Phosphate and Chemicals Limited. The first issue was first selected for deliberation in 1985 and then the committee kept continuing discussion on this issue through 1993 to 2000. Most of these issues were first selected by the COPU in 1997–1998 followed by submission of reports to the *Lok Sabha* in 1998–1999. The committee also considered and adopted reports on several issues such as the Role of Public Sector Banks in Self-Employment Schemes and Telecommunication Services in Rural Areas both of which were selected for detail examination by the COPU in 1996–1997. The committee took three years to produce reports on both of the deliberated cases. Action-taken reports are yet to be submitted to *Lok Sabha*.

Two fresh agenda of deliberations were dealt with by the COPU which ended with a committee report followed by an action-taken report. A fresh agenda of deliberation was Expansion and Modernization of Ports with special reference to Mormugao Port Trust which was selected by the committee in December 2001. The COPU took evidence of the representatives of the ministry of Shipping and Mormugao Port Trust and produced a report in April 2002. Later the committee submitted an action-taken report based on the replies rendered by the government on the recommendations contained in earlier report. 45.5 percent of the recommendations were accepted by the government (see Table 6.3 for details). Another fresh agenda by the COPU in the thirteenth *Lok Sabha* was Hindustan Petroleum Corporation Limited: infructuous expenditure on creation of a pipeline. The COPU also deliberated on issues such as creation of new demand for grants for Defense Research and Development Organization (DRDO) under the Ministry of Finance, shifting of north-western railway zonal headquarters from Jaipur to Ajmir, development of infrastructure for growth of tourism – Development of Ajmer City and so on. A survey of COE's agenda of deliberation in the thirteenth *Lok Sabha* suggests that the committee activities have largely confined to improving the organization and working of the administrative machinery rather than holding the government accountable.

Since CAG's reports are the mainstay of committee deliberation, the weakness of CAG (discussed earlier) also applies here and affects adversely the functioning of COPU. The examination of reports of CAG by COPU has also fallen into delays (Mukhopadhyay 2002: 7). For instance, in 1998–1999, COPU selected 2.5 percent of the paras included in the CAG's reports. In fact, there is no system of monitoring at government level for follow-up on the reports of CAG (Commercial). Action-taken notes have not been received regularly and in time. For instance, out of 57 reports of CAG (Commercial) presented to parliament from March 1993 to July 1998, action-taken notes in respect of as many as 865 paragraphs of various reports pertaining to 30 ministries/departments were pending as on December 16, 1998 (*Lok Sabha* 2000: 1). In short, the implication of COPU in ensuring executive accountability at the initiation and the recommendation level is moderate and minimal at the implementation stage.

Committee on Estimates (COE)

From the available data on the COE in the thirteenth *Lok Sabha* (see Table 6.2), we can see that on an average about 46 percent of the total members did attend the committee meeting. A quorum is one-third (ten) of the total number of members of the committee. Six out of an average of 14 members attending the committee meeting were from the opposition. The COE held 29 meetings. It spent an average of one hour 27 minutes per meeting. Average frequency of committee meeting (50 days) was disappointing compared to PAC. The PAC also submitted 19 reports in the thirteenth *Lok Sabha* of which 11 were original and eight action-taken reports. All 19 reports had been released to the internet for public consumption. It is pertinent to note that since its inception in April, 1950 until 2003, the Committee on Estimates has presented 888 reports covering almost all the ministries/departments of the Government of India. Out of these 464 are the original reports and 424 are reports on action-taken by the government on earlier reports of the committee.

AGENDA OF DELIBERATION

A major portion of agenda of deliberation was concentrated on reports on action taken by government on the recommendations contained in four earlier reports of the Committee on Estimates in the twelfth *Lok Sabha* such as closure of textile industry, crude oil – indigenous production and imports, public sector banks-bad debts. Most of these issues were first selected by the COE in 1997–1998 followed by submission of reports to *Lok Sabha* in 1998–1999. The committee also considered and adopted reports on several issues such as the role of public sector banks in self-employment schemes and telecommunication services in rural areas, both of which were selected for detail examination by the COE in 1996–1997. For both cases, the committee took three years to produce reports on both of the deliberated cases. Action-taken reports are yet to be submitted to *Lok Sabha*.

In the thirteenth *Lok Sabha*, a high 70 percent of the total recommendations contained in earlier reports submitted to COE were accepted by the government (209 out of 298, see Table 6.2). However, COE took an average of three years to finish off an issue without any concrete result. The COE met far less frequently than PAC. Furthermore, that mere acceptance of recommendations does not result into implementation of the same also applies for COE. In sum, the implication of COE in ensuring executive accountability at the initiation and the recommendation stage well and moderate at the implementation stage.

Operation of selected Departmentally-Related Standing Committees (DRSCs)

Departmentally-Related Standing Committee (DRSC) on Home Affairs

Three Ministries of government of India, namely Ministry of Home Affairs, Ministry of Personnel, Public Grievances and Pensions and Ministry of Law Justice and Company Affairs, have been placed under the jurisdiction of the Committee on Home Affairs. Based on data available from Table 5.6 on Standing Committee on Home Affairs, it is obvious that on average 49 percent of the total members attended the committee meeting. The committee spent an average of 2.20 hours for each committee meeting. Average frequency of committee meeting was eight days. The committee kept meeting regularly and frequently. It held a record number of 174 main committee meetings and five sub-committee meetings in four years and produced 64 reports. It also undertook six study visits. One study visit was undertaken in the state of Jammu and Kashmir to assess the situation of cross-border terrorism and insurgency. The committee also undertook two study visits for on-the-spot appraisal of the Administration of Union Territories without legislature (Chandigarh, Andaman and Nicobar Islands).

Table 6.4 Nature of committee operations (departmentally-related standing committees) in Indian parliament

	Name of committee	*Number of meetings held*	*Yearly average member turnout (%)*	*Total number of members*	*Average attendance (%)*	*Average duration of meetings*	*Average frequency of meetings*	*Number of reports presented*
RS (2000–2003)	DRSCOHA	174	33%/1	45	22 (48.9%)	2 hours 12 min	8 days	54
13th LS	DRSCOD	40	38%/3	45	21 (47.2%)	2 hours 15 min	27 days	21
13th LS	DRSCOA	69	26%/1	45	20 (43.6%)	1 hour 37 min	16 days	50

Source: compiled and calculated by the author from Indian *Lok Sabha* 2004. Resume of Work of 13th *Lok Sabha*, Indian Lok Sabha (2004d), *Rajya Sabha* Annual Report 2000–2003, Indian *Lok Sabha* (2001, 2002, 2003, 2003a, 2004) and Departmentally Related Committees: A Review (1999–2000, 2001 and 2002), Indian *Lok Sabha* (2001, 2003, 2003a).

Notes
DRSCOHA – Departmentally-Related Standing Committee on Home Affairs.
DRSCOD – Departmentally-Related Standing Committee on Defense.
DRSCOA – Departmentally-Related Standing Committee on Agriculture.

AGENDA OF DELIBERATION

The committee did huge volumes of work with respect to consideration of demands for grants, examination of bills referred to it by the parliament and deliberation of other general issues of importance. The committee considered the demand for grants of the related ministries/departments and presented three reports thereon to the parliament during budget session every year. During this time (2000–2003) the committee examined 47 bills and presented 33 reports to both the Houses of parliament. Among the important bills were, The Lotteries (Prohibition) Bill 1999, The Freedom of Information Bill 2000, The Lokpal (Ombudsman) Bill 2001, The Constitution (88th to 102nd) Amendment Bill, The Companies Bill (Amendment) 2001, The Contempt of Court Amendment Bill 2003, Illegal Migration Laws (Repealing and Amendment) Bill 2003, The Salaries and Allowances of the Judicial Officers of the Union Territories Bill 2003 and so on.

It deliberated on general issues of importance such as administration of Union territories, internal security situation in the country, economic and infra-structural development, Swatantrata Sainik Samman pension scheme (Independent Soldiers Honorary Pension Scheme) and the insurgency situation in the north-eastern region. Inland security was a major issue of discussion in committee meeting. "Cross-border terrorism and insurgency in Jammu and Kashmir" was one of the most widely publicized agenda of deliberation of the committee. The issue was taken by the committee in May 2000. A study group was constituted headed by the chairman which visited Jammu and Kashmir in July 2000. A committee report was laid to both Houses of parliament in July 2001. Action-taken notes were received from the ministry in November 2001 and an action-taken report was present to the parliament in July 2002. It is apparent from the above discussion that the committee took two years to finish off the issue.

The committee made a large number of recommendations in every committee meeting. Forty-five percent (see Table 6.5 for details) of the recommendations made by the committee were accepted by the government. Subsequently about 2 percent of recommendations were dropped at the action-taken stage on receipt of government's replies. The percentage of acceptance of recommendations by the government is low compared with other committees.

The recommendations/observations made by the DRSC on Home Affairs in its various reports have evoked positive response from the government. For example, the committee in its 38th Report on Demands for Grants (1997–1998) of Ministry of Personnel, Public Grievances and Pensions had recommended for early enactment of the "Right to Information Act". Subsequently, the government introduced the Freedom of Information Bill, on July 25, 2000. This bill was also examined by the committee and the report thereon presented to Parliament. The bill was passed by both Houses of parliament during the winter session 2002. The Lotteries (Prohibition) Bill 1999 has also been a sequel to the observations/recommendations of the committee contained in its 42nd Report on the Lotteries (Regulation) Bill, 1998. Similarly, the committee examined the

Table: 6.5 Statement showing analysis of action taken by government on the recommendations made by three selected DRSCs on earlier reports presented in the 13th *Lok Sabha* (2000–2003)

	Standing Committee on Agriculture	*Standing Committee on Defense*	*Standing Committee on Home Affairs*
Total number of recommendations accepted by the government	249 (53.8%)	194 (78.2%)	48 (45%)
Total number of recommendations which the committee did not pursue in view of government replies	20 (4.31%)	5 (2%)	2 (1.96)
Total number of recommendations in respect of which replies of government have not accepted by the committee	79 (17.05%)	43 (17.3%)	11 (10.78%)
Total number of recommendations in respect of final replies of were awaited	115 (24.84%)	6 (2.4%)	39 (38.24%)
Total number of recommendations	463	248	102*

Source: compiled and calculated by the author from *Lok Sabha* Secretariat, Departmentally Related Committees: A Review (1999–2000, 2001 and 2002), Indian Lok Sabha (2001, 2003, 2003a), Reports of Standing Committee on Defense (19th and 21st) Indian *Lok Sabha*, 2003d, 2003e, Reports of Standing Committee on Agriculture (46th – 50th) Indian *Lok Sabha*, 2004c) and from Annual/Administrative Reports of Rajya Sabha (Committee Section), *Rajya Sabha* Secretariat, 2000–2003, Indian *Rajya Sabha* (2001, 2002, 2003, 2003a, 2004).

Lokpal Bill, 1996 and presented its 40th Report thereon to parliament. The government accepted most of its observations/recommendations therein and brought out a revised bill, namely the *Lokpal Bill*, 1998 which was again referred to the committee for examination and report. Subsequently, the committee presented its 50th Report on the Bill and presented the same to Parliament. The bill was again revised in the light of the observations/recommendations of the committee and *Lokpal Bill*, 2001 was introduced in *Lok Sabha* on August 14, 2001. This bill was also referred to the Committee for examination and the 84th Report of the committee thereon presented to parliament. Due to the importance of its reports, these have received wide attention in the media and got wide publicity (*Rajya Sabha* 2003). This is definitely an improvement upon a system in which the legislature is simply understood to be an "approving and attesting institution". In short, the Standing Committee on Home Affairs performed well in initiation, recommendation and implementation levels and its impact in calling the government to account was substantial.

Departmentally-Related Standing Committee (DRSC) on Agriculture

Three ministries of government of India, namely the Ministry of Agriculture, Ministry of Food Processing Industry and Ministry of Water Resources have been placed under the jurisdiction of the Committee on Agriculture. Based on data available from Table 6.4, it is obvious that an average 44 percent of the total members attended the committee meeting. The committee spent an average of one hour 37 minutes for each committee meeting. Average frequency of committee meeting was 16 days. The committee kept meeting regularly and frequently. It held 69 committee meetings in three years and produced 50 reports including 25 action-taken reports. It also undertook eight study visits in the first three years of thirteenth *Lok Sabha*.

AGENDA OF DELIBERATION

The committee did huge volumes of work with respect to consideration of demands for grants, examination of bills referred to it by the parliament and deliberation of other general issues of importance.

The committee considered the demand for grants of the related ministries/departments and presented reports thereon to the parliament during budget session every year. The committee considered demand – for grants of each and every ministry/department under its jurisdictions every year and held a good number of committee meetings on it and presented reports to both the Houses of parliament. It also considered the action-taken reports on earlier recommendations. The committee was quite efficient to finish off the demand for grants of all five ministries/department within one year. The committee has been examining the budgetary allocations (demand for grants) every year and has been making recommendations with respect to modifications of budgetary allocations to various ministries/departments. Only two bills were referred to the committee for examination in the thirteenth *Lok Sabha*. Two bills were Aquaculture Authority Bill, 2000 and the Multi-State Cooperative Societies Bill, 2000. The committee submitted reports on these two bills to the parliament. It deliberated on general issues of importance such as drought situation in the country, national agriculture policy, rainwater harvesting and ground water recharge and flood management. These recommendations were advisory in nature.

The committee made a large number of recommendations on demand for grants, bills and general issues in committee meetings. Some 54 percent (see Table 6.5 for details) of the recommendations made by the committee were accepted by the government. Subsequently about 4.3 percent of recommendations were dropped at the action-taken stage on receipt of government's replies.

The recommendations/observations made by the DRSC on Agriculture in its various reports have evoked positive response from the government. For instance, in its tenth report on demand for grants (2000–2001), the Standing Committee on Agriculture expressed its unhappiness over the scaling down of the budget allocations for the Accelerated Irrigation Benefit Program (AIBP) at the revised estimates stage from Rs16,000 million to 14,000 million by the Ministry of Finance without even consulting the Ministry of Water Resources. The committee recommended that the allocations in this regard should be appropriately increased and released. In response to such repeated recommendations, the Finance Minister announced in his budget speech on 28 February that he proposed to increase the allocation for the AIBP from Rs2000 crore last year to Rs2800 crore in 2002–2003 (Malhotra 2003: 399). In short, the impact of the Standing Committee on Home Affairs in calling the government to account was moderate in initiation, recommendation and implementation levels.

Departmentally-Related Standing Committee (DRSC) on Defense

The Ministry of Defense is covered under the jurisdiction of the Standing Committee on Defense. Based on data available from Table 6.4, it is obvious that an average 47 percent of the total members attended the committee meeting. The committee spent an average of 2.25 hours for each committee meeting. Average frequency of committee meeting was 27 days. The committee kept meeting regularly and frequently. It held 40 committee meetings in three years and produced 21 reports including 11 action-taken reports. The main committee made six on–the–spot study visits and several study groups undertook six other visits in the first three years of thirteenth *Lok Sabha*. Among the spot visits were ordnance factories, air force stations, Defense Research and Development Organization (DRDO) scattered in different parts of India.

AGENDA OF DELIBERATION

The committee did huge volumes of work with respect to consideration of demands for grants, examination of bills referred to it by the parliament and deliberation of other general issues of importance. The committee considered the demand for grants of the Ministry of Defense and held a good number of committee meetings on it and presented reports to both the Houses of parliament. It also considered the action-taken reports on earlier recommendations. No bill was referred to the committee for examination in the thirteenth *Lok Sabha*. It deliberated on policy/general issues of importance such as self-reliance in defense, DRDO, quality assurance organizations under Ministry of Defense, manpower planning and management policy in defense, policy on nuclear weapons, deployment of army for counter-insurgency operation, modernization of Indian air force, the synergy between intelligence agencies and defense force and so on. These recommendations were advisory in nature. Most of the controversial issues on defense policies and expenditure were deliberated and dealt with by PAC. Most of the agenda were on strategies and means of improving the defense system in India. Given the warring relations with neighboring Pakistan, the committee focused more on how to refine and advance the defense system.

The committee made a large number of recommendations on demand for grants, bills and general issues in committee meetings. An impressive 78 percent (see Table 6.5 for details) of the recommendations made by the committee were accepted by the government. Subsequently about 2 percent of the recommendations were dropped at the action-taken stage on receipt of government's replies. In short, the impact of the Standing Committee on Defense in calling the government to account was good in initiation, deliberation, recommendation and acceptance levels. However, the committee sporadically followed up the status of implementation, in most cases the matter was left to the incumbent government to implement.

Conclusion

India has been a longstanding democracy since 1947 and parliament has remained at the heart of this democratic advancement. Parliament is regarded by the political parties in India not only as a symbol of legitimacy and democratic governance but also as a forum for deliberation and resolution of critical issues of national importance and holding the government to account. The formal institutional arrangements of the political system in India appears institutionalized and in good shape in checking and balancing the power and authority of the executive. All the major characteristics (strong opposition, independent parliamentary secretariat, institutionalized committee system and so on) of a functioning legislature are vibrantly present in India and it plays a vital role in governing the country and holding the government accountable. All the major political institutions including the parliament (and parliamentary committees), the presidency, the judiciary, the state assemblies, the local government units and other independent institutions are functioning well.

Political power is dispersed among many political institutions. Indian parliament is bicameral. To become law, legislation must pass each House and have the assent of the president. India has an organized and integrated system of local government having linkage from village to distract/division levels. Elections of major local government institutions have taken place at regular interval. There are many provincial parliaments (five have bicameral parliament) in India which provide political space for different political parties to act and be accommodated with the governance system as a whole. There is enormous scope for the opposition political parties to share the power through representations in different political institutions. Political parties over the course of time have learned how to behave with the opponents and have accustomed to share power and coexist with rival power holders. They are habituated to abiding by the rules of the game of politics.

Institutional arrangements are discernible in India which reflects dispersal of power as well as the incumbent government's willingness to leave space for the opposition. In India, the prime minister is not leader of the House. The Speaker is usually elected on consensus among different political parties. Committee memberships and chairmanships are based on the proportional representation of parties in the House. Ministers who belong to the executive branch are excluded from committees and thus the neutrality and relative independence of committees as institutions of legislative branch has been maintained. Moreover, there are a good number of institutions such as National Human Rights Commission (NHRC), Central Bureau of Investigation (CBI), Central Vigilance Commission (CVC) which may get institutionalized over time and serve the people. Thus the external context of the parliament and parliamentary committees has largely determined the way parliament and committees have performed in India.

Institutionally, the parliamentary committee system in India is mainly patterned on the Westminster system. The committee system in Indian parliament has reached its current state through a slow, lengthy and painstaking evolutionary process. In fact, many of the key[3] features of the committee system within the Westminster tradition which bear the potentials of checking the monopoly of governmental power and calling the government to account are vibrantly present in India. Parliamentary committees in India in general are not permanent (usually elected annually, although they have a permanent flavor) and functionally correspond to ministerial structure. Formally, their jurisdictions are comprehensive ranging from legislation to oversight to investigation and their role in doing that job is significant. Formally committees cannot select their chairs and members. Selection and appointment of committee chairs and members are done by the Speaker in consultation with the political parties. Committees meet in camera and decide on the basis of majority. Committees cannot set their own agenda and have the power to send for papers, persons and documents with the exception that government may decline to produce a document on the ground that its disclosure would be prejudicial to the safety or interest of the state. They can consider legislative bills referred to them by the House and have significant role in budget allocation and demands for grants. Notwithstanding the institutional arrangement of committee system in India places the government (the major party) in an advantageous position to be the ultimate arbiter on any issue of governance, committees function on consensus and views of the opposition are very often respected and accommodated.

Formally committee recommendations are not binding on the incumbent government but a high number of (60 percent or so) of recommendations are accepted by the government and those that are not accepted are explained the government by proving explanatory notes. The committee system is highly institutionalized and there is a link between and among all the stages of committee operations i.e. committee formation, deliberation, recommendation and acceptance. The matter of implementation of recommendations is left to the government to act on. This is an institutional limitation of committee system in a parliamentary system of government and India is not an exception in this case. Hence the job of committees is usually done once their recommendations are accepted by the government. In sum, institutionally India has got a working parliament and therefore a working committee system with significant scope in ensuring executive accountability.

In terms of ensuring government accountability, the role of the PAC, COPU and COE is confined largely to the initiation and the recommendation stages with lukewarm implications at the implementation level. Sometimes these took several years (five to seven years are common) to finish off a contentious issue without any concrete result. It is obvious from the operations of three selected DRSCs that their endeavor to ensure executive accountability is mainly confined to the initiation, recommendation and acceptance stages. At the implementation stage, their role to ensure executive accountability is hard to judge. Committee deliberations have largely been confined to improving the organization and working of the administrative machinery rather than holding the government accountable. The media in general and the print media in particular had played a vital role in calling the executive to account by exposing divergent cases of malpractices and irregularities to the public and compelled the parliament/parliamentary committees and other anti-corruption agencies to get into action.

Limitations of committees in Indian parliament are numerous. Parliamentary committees have a restricted role in law-making. In India, average turnover of committee members is high i.e. 33 percent. This deters committee members from developing specialized knowledge and expertise to make committee more effective. DRSCs have 45 members and short lifespans (one year). The large size of the DRSC makes effective functioning difficult. Currently there are too many committees in Indian parliament to run efficiently and effectively. While India has significantly broadened committee involvement in various parliamentary businesses over the last decade, a coordination mechanism is currently lacking. Committees operate in a fragmented manner.

Very often, recommendations that are really important or of some consequences (as we have seen in the case of Bofors scandal, coffin scam, sleeping bags scam) were not accepted by the government. Ministries have rarely accepted the recommendations/observations of the committees when they relate to substantive issues like changing procedures, taking action against errant employees or disturbing the status quo. Sometimes, government ministries simply decline to provide documents to the committee in the pretext of national security as we have seen in case of coffin scam in the thirteenth *Lok Sabha*. So far as the administration is concerned, committee recommendations provide a corrective future action. Moreover, the mere existence of these committees works as a deterrent against irresponsible actions.

A well institutionalized parliament and parliamentary committees have evolved over time and taken root in India. Parliamentary committees have developed their own distinctive identities guided by their own institutional values and culture of work. Thus the current state of securing executive accountability by parliamentary committees in India hinges upon the prevailing macro-political context of the country and the institutionalized committee system originating mainly from the political context and shaped in part by the prevailing hierarchical culture of India.

7 Parliamentary control and government accountability in Sri Lanka

The role of parliamentary committees

Sri Lanka, a former British colony, is one of South Asia's most established democracies. It was the first British colonial territory in which elections under universal suffrage were held prior to independence in 1931, 1936 and in 1947 (Silva 2000: 48).The military has never been deemed a serious threat to civilian government and has kept on the periphery of the public policy-making arena. However, despite its democratic tradition, since 1971 Sri Lanka has been under emergency rule[1] for longer than it has been under democratic rule. The Sinhala-Tamil ethnic crisis in Sri Lanka climaxed in 1983 into a civil war. This civil war has already claimed 65,000 lives and displaced more than 670,000 people from their homes (Herath 2002). For a systematic presentation, this chapter is further organized into three parts, i.e. the Sri Lankan parliament in its political context, the historical evolution of the parliamentary committee system in Sri Lanka and the formal arrangement of committee system and its real-world implications in calling the government to account.

The Sri Lankan parliament in its political context

The Soulbury Constitution of 1946 established a bicameral parliamentary system composed of the House of Representatives and a Senate with the Governor-General as nominal head of state. With the adoption of a new constitution in 1972, Ceylon became the Republic of Sri Lanka. The Governor-General was replaced by the president as the nominal head of the state. The bicameral system was succeeded by a unicameral type. The new constitution of September 1978 declared the country as Democratic Socialist Republic of Sri Lanka. This third constitution introduced a semi-presidential system following the model of the Fifth French Republic. The plurality electoral system was replaced by proportional representation in multi-member constituencies (Wagner 2001: 699). Each of these changes had the effect of extending the ruling party's length of time in power.

The constitution of 1978 was revolutionary in that it shifted the seat of executive power away from a cabinet that was part of the parliament to an executive president who is elected independently of it and is not accountable to the legislature. The president has the right to attend, address and send messages to parliament at any time. He or she makes statements of government policy in parliament at the commencement of each session. In fact, the president cannot be criticized by parliament in the floor of the House. Thus the powers of the executive are formidable under the 1978 constitution and its relationship with the legislature is an unequal one (Welikala 2002: 3).

The president is the head of the executive, the head of the government and the Commander-in-Chief of Armed Forces. Cabinet is appointed by the president in consultation with the prime minister. The president appoints and dismisses cabinet ministers, including the prime minister and even presides over cabinet meetings. He/she can hold selected portfolios too. All four executive presidents invariably held the most crucial ministerial portfolios such as defense, finance or foreign affairs. He/she appoints members of higher courts including Supreme Court and Appeal Court judges. More importantly, the president can dissolve the parliament after one year under presidential powers and may submit to national referendum matters of national importance (Derbyshire and Derbyshire 2000). Dissolution of parliament by the president at will has been commonplace in Sri Lanka. For instance, former president Kumaratunga had suspended the Sri Lankan parliament twice and called for new elections before schedule. President Kumaratunga commented, "Under our constitution the prime minister is merely a glorified minister. It takes just a one-sentence letter from me to dismiss the prime minister and his entire cabinet" (*International Herald Tribune*, October 15, 2003). Since 1978 when the executive Presidency was created it is undeniable that the role of parliament has declined considerably and with it oversight of the executive (CPSU 2000).

All the respondents (100 percent, with mean score 4) in our questionnaire survey (see Appendix, Table A1.1 for detailed survey results), were of the view that a strong parliament is a prerequisite for a strong committee system and vice versa. They admit that within the prevailing political framework, parliament is very weak vis-à-vis the executive and so is the parliamentary committee system. One opposition MP expressed his disappointment by saying that "parliament itself let alone committee system has become next to useless and it does not really add any value to the progress of the nation".

Parliament, known as the National State Assembly, is unicameral parliament and has supreme legislative authority. An argument in defense of the unfettered legislative power over the executive is that power of appropriation or raising money remains with the parliament. Moreover, any treaty or agreement between Sri Lanka and any foreign state has to be approved by parliament by a two-thirds majority. But this argument sounds hollow. In the past 26 years since the semi-presidential form of government has been in operation, the president and the majority party in the House belonged to the same party except for some 29 months. For the first time in Sri Lanka, the prospect of co-habitation, inherent in the Gaullist presidential system became a reality when UNP (United Nationalist Party) won the parliamentary elections held in December 2001 and became major party in the parliament while the presidency was held by the PA (People's Alliance). But this co-habitation in Sri Lanka did lasted for only 26 months.

Moreover, Article 85(2) of the Sri Lankan Constitution provides that the president in his/her discretion submit to the people by referendum any bill which has been rejected by parliament; even appropriation bills are not an exception. The only condition to be satisfied for such bills to become a law are that these must be approved by an absolute majority of the valid votes cast must add up to at least two-thirds of the whole number of electors entered in the register (Wilson 1980: 74). Moreover, under a state of emergency the president has the power to pass legislation without parliamentary consent.

Of the survey respondents, 70 percent disagree with the statement that institutionally committees are much weaker in parliamentary systems than in the presidential system. The mean score is 0.5 only. They opined that the semi-presidential system introduced in Sri Lanka in 1978 had not been at all conducive to the emergence of a strong parliament and parliamentary committee system. They were unanimous in their opinion that at least the provision of the president's power to dissolve parliament after one year of parliament's life at his/her will or convenience must be abolished in order to keep the parliament alive. Parliament was dissolved by the former president Kumaratunga twice in four years. This provision has undoubtedly made the parliament vulnerable to the president. They believe there is a strong public demand to revert to the parliamentary system in Sri Lanka including the switching of electoral system from preferential vote system to "first-past-the-post" (FPTP) or mixed "German-type-system". They strongly believe that the current electoral system which prevents any party from garnering a two-thirds majority (that is a requirement to bring necessary amendments to the constitution) in the parliament has stood the way to take this country forward as well as to dissolve ethnic conflict with the Tamils. A number of MPs defended the utility of the semi-presidential system. They thought that this system had served well in maintaining the integrity of a united Sri Lanka.

On the question of the restoration of the second chamber in Sri Lankan parliament in a bid to make the executive accountable, 70 percent of the respondents answered in the positive on condition that the shift of the system of government from semi-presidential to the parliamentary system must precede the restoration of the second chamber. Most of the MPs believe that attempts have been made in Sri Lanka to promote substantial autonomy (by creating nine elected provincial parliament) within a united country without regional representation (in the form of Senate or council of provinces) at the center. A second chamber can fill this void. It is important that the regional politicians and party groups are made to feel part of the whole, stakeholders in a united nation. Within the current political framework, introduction of a second chamber will make things further complicated.

Formally, the parliament of Sri Lanka does have the power of the purse. Each year, the budget is passed by parliament and allocations confirmed in the Annual Appropriation Act. The first reading of the bill is a formal one and confined to tabling of the bill. The second reading usually commences one month later. This is followed by the debate on the second reading, which does not last for more than seven days. The second stage of the second reading is done in the Committee of the Whole House, which must get its business done in a maximum of 22 days. The program for the committee stage debate is drawn up by the opposition, which decides the allocation of time for each ministry (Wijesekera 2002: 69–70). Thus the opposition gets a chance to vent their grievances and review the operations of administration. In the course of the committee stage, proposed allocations can be reduced but cannot be changed in any other way. No amendment can be moved to increase the allocated sums. The final approval for appropriation bill is given at third reading with no debate allowed. The importance of the appropriation bill is evident by the fact that on its rejection on the first occasion results in the dissolution of the Cabinet of Ministers stand dissolved and on the second occasion the parliament itself stands dissolved.

In reality, parliament's control over public funds is very weak. Actual expenditure often exceeds budget estimates, revenues are under-realized and there is insufficient information on assets and liabilities of the state. As a result, budget deficit targets for the past several years have not been met. The frequency of budget revisions and significant supplementary estimates are additional indicators of weak parliamentary control. During year 2000, supplementary provisions amounting to US$457 million or 9.2 percent of the budget expenditure estimates were approved by the parliament. Further evidence is the amount of time spent by the Committee on Public Accounts (COPA) on routine regularization of budget excesses, when it examines the audited appropriation accounts several years after the event. Aside from this, treasury controls over the release of funds, because of insufficient cash flow, further erodes parliamentary control (The World Bank 2003: 5).

Currently the Sri Lankan parliament comprises 225 members who are directly elected by a "modified" system of proportional representation (PR) involving preferential voting for six-year terms. The Department of Elections is a highly independent body, which conducts elections. It has the power to take over electronic state media during elections if necessary. The country is divided into 22 multi-member constituencies (that comprise between four and 20 seats) from which 196 deputies are returned with the remaining 29 being elected from party lists on the basis of the total national vote of each party. Each voter votes for a specific party and three of its candidates. A party must win at least 5 percent (it was reduced to 5 percent in 1987 from 12.5 percent in 1978) of the votes in a constituency to claim seats. Although this system creates a closer correspondence between vote percentages and parliamentary representation, the equitable nature of proportional representation is diluted by constitutional provision that grants the party with largest percentage of votes in each district a bonus seat in addition to those gained through proportional representation (U.S. Library of Congress 1986). Moreover, while PR has succeeded in putting an end to the lopsided parliamentary victories resulting from the "first-past-the-post" system, it has also led to increased representation of ethnically based or extremist minor parties. Since these minor parties were critical to building majority coalitions, the main political parties tended to adopt the minor parties' agenda, exacerbating the country's division (NED 1997). According to the prevailing version of proportional representative system, the constituency votes for the party first and the individual later. The party hierarchy is empowered to expel any of its members who cross the floor or vote against the party and replace him/her with another member of the party. An expelled MP automatically loses his/her seat. The second amendment to the constitution passed in 1979 allows the whole parliament to decide whether a member of parliament can be expelled by his or her party or change his or her party allegiance. This has placed the governing party in an advantageous position and invariably encouraged the members of the opposition to defect from the opposition to the majority party/coalitions. Moreover, there are no by-elections, with parties being able to appoint successors to deputies who retire or die. This electoral system has undoubtedly strengthened party's grip over an individual MP. A leading Sri Lankan daily comments:

> The existing Preferential Voting system is a disaster. This system will automatically encourage jealousy and hatred. In the Preferential Voting system it is not the two parties that are contesting but those in the same parties. Hatred, jealousy, grows within the parties. If we are to hold a referendum on this system, whatever party they may belong to, 95 per cent will opt to changing the system.
>
> (*The Island*, August 12, 2003)

Most of the respondents have expressed their opinion in favor of reintroduction of the first-past-the-post or mixed "German-type-system".

Committee members were asked about the anti-defection law and its impact on the behavior of an individual MP in committee sessions. 40 percent of the respondents completely agree that anti-defection law circumscribes individual freedom of an MP and it certainly has an impact on the functioning of committees. About half of the respondents, having disagreed with the statement claimed that this anti-defection law had more merits than demerits considering the political situation in Sri Lanka where despite the restrictions, floor-crossings and horse-trading had been frequent. This law is necessary for political stability of the country. They think that even the existing law has failed to prevent MPs crossing the floor in Sri Lanka and hence they want to see the law made more stringent like the one in India.

An analysis of the view of respondents concerning the relationship between the control of their parties over them and the level of committee strength, 90 percent hold that there is a strong correlation between these two variables. However, almost all of the respondents, irrespective of party affiliation, are of the view that in Sri Lanka, the influence of party over the committee member is not substantial and once they are in the committees, they work on their personal capacities as an MP rather than as a party representative. They observe that even when a ruling party cabinet member presides over a consultative committee meeting, backbenchers from the treasury bench and the opposition are allowed to express their views on the deliberated subject. Sometimes the minister entertains harsh criticisms of government from the opposition members too.

When asked about the role of opposition in holding the government accountable, an overwhelming 100 percent of respondents maintained that a strong but disciplined opposition was at the heart of parliament and parliamentary committees. They believe that it is the opposition in the parliament who keeps a watchful eye on the functioning of the government and criticizes the government whenever it gets a chance to do so. Opposition members make committees vibrant. There was very strong opposition (an average 49 percent of the total 225 seats were occupied by the opposition) in the last three parliaments (fourth, fifth and sixth). Frequently dissolutions of parliaments marred their potentials of becoming strong parliament vis-à-vis the executive. They opined that there must be some sorts of agreement and consensus between the government and the opposition on nationally significant matters like resolving the ethnic conflicts in Sri Lanka. The relationship between the two top leaders of the two major parties has been disappointing over years. Some respondents attribute this troubled relationship between the two to the hereditary democracy (two top leaders coming from two distinguished families whose ancestors alternated power) in Sri Lanka. They feel that the two leaders must reach a consensus before embarking on resolving ethnic conflicts in the north-eastern part of the country.

Sri Lanka has a written constitution. At least nine articles of the constitution especially those dealing with the structure of the government, the national anthem, the national flag and Buddhism have been made protective articles. Those proposing to amend these provisions not only have to muster the support of two-thirds of total members; proposals for amendment have to be vetted in a national referendum (Warnapala 1980: 927). The constitutional requirement for a two-thirds majority support in the legislature to change the system of government has become another problem (due to the PR electoral system) in resolving the ethnic problem. This is the reason why the devolution package tabled in the legislature by Kumaratunga government in the year 2000 was not passed (Herath 2000).

The Supreme Court has the power of judicial review; it can determine whether an act of parliament is consistent with the principles of the constitution. However, the power of judicial review is to be exercised before the enactment of the law. More importantly, the judiciary's opinion can be waived through a two-thirds majority vote in the parliament (Phandis 1989: 165). However, once a bill has been passed by the legislature and becomes an act, no court or tribunal can invalidate such an act. Thus the power of judicial review is limited to a certain extent.

Up to the year 1987, Sri Lanka had a highly centralized form of government. Under the 13th amendment to the constitution, passed in November 1987, extensive powers have been devolved to nine directly elected provincial councils (parliaments), primarily with a view to meeting Tamil demands for greater autonomy. Each province is headed by a governor, who is appointed by the president. Local government also includes district councils, municipal councils, urban councils and village-level councils. All local governments have limited powers, and the president of the republic has the power to dissolve them at will.

Historical development of parliamentary committee system in Sri Lanka

In the history of legislatures in Sri Lanka, committee tradition had existed and a novel experiment in semi-responsible government was attempted through the executive committee system of the Donoughmore period (1931–1946). Each executive committee elected a chairman who acted as the minister. The minister could not take executive decisions all by himself. The executive committee members collectively took decisions. It was a system of committees devised to work in a political environment where no political parties existed, and therefore the private member in the case of ordinary state councilor was able to exercise some influence in the matters of legislation and the administration but the whole exercise fell on the chairman of the committees.

In 1947, the new parliamentary system which came to be created on the traditional Westminster model, contained a traditional system of committees (consisting of standing committees, the select committees, Petitions Committee, Committee on Public Accounts, Committee on Public Enterprises, High Post Committee and so on) which functioned effectively and served the intended purpose largely because of the fact that the parliament remained supreme till it was devalued in 1978 by the introduction of executive presidency in the constitution. In addition to traditional structure of committees, the consultative committees on ministries were introduced in 1978 to oversee the activities of ministries. They were introduced in the context of the decline of the legislature – a unicameral legislature for that matter – which occurred as a result of the introduction of a constitution under which the executive enjoyed enormous power and this is the primary cause of existing constitutional crisis in the country. It was because of this feature in the new constitution that even the traditional parliamentary committees began to decline in their effectiveness; they performed a useful function in the past as committees of scrutiny (Warnapala 2003). No major parliamentary reform for rationalizing or strengthening the committee system was introduced in Sri Lanka since 1978.

Some 17 oversight committees were proposed by the Ranil Wickremasinghe Government in the fifth parliament (2002–2003). All oversight committees would be established on a sectoral basis. The committees will consist of between four and eight members and will be chaired by an opposition member. Each sectoral committee will have the power to send for and examine any persons including cabinet ministers and government secretaries. Up to three non-parliamentary specialists will be allowed to sit on those committees. Of course, they would have no voting right (*Daily News*, May 22, 2003; *The Island*, May 30, 2003). This proposal could not be materialized due to the early dissolution of the parliament by the president which put an end to Wickremasinghe regime.

The institutional arrangement of committee system in Sri Lanka and its real-world implications

The power to appoint committees has been recognized under Article 74 of the constitution. The composition, functions, terms of office, quorum and procedure in conducting business in the committees are regulated under Standing Orders and the directions by the Speaker issued under Standing Order.

Typology of committees

According to the Standing Order, the Sri Lankan parliament apart from the Committee of whole House has four broad categories of committees:

- select committees;
- consultative committees;
- standing committees; and
- committee for special purposes.

Select committees

These are ad-hoc committees. They are appointed by the Speaker to inquire into matters which may be referred to them by the parliament. A select committee consists of not more than 12 members. four members of a select committee usually form the quorum. In the past, select committees have been appointed to prove various matters like the motion for removal of a judge, to recommend laws relating to media reforms and constitutional reforms.

Consultative committees

Consultative committees which exactly correspond to the number of ministries are constituted at the commencement of each session by the Committee of Selection. The concerned minister (deputy ministers in case of the ministries which are under the president) is the ex-officio chairman of each consultative committee. The functions of a consultative committee are to "to inquire into and report upon such matters as are referred to it by the chairman or by parliament including any proposal for legislation, supplementary of other estimates, statements of expenditure, motions, annual reports or papers". It has the power to initiate through the chairman any bill or motion. They are expected to meet at least once a month. It is the duty of the secretary to the ministry to make arrangements for the meeting of the consultative committees in consultation with secretary–general of parliament.

An ambiguity at first glance with regard to the system of consultative committees now obtaining relates to the conflict between Article 45(1) of the Constitution which provides for appointment of ministers of non-cabinet rank who are nonetheless responsible to parliament and Standing Orders that only provide for the establishment of consultative committees corresponding to the number of cabinet ministries (Welikala 2002: 25). Thus non-cabinet ministries remain outside the regime of parliamentary committee scrutiny. In the fifth parliament, there were 32 cabinet ministries and 31 non-cabinet ministries. The working of those 31 non-cabinet ministries remained precluded from the committee control and scrutiny.

Standing committees

The Committee on Selection, at the commencement of every session, appoints the standing committees. Each standing committee consists of 20 members. The function of a standing committee is confined to the consideration of bills referred to it by the parliament.

Committees for special purposes

In Sri Lankan parliament, there are a number of committees for special purposes. They are the Committee on Selection (which is a 22-member all party committee headed by the Speaker is appointed at the commencement of each session to consider the number, the function, the composition and quorum of the committees), the House Committee, the Committee of Standing Order, the Business Committee, Committee on Public Accounts, Committee on Public Enterprises, the High Post Committee, the Disciplinary Committee, Committee on Privileges and Committee on Public Petition. Contrary to practices in more developed Commonwealth countries, Sri Lanka does not have a budget or Estimates Committee.

COMMITTEE ON PUBLIC ACCOUNTS (COPA)

This is one of two financial committees in the parliament. Currently it consists of 19 members nominated by the Committee on Selection. The prime function of this committee is to examine the appropriation of sums granted to all ministries, departments, and local authorities by parliament to meet the public expenditure. It examines the report of the Auditor General.

According to Section 149(1) of the constitution, all public revenue and expenditures have to be channeled through the Consolidated Fund but there are a number of off-budget funds such as the President's Fund, Lottery Funds and Gam Udawa Funds (Rural Awakening Funds) and the failure to bring them under the purview of Public Accounts Committee has resulted in an erosion of public accountability (Warnapala 2004: 135).

COMMITTEE ON PUBLIC ENTERPRISES (COPE)

This is the other financial committees in the parliament which consists of 19 members nominated by the Committee on Selection. COPE examine public enterprises. These examinations are based on the current performance aspects and queries raised by the Auditor-General (AG) on the activities of such enterprises. The Chief Accounting Officers (CAO) and the Accounting Officers (AO) are examined in depth on the submission of annual reports to parliament, preparation of annual budgets, corporate plans and implementation of such plans.

THE HIGH POST COMMITTEE (HPC)

A high-level parliamentary committee which is headed by the prime minister (by the Speaker from the fifth parliament) and made up of the Leader of the Opposition, the Deputy Leader of the Opposition and the Minister for Finance and Planning as members, examines the suitability of candidates to be appointed as secretaries to the ministries, heads of diplomatic missions, chairmen and members of boards of state institutions such as corporations in Sri Lanka. There have been occasions when the committee has rejected ministerial nominees for higher positions.

Structure

Committees are supposed to be constituted at the commencement of each session of parliament. There is nothing mentioned about the formation of committees in the inaugural session of a new parliament. However, parliaments in Sri Lanka took two months on an average to form the committee and an average of three months to get its business started with. On the question of the formation of all committees in the inaugural session of a new parliament, 91 percent of the respondents were in favor of such an idea. The terms of earlier Sri Lanka parliaments (third, fourth and fifth) were invariably curtailed due to dissolution (normal life is six years) by the president. An interesting point to note is that since the date of dissolution of parliament, it takes an average 2.5 months to get started with a new parliament. Thus in four years (2000–2004), due to early dissolution of parliament twice, the executive had been immune from any parliamentary control for five months.

In Sri Lanka, committee members/chairs are nominated/elected for a session that span over a year or so. Usually chairmanships of the committee remain the same as they are usually reelected or reappointed. Problems remain with the turnover of the membership. In Sri Lanka, average turnover of committee members is 25 percent due mainly to absenteeism for three consecutive meetings. This deters committee members to develop specialized knowledge and expertise to make committee more effective. Most of the respondents (80 percent, mean score is 3.5) think that the terms of committees should be coterminous with lifespan of the parliament to give members enough time to develop expertise and expand their horizon of knowledge on different aspects of governmental and legislative activities.

In Sri Lanka, consultative committees parallel the structure of government ministries. Respondents were sharply divided on issue of consultative committees' correspondence to government ministries. Some 51 percent of the respondents think that consultative committees should parallel the structure of government structure. However, they feel that in Sri Lanka there are too many ministries (35 cabinet ministers and 30 non-cabinet ministers) to have control and run efficiently. They favored the reduction of the number of ministries from 35 to 20 or so. A good number of respondents (30 percent) disagreed with the proposal and suggested that given the situation that number of reduction of ministries is impossible in Sri Lanka, it is better to group several the consultative committees into one like the system in India based on the nature of functional operations for effective functioning of the committees. For instance, the Ministry of Energy, Forestry and Environment can be grouped under one committee which will help to reduce the number of consultative committees. Currently there are too many committees (35) to be provided with secretariat supports. Some respondents suggest that irregular committee meetings and poor member attendance can sharply abate if the number of consultative committees can be axed.

The size of most of the committees in Sri Lanka ranges between 15 and 20. Membership of some select committees and standing committees on legislation may exceed 20. The memberships of certain committees are specified in the standing order. However, the House on various occasions adopted resolution to vary the composition of committees which is an irregular procedure (Wijesekara 2002: 76). Majority (91 percent) of the respondents agree that small committee (consisting of 15–20 members or so) enhances committee specialization and dilutes party division. However, poor attendance of committee members hinders the efficacy and full potential of committees. Some respondents raised a very important issue related with the small size of committees i.e. the number of the committees. They think that currently there are too many committees in the Sri Lankan parliament to run efficiently and effectively. They feel that select committees and standing committees on bills are redundant. Their functions can easily be handed over to consultative committees on ministries which should be reorganized, reformed and renamed (as oversight or departmentally-related committees).

In Sri Lanka, the interest and preferences of members are usually obtained before they are appointed into a committee by their own political parties. In doing so, it is ensured that the interest of the individual MP does not conflict with that of the political parties. On the question of selection of members based on their own interest and expertise rather than the government or the political parties, 60 percent of the respondents completely agreed. This is conducive to committee specialization.

Usually chair of a committee is appointed by the Speaker. However, committees for special purposes have been given the right to elect their chairs. Nothing is mentioned in the Standing Order regarding the distribution of committee chairs. The chairmanship of a committee normally goes to a minister. All the consultative committees are headed by concerned ministers. Since independence, the practice of appointing an opposition member as chairman of COPA was followed in the first decade after independence. Since then, successive governments have kept control of chairmanships of two financial committees – COPA and COPE. However, in the fifth parliament (January 2002–February 2004), COPA and COPE were headed by opposition MPs. This has taken the shape of a convention as the sixth parliament has followed the precedents of the fifth. The Speaker is the chairman of committees such as House Committee, Committee on Standing Order, Committee on Parliamentary Business and Committee on Selection etc.

Members were divided on the question of proportion distribution of chairmanship among the parties. Of the respondents, 50 percent have reservations about this proposal. Proportional distribution of memberships in the committee is already in practice in Sri Lanka. Given the immature and confrontational political culture in Sri Lanka most of the respondents thought that chairmanships of committees (except COPA and COPE) should remain with the ruling party or coalitions unless and until a congenial political culture evolves in Sri Lanka. Some 30 percent of the respondents who agree completely with the statement have their own arguments. They argue that a committee is a mini-parliament and in term of chair selection attention must be given to uphold the representative character of the House. They think that the distribution of chairmanships of committees based on the proportional representation of the parties in the House will help the opposition feel that they are accommodated within the governance system which may contribute to lessening the political bitterness and confrontation between the two major parties.

Unlike elsewhere, ministers/deputy ministers are entitled to become members/chairs of all committees including financial committees (COPA and COPE) in Sri Lanka. In response to a question eliciting their opinion on the exclusion of ministers (as chairs and members) from committees, the majority of the respondents answered in the negative. They argued if the minister chaired the committee, it would be easier for him/her to implement committee recommendations. They referred to Australia as a case where committees are usually headed by ministers. A small group of respondents (23 percent) agree that in order to maintain the separation of power, ministers who are from the executive branch should be excluded from committee. Even they should not be allowed to continue as committee members. For some respondents, this was a radical reform proposal. They preferred to follow the system in Bangladesh which allowed ministers to be in committees as members only.

All the respondents (100 percent) expressed their satisfaction that COPA and COPE were headed by senior opposition members and were of the view that this should be continued so. They believe that COPA and COPE are the most prestigious committees in Sri Lanka which deal with the oversight of the financial affairs of the executive can be exemplars to offer chairmanship of consultative committees based on party composition in the House in the coming years.

Almost all (96 percent) the respondents felt the necessity of forming a Liaison Committee consisting of the chairmen of different committees chaired by the Speaker to ensure proper coordination and avoid unnecessary overlapping or duplication of work to save money, resources and time. The Sri Lankan parliament currently does not have a committee of this kind. The respondents felt that this committee can help the Speaker to keep track of the over all activities of committee system as whole.

Procedures

Parliamentary committees in Sri Lanka can not choose their own agenda of deliberations. Their operations are confined to matters (bills or other issues) which are referred to them by the House. The current Standing Orders restrict the potential scope of the consultative committees as monitors of administration by specifically listing the matters that may be referred to them. Thus the committees are constrained to consider only those matters that may be properly directed to them such as proposed legislation, estimates, motions and annual reports that come within the purview of the particular ministry. Moreover, there is no tradition of the executive submitting statutory instrument/subordinate legislation for parliamentary scrutiny and ratification.

When asked about the agenda-setting capability of parliament 59 percent of the respondents agreed that committee's ability to set its own agenda is a crucial power to constraint government. They report that in Sri Lanka, committees deal with matters referred to it by the House where the decision of the majority party usually prevails. This is a major limitation of the committee system in Sri Lanka.

That committee stage of bill consideration should precede floor consideration was favored by over 50 percent of the respondents. They think that this is an extreme legislative reform proposal considering the vulnerability of parliament to the wishes of the president. They reported that usually there were no committee stages of government bills during the last few years.

The sittings of the committee are held in camera in Sri Lanka. The deliberation of the meeting is, as per the Standing Order, confined exclusively to committee members and officers of parliamentary secretariat. However, in the meetings of consultative and financial committees, officials including the secretary of concerned ministries and relevant public bodies remain present to clarify, explain and account for specific matter. Moreover, Speaker/chairman can allow strangers (experts, media, witnesses from public) to participate in committee meetings. But they must be withdrawn during committee deliberation. Evidence, oral or written report or proceedings of the committee is confidential until its placement to the House.

On the question of the nature of committee session (open or closed) 93 percent of the respondents agree that it should be closed which will help foster inter-party compromise and relax party discipline. Currently there is a proposal on the table regarding whether opening up of committee session to media. Most of the respondents believe that considering the socio-political culture in Sri Lanka, committee sessions must be closed. In the committee sessions, high government officials remain present who have to account themselves before the committee. Sometimes, the Chief Accounting Officer (CAO) and Accounting Officers (AO) have to face very tough time in committee sessions. Some MPs are afraid that the media may not be able to publish objective reports of committee sessions at this moment. They may publish reports which may embarrass the officials as well as the government. Sharp party division within the committee sessions is hardly seen. That will disappear once committee sessions are open to media. MPs would like to play the same as they do in the House and consensus which is common in committee sessions will shift to confrontation.

Committees can hold public hearings on bills or any other matter in committee sessions which has hardly been practiced in Sri Lanka. The proposal of public hearings on legislative bills and other oversight matters was supported by 95 percent of the respondents. They felt that this kind of public hearings would add valuable information and inputs which would help the parliament to get public reactions on the bill and thus get the chance to improve the contents of the bill or the matters discussed prior to be passed by the House.

In Sri Lanka, the committees have the right to send for papers and persons and usually the request of committee are complied with. But the government has the right to decline to provide papers to the committees on the ground that its disclosure would be prejudicial to the safety or interest of state. Some 80 percent of respondents supported the continuation of the committee's right to send for paper and persons. Some respondents felt that ministers should be excluded from summoning to the committees. It is the House where he/she should better be asked questions regarding the performance of his/her ministry.

Functions

The prime functions of parliamentary committees include legislation, allocation and review of budget and oversight of the executive. Committees in Sri Lanka have no role in budget allocation, which is a preserve of the House. The second stage of the second reading on appropriation bill is done in the Committee of the whole House. COPA and COPE are empowered to examine the financial propriety of the money granted to government department and public corporations. But if anything goes wrong in between budget allocation to review of financial statements by COPA and COPE, no committee level oversight is done. However, if a newspaper reports about financial misappropriations or other irregularities of government bodies, the parliament can appoint a select committee to look into the matters that are hardly done.

In Sri Lanka, the parliamentary committees play no major role in law-making. Government bills are rarely refereed to committees for scrutiny. From October 2001 to December 2004, none but five private members' bills (see Table 7.1) were sent to committees for scrutiny. 75 percent of the respondents (the mean is 3.1 out of maximum four) completely agreed that committees

Table 7.1 Bills introduced and passed (2000–2004)

	Number of bills tabled and passed				*Total number of bills sent to committees for scrutiny*
	Government bills		*Private members' bills*		
	Tabled	*Passed*	*Tabled*	*Passed*	
Sixth (April 2004–	42	30	9	0	0
Fifth (Dec. 2001–Feb. 2004)	184	72	44	5	5 (private members' bills)
Fourth (Oct. 2000–Nov. 2001)	44	18	12	0	0

Source: compiled by the author from Bills Register/Acts Register, Parliament Secretariat, Sri Lanka (2000–2004), Parliament of Sri Lanka (2004).

should have exclusive jurisdiction over legislation and oversight of the executive. They think that committees should play a significant role at various stages of law-making – from review of bill to review of act. They think that committees should have major role in the oversight of administration too. Some respondents expressed their reservation about giving the committee exclusive jurisdiction over law-making and oversight of executive which may cause the executive and the legislative branch to dive into power wrangling.

Committee reports are usually presented to the House but never debated. Asked whether committee reports should be presented to the House regularly and debated as well, 60 percent of the respondents answered in the positive. Some respondents do not have any opinion about this matter. As the committee reports were not regularly published (because committee meetings were not held regularly and parliament was not there on regular interval), regular deliberations of committee reports had never been felt strongly. Committee deliberations are held in camera. Neither public nor the media are allowed to witness the proceedings of committees in Sri Lanka. The specific Standing Orders do not permit publication of any proceedings of committees of parliament before they are reported to the House. The earlier practice of printing the minutes of evidence of the proceedings (verbatim recording) was abandoned over a decade ago. Committee reports are hardly published. Even the very few committee reports which have been published so far do not contain minutes of committee meetings. As a result, currently, the public and MPs (except those who are members of that particular committee) have no access to the examinations of committee operations and remain largely ignorant of these deliberations.

In Sri Lanka, if a committee member does not agree with the decision of the majority members of the committee he or she can record a note of dissent that is included in a single minute. Respondents were sharply divided on a question about the presentation of minority report in case of dissention in the committee meeting. 45 percent of the respondents agreed that the minority should be allowed to present their own reports which would reflect that the committees were not dominated by the government. They reported that in Sri Lanka, decisions in committee sessions are made on consensus basis. However, in the past, the minority were allowed to present their own report in case of dissention. Those who opposed the proposal argued that, if necessary, the same report could contain the dissent of the minority and serve the same purpose.

In Sri Lanka, committee recommendations are not mandatory for the executive to comply with. However there is a formal provision which requires the government departments to come up with treasury minutes following the recommendations of committee meetings. That requirement is rarely fulfilled. The government is not required to respond to the recommendations of these committees within any stipulated period of time. This leaves the accountability loop open. Respondents were asked about the issue of enforcement of committee recommendations. Some 60 percent of the respondents agree that committee recommendations must be made mandatory for the incumbent government. Implementation of committee recommendations, regardless of their contents, shall have a salutary impact on the improvement of the performance of the government bodies, they believe. But those who opposed (20 percent disagreed completely) the proposal thought that recommendations should be advisory as is the case in most of the countries. The executive has been mandated by the people to rule the country and the implementation of the recommendations of committees should be left to the executive. Otherwise, the parliament would encroach or obstruct the affairs of government. However, they agree that the government should comply with the recommendations as a convention.

A proposal was presented before the respondents that in order to monitor the state of implementation of the committee recommendations, an action-taken sub-committee should be formed and, in case of failure to comply, the government offices should submit an explanatory note. All the respondents (100 percent) were in favor of the proposal. They believe, given the situation in Sri Lankan parliament, where there is no institutional mechanism to monitor and thus there is no track of past recommendations and discussions and hardly any follow-up of previous issues, this may be a good proposal to introduce.

Committee resources

Interviews with the deputy Speaker and a deputy minister in the sixth parliament manifested that 50 percent of the MPs are new in the current parliament. Over 50 percent of the MPs in the parliament are graduates. The educational background of the Sri Lankan parliament, which at independence had a good set of educated parliamentarians, experienced a comparative decline (*Lok Sabha* 1997). 80 percent of the respondents agreed completely that full-time professional and experienced legislators, coupled with low turnover of committee membership, can help active and powerful committee to emerge. The respondents opined that an MP's educational and professional background as well as experience in government and committee work really matter for his performance in committee. Most of the respondents expressed their dissatisfaction with the salary and benefits they used to get from the parliament which they believed had prevented them from becoming full-time politicians. Data from minutes of five selected committees in the fifth parliament manifests that the average turnover of committee membership is 25 percent, that deters the development of a stable committee. However, chairmanships of committees are quite stable. While chairs are elected/nominated for a session, they usually are reelected/reappointed to continue for the life of a parliament.

The secretarial and staff services necessary for the working of the parliament are provided by the Office of the Secretary-General of Parliament. The post of Secretary-General is constitutional one and he/she is appointed by the president. It is an autonomous office independent of the executive which is put under the Staff Advisory Committee (SAC) in Parliament. The Secretary-General is assisted and supported by a deputy Secretary-General and an assistant Secretary-General. The SAC consists of the Speaker (Chairman), the Leader of the House, the Leader of the Opposition and the Minister of Finance. The parliamentary secretariat consists mainly of six departments. The staff of the Parliamentary Secretariat is appointed by the Secretary-General with the approval of the Speaker. The total permanent staff is 786 as per the 2001 cadre. Of note, the Secretary-General of parliament is the ex officio secretary of all parliamentary committees. All parliamentary staffs are recruited by the parliament secretariat and their promotion and personnel policies are regulated by the secretariat. The secretariat staffs are independent of executive control. In response to a question about the necessity of a separate committee secretariat supported with a healthy budget, sufficient number of specialized/competent staffers and logistic supports, 64 percent of the respondents answered in the positive. Thirty percent of the respondents expressed their reservations about the first part of the question but favored the second one. They felt that committee branch could be strengthened within one parliamentary secretariat and the establishment of a separate committee secretariat was unnecessary.

Committee officials (who were interviewed) report that lack of secretariat resources serving three sections (COPA and COPE under one section, consultative committees are under another and the rest are placed under another section) of committees is a crucial factor affecting the quality of deliberations in committee sessions. Each section consists of six/seven officers headed by an assistant director whose educational background and experience are not in par with specialized knowledge required for committee activities. There is neither any major research unit in the secretariat nor sufficiently trained professional staff who can interpret audit reports, annual reports and corporate plan and provide briefings to the members so as to enable them to participate in meaningful discussions. Logistics supports (books, research materials, computers, internet etc.) are also inadequate in committee offices.

In Sri Lanka, committees are allowed to obtain advices from experts (can attend as strangers but are excluded during deliberation) in their respective fields if required. Earlier, committees have been benefited from the hearings of external experts on many occasions. However, experts can render their advice only, the final decision regarding the matter consulted rests exclusively with the committee. All respondents (100 percent, with mean score four) were of the view that committees would be benefited from the expertise and knowledge of external experts who are relatively independent of the executive and political influence.

Real-world operation of selected committees

The following section is an account of the practical functioning of several committees in Sri Lankan parliament. Five committees – three committees for special purposes – COPA COPE, HPC and two other consultative committees on ministries (Public Administration and Defense) have been picked up to illustrate the real-world functioning of parliamentary committee system in Sri Lanka. Attendances at committee meeting, frequency of meetings, average time spent for each meeting, agenda of deliberation, production of reports etc. have been applied as benchmarks for evaluating committee performances.

Three selected committees for special purposes

Committee on Public Accounts (COPA)

COPA is thought by many as the most prestigious and most active parliamentary committee in Sri Lankan parliament. From the available data on the COPA in the fifth parliament (see Table 7.2), it was obvious that on an average only 36 percent of the total members attended the committee meetings. A quorum for committee meeting is four. Of an average of five members attending the meeting two were from the opposition. So the treasury bench members had a natural edge over the opposition to make the decision according to their preferences.

Table 7.2 Nature of committee operations in the fifth Sri Lankan parliament (committees for special purposes)

Name of committee	*Number of meetings held*	*Total number of members*	*Yearly average member turnout (%)*	*Average attendance (%)*	*Average duration of meetings*	*Average Frequency of meetings*	*Number of reports presented*
COPA	61	15 (19)	27	36	110 mins	7 days	1
COPE	70	15 (19)	25	47	150 mins	3 days	1
HPC	27	27	24	38	37 mins	25 days	0

Source: complied and calculated by the author from Minutes of Committee on Public Accounts of first and second session of the fifth parliament, Parliament of Sri Lanka (2003), Minutes of Committee on Public Enterprises of first and second session of the fifth parliament, Parliament of Sri Lanka (2003a), Minutes of the Committee on High Post of the first session of fifth parliament (Vols 1–3), Parliament of Sri Lanka (2003b).

However, decisions in the committee were made on consensus. COPA used to meet frequently and regularly. Within two years time, it held a total of number of 66 meetings. Average frequency of committee meetings was seven days. It spent an average of one hour and 50 minutes per meeting.

AGENDA OF DELIBERATION

The committee discussed audit objections of different public organizations under different ministries regarding financial irregularities in different financial years involving billions of Sri Lankan rupees. The report of the Auditor General focuses on the following main areas (Warnapala 2004: 122):

- excesses of programs and projects;
- non-compliance with advance accounts limits;
- unauthorized working losses;
- audit observations on noncompliance with rules, regulations and statutes etc.;
- value-for-money audit.

COPA deliberations tend to focus mainly on the minor matters such as trivial budget excesses (or revenue deficits) and instances of non-compliance with government procedures. Apart from the review of performance and audit queries pertaining to different government offices COPA also deliberated on delay in printing of AG reports, poor attendance in committee meetings, and utilization of foreign aid by the Department of External Resources so on. The problems of ensuring executive accountability by the PAC can be broadly categorized into three – problems at the initiation level, problems at the deliberation level and problems at the implementation level.

PROBLEMS AT THE INITIATION LEVEL

Since COPA bases its actions entirely on the reports of the AG, its shortcomings have a baneful effect on the performance of the COPA. The AG is the first line oversight agency, empowered to examining all public accounts while others like the committees, the Permanent Commission to Investigate Allegations of Bribery or Corruption and the Ombudsman are selective investigatory agencies. The AG cannot perform satisfactorily for a number of reasons:

Although the Auditor General (AG) of Sri Lanka is a constitutional post, it is not fully independent of the executive in terms of budgetary allocation and staff recruitment. Article 153 of the constitution provides for the appointment of the Auditor General by the president. The removal thereafter is by parliament and or by a special address by the president to the parliament. Though the functional independence of the Auditor General has been hitherto safeguarded by this Article, his financial and administrative independence, due to the absence of constitutional and legislative provisions on the subject, is constrained by the executive arm of government.

The Auditor General depends on the General Treasury coming under the Ministry of Finance for his budget, and the resource allocation for his department. Unlike in other advanced Commonwealth countries, the budget of the Auditor General in Sri Lanka is not subject to scrutiny or approval by a legislative committee, nor are there any safeguards against executive control over his budget. Similar to the problems faced by other government departments, the Auditor General's department too has budget cuts imposed on it by the General Treasury and often encounters delays in obtaining the approved funds. Currently, about 25 percent (the approved audit strength is 1318 of which 328 are vacant) of the staff positions in the Auditor General's department are vacant due to lack of funds.

Due to resource constraints, it is unable to attract, train and retain professionally qualified staff. The outcome, as currently evidenced, is that the audit information is not timely, lacks materiality, and the audit programs focus on compliance and financial (attestation) audits, which are not on par with international best practices. It is interesting to notice that the Auditor General's (who is not a parliamentary officer) department itself is not audited by any external agency (World Bank 2003: 18).

Control over administrative matters relating to the appointment, promotion, transfers, disciplinary issues and overseas training of staff of the Auditor General rests with the secretary to the president. The recent amendment to the constitution has vested those powers of staff appointment to the Public Service Commission, which is yet to be operational. Further, as the constitution does not include Auditor General in the "public officers" exception list, all administrative regulations of the government, as described in the Establishment Code, are applicable to the Auditor General himself and to his staff. This further constrains the administrative independence of the Auditor General.

The Auditor General has made considerable progress in recent years in clearing the backlog of audits and expediting preparation and submission of reports to parliament. Nevertheless, audit reports are not available to the public on a timely basis. A World Bank Assessment found delays across the entire audit processes which were essentially due to factors beyond the control of the Auditor General. Less than 50 percent of the government agencies rendered their 2000 accounts for audit on time. Thereafter, numerous and inordinate delays are encountered in translation, review by parliamentary committees and eventual printing by the government press. On average, audit reports are not available in the public domain until five to six years after the end of the financial year to which they relate (World Bank 2003: 18).

Information contained in most of the audit reports is not relevant for assessing the overall performance of government agencies. The Auditor General's focus is on compliance audits, the occasional value-for-money audit (16 done so far) but there is an absence of system-based audits where an organization's effectiveness and its system of operations are audited. Equally absent are project audits and surprise audits. The format of audit reports is not appropriate for triggering debate or discussion. Not only are they excessively lengthy but they also fail to highlight pertinent issues (Transparency International 2004: 19).

Another significant lapse is the level of coverage of public audit. The constitution provides for public audit of all government agencies, public corporations, provincial councils, local authorities and commissions – a total of over 1500 institutions. However, in the recent past, defense expenses, which accounted for 15 percent of government expenditure in the year 2000, were exempted from audit. A special provision in the government's financial regulations was invoked, citing the national security interests as the reason. As a result, the Auditor General was denied access to records and had to be content with only a certification by the president and Minister of Finance as regards defense expenditure. Further, companies in which the government has significant financial exposure, by way of commitments or government guarantees, are also not covered by public audit (World Bank 2003: 19).

PROBLEMS AT THE DELIBERATION LEVEL

In fact, there are numerous instances where scheduled committee meetings had to be cancelled because of lack of a quorum. This also adds to the backlog of audit reports to be reviewed by the committees. Consequently, there is a tendency to bunch reviews. On review of a COPA agenda for a particular meeting, it was revealed that just over an hour was allocated for reviewing the audit reports of four agencies with expenditure over Rs11.5 million (US$115,000) (World Bank 2003: 22).

An examination of the records shows that COPA on no occasion had the participation of all of its members. Normally five or six members attend the meeting and even this depleted attendance does not mean that members are there all or even most of the time. The practice has been for the members to walk inside the committee room in order to mark present and remain till the quorum formed; four members of the committee constitute the quorum and thereafter members come and go freely. Finally, the experience shows that it was the chairman and one or two senior members who attended regularly while others attend half or less of the meetings (Warnapala 2004: 115–116).

Lack of secretariat resources serving COPA is another factor affecting the quality of deliberations. There is no research capacity in the secretariat nor experts who can interpret audit reports and provide briefings to the members so as to enable them to engage in meaningful discussions. Another impediment to quality deliberation is the inordinate delays in the committees' examination of audit reports. On average, if an audit report is to be reviewed at all, it is late by at least five to six years. As the responsible government officials are most likely to have moved on since then, very often, the budget excesses are retroactively approved and explanations for non-compliances accepted. This negates the value of such an examination.

PROBLEMS AT THE IMPLEMENTATION STAGE

The committee made some important recommendations to resolve the objections raised by the AG. Typical recommendations by the committee included directions towards the CAO (Chief Accounting Officer)/AO (Accounting Officer) to inquire and investigate irregularities and submit a report within two months or so and no further follow-up action was conducted. Recommendations were made to take stern action against a director of education department, take action to recover uncollected revenue from survey department and to surcharge errant officials of different departments. Despite this, the committee expressed its dissatisfaction repeatedly with the non-implementation of committee directives in previous meetings, the fate of most recommendations were unknown.

In the early phase of parliamentary democracy in Sri Lanka, COPA used to prepare comprehensive reports which included the verbatim reports of evidence as well. This practice has been abandoned now and the committee issues three or four reports within a year where they are referred to the Treasury with whom lies the responsibility of financial rectitude of all public offices. The committee on its own has resolved to exclude the minutes of proceedings/evidence from the report and they are kept in the parliamentary secretariat (Parliament of Sri Lanka 1995: 25).

The Treasury issues a minute in reply to the observations made by the Public Accounts Committee and sometimes makes changes as a result of the criticisms of some procedure or action. The Treasury minutes are not published regularly and this in a way make the recommendations of the committee redundant. In 1990, the COPA in its report made a reference to the commencement of issuing treasury minutes after a lapse of two decades (Parliament of Sri Lanka 1993: 23).

In addition, there is no facility for monitoring and, thus, there is no track of past recommendations and discussions and hardly any follow-up of the issues of the prior year. In two years COPA came with only one report of 11 pages on Measurements Units, Standards and Services Departments. As in the case of many reports tabled in parliament, the report of COPA is not debated in the House and thus its keeps going unnoticed. This was particularly due to the fact that the report comes a few years later after all the interest in a particular year has vanished (Perera 1958: 30). This is one reason why the reports of COPA do not evince much interest from the bureaucracy and the public.

Hence, the COPA in the fifth parliament of Sri Lanka had played a commendable role in ensuring financial accountability of the executive at the initiation and recommendation levels despite numerous limitations. But the impact of COPA operations at the implementation stage – the most important stage of committee involvement in ensuring executive accountability – was unknown.

Committee on Public Enterprises (COPE)

COPE is an important financial committee in the Sri Lankan parliament. From the available data on the COPE in the fifth parliament (see Table 7.2), it was obvious that on an average only 47 percent of the total members attended the committee meeting. A quorum for committee meeting is four. Of an average of nine members attending the meeting four were from the opposition. Decisions in the committee were made on consensus. Average duration of COPE meetings was two hours, 30 minutes, which was even higher than that of COPA.

AGENDA OF DELIBERATION

The committee examined the performance aspects and queries raised by the Auditor General on activities of public enterprises. The CAOs and AOs were examined in depth on the submission of annual reports to parliament, preparation of annual budgets, corporate plans and implementation of such plans. Apart from the review of performance and audit queries pertaining to different enterprises, COPA also deliberated on follow-up of committee recommendations and deliberation of committee reports by the House, defiance of recommendations by several public enterprises, various financial irregularities and made recommendations. The CAO and AO were frequently directed to submit reports on many issues.

PROBLEMS AT THE INITIATION LEVEL

Since the Committee on Public Enterprises (COPE) bases its actions on the reports of the AG, its shortcomings (as we have seen with COPA earlier) have an adverse impact on the performance of the COPE too. Accounts of all public corporations, except companies, are audited by the Auditor General, who at times uses the services of a private auditor. Audited financial statements, except companies, are reviewed by the parliamentary committee on public enterprises (COPE). Government-owned companies (numbering around 35) range from wholly owned to majority owned companies that carry on commercial activities. Government-owned companies are expected to comply with the requirements in the Companies Act and are not subject to scrutiny by COPE. These majority owned companies came about when the government divested or privatized previously state-owned enterprises. There is no oversight of companies where the government has a significant financial interest or exposure, but has transferred management to a third party. Most notable of these are Sri Lanka Telecom Limited and Sri Lankan Airlines Limited.

In addition, although the Auditor General has considerable autonomy in planning the scope of his audit work, he is not able to carry out value-for-money audits or to provide material and relevant observations on the performance of these enterprises. Consequently, the COPE too is unable to meaningfully assess the achievements of these enterprises.

The majority of the COPE and COPA members are obliged to the chairmen and directors of the corporations and to other high ranking government officials whose corporations and government accounts are being examined, for various favors extended to them from time to time such as finding employment for the constituents, relations and loyalists and for many other favors. Moreover, the corporation chairmen and working directors are frequently defeated candidates or loyalists of the incumbent government and are influential with the MPs who sit on COPE and COPA. In some instances the chairmen and the directors may not be holding office at the time the audit reports are examined as the political parties who appointed them at that time are no longer in power or the directors have fallen out of political favor and as such new directors have been appointed as replacements. As a result, hardly any action is taken on the audit reports and consequently the defaulting chairmen and other directors go free in spite of plundering the assets of the state (*The Island*, July 15, 2002).

PROBLEMS AT THE DELIBERATION LEVEL

COPE used to meet frequently and regularly. Within two years time, it held a total of number of 70 meetings. Average frequency of committee meetings was three days. In fact the committee used to meet too frequently to get any result. At one point, it was holding meetings everyday. The committee met 29 times without giving one calendar day break between two consecutive meetings. On review of a COPE agenda for a particular meeting, it was revealed that the COPE, for just one day, summoned 15 corporations. Due to lack of quorum, scheduled COPE meetings were cancelled at least four times in the fifth parliament. However, there was a pause of 134 days between the 48th and 49th meeting of COPE in the first session of fifth parliament which manifested the impotence of the committee.

PROBLEMS AT THE IMPLEMENTATION LEVEL

The committee made a number of recommendations to resolve the deliberated problems in all the committee meetings. The implementation status of most of the recommendations has remained unknown due to lack of any institutional mechanism to follow-up. In short, the implication of COPA in ensuring executive accountability at the initiation level and at the deliberation level is moderate but missing at the implementation stage.

High Post Committee (HPC)

The High Post Committee in Sri Lankan parliament is unique in South Asia and modeled, to some extent, on the US Senate which approves presidential appointments. However, this committee examines the suitability of high government officials only. From the available data on High Post Committee in the fifth parliament (see Table 7.2), it was obvious that on an average only 38 percent (ten) of the total members attended the committee meeting. A quorum for committee meeting is three meaning only, one-ninth of the total membership is required to hold a meeting. However, decisions in the committee were made on consensus. The HPC did not sit frequently and regularly. Within two years time, it held a total of number of 27 meetings. Average frequency of committee meetings was 25 days. It spent a surprising average of only 37 minutes per meeting, the lowest average time spent by any committee in Sri Lanka. At one point, the committee did not hold any meetings and remained inactive for over three months. There was a big pause of 96 days between the 24th and 25th committee meetings. Since June 2003 to February 2004, the committee had met only four times (in seven months and 20 days).

The High Post Committee has no staff of its own, let alone having investigative staff. The committee does not conduct its independent investigation into the suitability of a candidate. The committee informs the public through the medium of newspapers that certain persons whose names are given in the notice are to be appointed to the posts mentioned against their names and invites the public to bring to the notice of the committee if they have any cause to object to any appointment. No anonymous petitions are entertained. Fearing the consequences for exposing officials, people become reluctant to respond to the committee's call. Consequently, there is invariably no response to the advertisement and the candidate get past or through the High Post Committee without much difficulty. Thus it would appear to defeat the purpose of the committee.

In the fifth parliament, the committee examined the suitability of a large number of candidates for appointment to state services and state corporations and found each and every candidate suitable for higher posts. In the many years of its existence, High Post Committee has only rejected one candidate – Mr. Upali Wijewardene, the nominee of the president himself to the post of Chairman and Director General of the Greater Colombo Economic Commission (GCEC). But Wijewardene held this post for many months after the committee reported adversely against him. Despite all shortcomings, this committee has symbolic value. There is an institutional mechanism at least to examine the suitability of appointments of people in high positions.

Consultative committees on ministries

Consultative Committee on Public Administration Management and Reform (CCOPA)

From the available data on the Consultative Committee on Public Administration Management and Reform (CCOPA) in the fifth parliament (see Table 7.3), it was obvious that on an average only 30 percent (six) of the total members attended the committee meeting. A quorum for committee meeting is three, meaning only one-sixth of the total membership is required to hold a meeting. However, decisions in the committee were made on consensus. Within two years time, it held a total of number of only ten meetings. The committee is formally required to meet once a month. However, the average frequency of committee meetings was 50 days. It spent a low average of only 40 minutes per meeting. At one point, the committee did not hold any meetings and remained inactive for over three months. There was a big pause of 99 days between the fifth and sixth committee meetings.

The committee deliberated on many issues including the request of an MP to provide distant education for public officials, amendment of the Public Services

Table 7.3 Nature of committee operations (consultative committees on ministries) in the fifth Sri Lankan parliament

Name of committee	*Number of meetings held*	*Total number of members*	*Yearly average member turnout (%)*	*Average attendance (%)*	*Average duration of meetings*	*Average frequency of meetings*	*Number of reports presented*
CCOPA	10	18	28	30	40 mins	50	0
CCOMOD	8	19	27	39	90 mins	70	0

Source: compiled and calculated by the author from Parliament of Sri Lanka (2003c), Minutes of the Consultative Committee on Ministry of Defense of the fifth parliament and Parliament of Sri Lanka (2003d), Minutes of the Consultative Committee on Public Administration, Management and Reform of the fifth parliament.

Management Act, newspaper reports regarding rental for houses given to MPs, recruitment of officials in Sri Lankan Administrative Services, non-use of official quarters by district/divisional secretaries and so on. It deliberated a lot of issues and frequently asked the CAO/AO to submit a report on investigation within a given time but never did follow it up. It made innumerous recommendations, the implementation status of which is unknown.

Consultative Committee on Ministry of Defense (CCOMOD)

Within two years, the committee held only eight meetings (see Table 7.3). It met irregularly and infrequently. The average frequency of committee meeting was 70 days. The average attendance of members in the committee meeting was 39 percent (seven). A quorum for committee meeting is three, meaning only one-sixth of the total membership is required to hold a meeting. Decisions in the committee were made on consensus. It spent an average of one hour and 30 minutes per meeting for deliberation. The committee used to deliberate a large number of agenda in a single session. For instance, in the fourth meeting of the committee, it deliberated 36 cases in two hours. No meeting of consultative Committees on Defense on was held since early February 2003 (till early February 2004 when the parliament was dissolved) when the defense ministry was taken over by the president and no deputy minister was appointed. The president never attends any committee meeting. In the absence of a deputy minister, the chairman of the committee could not be reappointed. Hence the committee had remained inactive for the concluding three months of the fifth parliament.

AGENDA OF DELIBERATION

Committee deliberation was mainly confined to police services. Major deliberations focused on the appointment of an Assistant Superintendent of Police for the Naththandiya division, building facilities for police staff at Kantale area, promotional scheme of police department, transfer of platoon police, appeals from female members of the police with regard to promotions and so on. Most of the agenda were related to routine discussion on administration. The committee deliberated on security issues in the north involving Tamils in several meetings the minutes of which were not made available to the author due to formal restrictions.

Although the members deliberated on a number of defense-related issues (such as providing data with regard to the relocation of army camps in the north-east, frauds, corruptions and malpractices at Gemunu Regiment, refilling of used bullets, school buildings occupied by the army) the attempts yielded no substantial result. The committee made some important recommendations, whose implementation status was unknown.

Air Vice-Marshall [retired] Harry Goonatilleke describes what it is like appearing before the committee: "It's a big laugh, nothing happens. I don't think any committee meeting has had any successes, and the system is so rotten that it'll be a waste of time trying to change it". Goonatilleke once appeared before the committee to testify over procurement in the air force. "I turned up, took the oath, and said I knew of certain people involved in profit-making. People's eyes glazed over. I turned to the Chairman and asked in his ear if he'd like me to name names – the son of a very important person was allegedly involved – and he said 'No, no, no! We don't want any names' " "But if opposition figures are involved", Goonatilleke adds, "well, then the Committee is interested" (CPSU 2000: 6).

The role of the Consultative Committee on Ministry of Defense in ensuring government accountability was therefore mainly confined to the initiation and recommendation stages and unknown at the implementation stage. The committee's endeavor to ensure transparency and responsiveness of government were thwarted by the government's denial to provide necessary documents on state security grounds.

A consultative committee designed to oversee the administration of a particular branch of the executive is fatally inhibited by the presence of its political head as chairman of the committee. Presently, consultative committees face difficulties in organizing and conducting regular meetings. Members are not sufficiently motivated to attend hearings and put their views on record. Consultative committee meetings are usually marked by poor attendance of members. On many occasions, consultative committee meetings had been cancelled for want of quorum. Former Parliamentary Affairs Minister A.H.M. Azwer informed the fifth parliament, "MPs do not attend Consultative Committee meetings when parliament is not in session. My Ministry Consultative Committee was called recently. I was the only member present on that day" (*Daily News*, June 5, 2003).

In addition, in the name of oversight of the executive, the committee provided opportunities for the MPs to raise matters pertaining to their constituencies and in the last two decades, interestingly, it was this aspect of constituency needs which dominated the proceedings of most of the consultative committees.

In other words, the committee members manifested very little interest on matters of public policy formulation and implementation. On the contrary, constituency-based issues such as the construction of a school, hospital and shortage of teachers for rural schools dominate the proceedings of the committee (Warnapala 2004: 48–49). Attending committee meetings enable the committee members to come in contact with the ministers and the bureaucracy who are inexorably involved with the public resource distribution system and get the work of the electorate of their constituencies done. In short, committee members' prime task of legislation and administrative oversight is replaced by their constituency interest.

From the preceding discussion on the operations of two ministerial committees, it is evident that these committees have not been successful in ensuring government accountability. Their endeavor is half-heartedly confined to initiation and recommendation stages. At the implementation stage their role to ensure government accountability is virtually redundant.

Conclusion

The formal institutional structure of the political system in Sri Lanka appears seriously disadvantaged in checking the unbridled power and authority of the executive and virtually unable to hold the government to account. All the major characteristics of a strong legislature are, in practice, absent in Sri Lanka and the parliament plays into the hands of the president even in time of cohabitation. The president is all-powerful and can dissolve the parliament at will after one year of its life. All the major political institutions including the parliament (let alone parliamentary committees), the judiciary, the provincial parliaments and the local government units are made captive to the vagaries of the president.

There is a strong public demand to revert to the parliamentary system in Sri Lanka including the switching of the electoral system from preferential vote system to first-past-the-post (FPTP) or mixed "German-type-system". The current electoral system which prevents any party from garnering a two-thirds majority in the parliament has paved the way to take this country forward as well as to dissolve ethnic conflict with the Tamils. Thus the external environment of the parliament and parliamentary committees has largely determined the way parliament and committees have performed in Sri Lanka.

Still within an executive dominated political framework, some institutional arrangements are discernible in Sri Lanka which reflects dispersal of power as well as the incumbent government's willingness to leave space for the opposition. Instances are numerous. In Sri Lanka the prime minister is not leader of the House. Currently, the Speaker and chairman of committees are from the opposition and the deputy Speaker is from the government. The High Post Committee which examines the suitability of high officials in Sri Lanka which was earlier headed by the prime minister is currently replaced by the Speaker. In terms of chairs and membership selection of committees the leader of the opposition is always consulted with. Chairs of COPA and COPE are from the opposition.

Institutionally, the parliamentary committee system in Sri Lanka is mainly patterned on the Westminster model. In fact, many of the key[2] features of the committee system within the Westminster tradition which at least bear the potential to check the monopoly of governmental power and call the government to account are unfortunately missing in Sri Lanka. Parliamentary committees in Sri Lanka in general are permanent and correspond to governmental structure. Formally, their jurisdictions are comprehensive, ranging from legislation to oversight to investigation but in reality their role in doing that job is marginal though not insignificant. Formally committees cannot select their chairs and members. Selection and appointment of committee chairs and members are done by the Committee of Selection and the Speaker in consultation with the prime minister and the leader of the opposition. Committees meet in camera and decide on the basis of majority. Committees cannot set their own agenda, however they have the power to send for papers, persons and documents with the exception that government may decline to produce a document on the grounds that its disclosure would be prejudicial to the safety or interest of the state. They can consider legislative bills referred to them by the House and do not have any role in budget allocation and demands for grants. The institutional arrangement of the committee system in Sri Lanka thus places the government in an advantageous position to be the ultimate arbiter on any issue of governance. However, during cohabitation, it is difficult to determine who the executive is. Is it the prime minister and his cabinet or the president? In sum, institutionally Sri Lanka has got a weak parliament and therefore a committee system with marginal scope in ensuring executive accountability.

In terms of ensuring government accountability, the role of the COPA and COPE is confined largely to the initiation and the recommendation stages with unknown implications at the implementation level. The implication of High Post Committee in securing executive accountability at the initiation and the recommendation stage is minor and missing at the implementation stage. Notwithstanding, it has a useful symbolic effect on the behavior of high officials in the Sri Lankan government.

It is obvious from the operation of two other selected consultative committees on ministries that their endeavor to ensure executive accountability is half-heartedly confined to the initiation and the recommendation stages. At the implementation stage, their role to ensure executive accountability is utterly missing. The major thrust of all these committees was on regularity and financial propriety. Meetings were held irregularly, and member attendance was poor. Sometimes committees suffered from quorum crisis too. The duration of committee deliberations was short. Committee reports were seldom produced. Minutes had been kept secret until they had been published. The opposition MPs very often had leaked the issues of discussion and the deviated actions of public officials to the media disregarding the formal restrictions to do so and thus played a significant role in making the working of committees more visible.

The decisions of committees are not binding on the government agencies and no mechanisms and initiatives are in place to keep track of the implementation of committee recommendations. No punitive measure is taken on account of non-compliance of committee recommendations. The implementation of the recommendations made by the committee is also contingent upon the willingness of the government of the day.

The domination of the ruling party is evident in the structural and functional arrangement of the committee system in Sri Lanka. Structurally the committee has been arranged in such a way that without the assent of the party in power no action can be taken to make the executive accountable. The frontiers (including the party chief) of the ruling party have enormous influence from the formation of committee to the implementation of committee recommendations. The institutional domination of the ruling party has also been reflected in the real-world functioning of the committee in securing executive accountability in Sri Lanka.

The aspiration of governments in maintaining political stability and territorial integrity of the country has persuaded them to continue with strong executive. This hard stance of government is also prompted by the prolonged ethnic conflict with Tamils. Parliament is being understood by the ruling regime as a symbol of legitimacy and democratic governance rather a forum for deliberation and resolution of critical issues of national importance and holding itself to account. The lack of bipartisanship in Sri Lankan militarized politics is a serious obstacle for parliament (and its committees) to carry out legislative and oversight functions and also to the present military conflict being brought to an end (CPSU 2002: 11).

8 Conclusion

This chapter makes a comparative review of the role of committees in Bangladesh, India and Sri Lanka and reports the findings of the study based on the observations and results drawn from the previous chapters. The objective of this research is to analyze the role of parliamentary committees in securing government accountability in contemporary Bangladesh, India and Sri Lanka. The dependent variable in this study is government/executive accountability, which is believed to be dependent upon certain factors such as political context, institutional evolution, design and rules and cultural configuration of a society.

This study presents two major sets of findings. One is concerned with the extent to which parliamentary committees in Bangladesh, India and Sri Lanka have been able to hold the government to account. The other relates to the methodological approaches of studying parliaments.

In general, the study finds that parliamentary committees in Bangladesh, India and Sri Lanka do not perform at par with their counterparts in the Western world in controlling the government and holding it to account. They lag far behind other parliamentary democracies in Western Europe and Commonwealth countries in term of institutional arrangements and practical implications in securing government accountability. However, committees' role in securing government accountability in these three countries cannot be overlooked. They are weak but not irrelevant. The mere existence of committees in these countries does matter. Committees are there to oversee the executive and they have been successful to some extent in making an impact on holding the government to account.

India has got the most institutionalized and assertive committee system in South Asia. It is clearly ahead of Bangladesh and Sri Lanka with respect to institutional arrangements and real-world implications in holding the government accountable. In terms of ensuring government accountability, the role of committees is largely confined to the initiation and the recommendation stages of committee involvement with limited implications at the implementation level.

When comparing Bangladesh with Sri Lanka in terms of committee strengths to hold the government accountable, it is hard to judge which one is better and in what respects. Committees' role in securing executive accountability in Bangladesh and Sri Lanka is largely confined to the initiation and the recommendation stages of their operations with unknown implications at the implementation level. The poor performance of the committee system in holding the government accountable in Sri Lanka emanates from the prevailing political system. In Bangladesh, it is the confrontational political culture which is causing problems for parliament and parliamentary committees to get institutionalized and perform to their potential.

This study also has implications for the study of parliaments worldwide. In contrast to the existing approach of studying parliaments advocated by many Western scholars, the study argues that the point of departure for categorizing parliaments should be from society, economy and political regime to intra-institutional political system.

In order to investigate the ways in which scholars have sought to capture or measure parliamentary strengths in holding the government accountable, the study presents a series of basic typologies of legislatures. However, as these typologies are rather crude (to appreciate the variations and divergences within a specific category of parliament), it then focuses on additional factors (socio-economic, political and intra-institutional) that are relevant in determining parliamentary strengths to make the government accountable. Thus the study offers a blend of macro-societal and micro-institutional factors that determine parliaments' strengths in holding the government accountable. The dissertation has two additional observations that add value to the study of parliaments, committees and government accountability.

The first is that the more governing power is diffused and shared between and among contending veto players regardless of the system of government, the more the system bears the potential of having a strong parliament to hold the government to account.

The second is that a strong parliament is a prerequisite for a strong committee system and vice versa, and a strong committee system is a prerequisite for calling the government to account irrespective of whether the political system is parliamentary or presidential.

In order to explore the factors that influence government accountability in Bangladesh, India and Sri Lanka, we have tried to answer the following four core questions:

- Does history shape institutional performance?
- Does context influence institutional performance?
- Do institutions (rules, procedures) matter for the way they perform?
- Does culture matter for institutional performance?

Institutional performance in this study is referred to the extent to which parliamentary committees are able to ensure government accountability. The four major questions are addressed in the light of institutional theory (historical institutionalism and regulatory institutionalism, new institutionalism) and cultural theory as propounded by Thompson (1990) and Hofstede (1991).

Institutionally, the parliamentary committee systems in Bangladesh, India and Sri Lanka are prominently modeled on the Westminster system which is characterized by strong executives and weak legislatures and legislative committees. In fact, many of the key features (mentioned in earlier chapters) of the committee system within the Westminster tradition, which at least bear the potential of checking the monopoly of governmental power and calling the government to account, are unfortunately missing in Bangladesh and Sri Lanka. However, there are commonalities as well as divergences with regard to the institutional arrangements and practical working of committees in these three countries.

Parliamentary committees in all these three countries meet in camera and decide on the basis of majority. Formally committees cannot select their chairs and members. Selection and appointment of committee chairs and members are done by the Speaker (and the Committee on Selection in Sri Lanka) in consultation with the political parties. In Bangladesh, the final list of committee chairs and members of different committees must win the nod of the prime minister, who is the executive head of the government.

Committees cannot set their own agenda (in Bangladesh they can do partially) and have the power to send for papers, persons and documents with the exception that government may decline to produce a document on the grounds that its disclosure would be prejudicial to the safety or interest of the state. They can consider legislative bills referred to them by the House and do not have any role in budget allocation and demands for grants. India is an exception in this case. However, the financial committees can make *ex post* financial scrutiny of government expenditure. Formally, their jurisdictions are comprehensive, ranging from legislation to oversight to investigation and their role in doing that job in India is significant. Parliamentary committees in India and Sri Lanka in general are not permanent (they are usually elected annually but have a permanent flavor). However committees in Bangladesh are permanent and formed for the life of parliament.

Committees in Bangladesh and Sri Lanka exactly parallel ministerial structure. In India committees functionally correspond to government ministries. Committee recommendations are advisory in all three countries. The media in general and the print media in particular have played a vital role in calling the executive to account by exposing divergent cases of malpractices and irregularities to the public and compelled the parliament/parliamentary committees and other anti-corruption agencies to get into actions in all three countries. The parliament secretariats (it is not independent of the influence of the executive in Bangladesh) in India and Sri Lanka are independent of the executive which function under the guidance and control of the Speaker. However, the Indian parliament secretariat has more resources i.e. staff, committee officials, books and materials than Sri Lanka.

India has got the most institutionalized and assertive committee system in South Asia. In India, committees are formed shortly after the inauguration of a new parliament. Committee memberships and chairs are distributed among the political parties proportionally based on their strengths in the House. The PAC is by convention headed by an opposition MP. Ministers are excluded from committee chairmanship/membership. Committee meetings are held regularly and frequently and reports are produced and submitted to the House regularly. Committees have a significant role in budget allocation and demands for grants.

In terms of ensuring government accountability, the role of committees is largely confined to the initiation and the recommendation stages with lukewarm implications at the implementation level. Sometimes committees took several years (five to seven years are common) to finish off a contentious issue without any concrete result. At the implementation stage, their role to ensure executive accountability is hard to judge. A high percentage (60 percent or so) of recommendations are accepted by the government and those that are not accepted are explained by the government by providing explanatory notes. The committee system is highly institutionalized and there is a link between and among all the stages of committee operations i.e. committee formation, deliberation, recommendation and acceptance. The matter of implementation of recommendations is left to the government to act on. This is an institutional limitation of the committee system in a parliamentary system of government and India is not an exception in this case. Notwithstanding that the institutional arrangement of the committee system in India places the government (the major party) in an advantageous position to be the ultimate arbiter on any issue of governance, committees function on consensus and views of the opposition are very often respected and accommodated.

Limitations of committees in Indian parliament are numerous. Parliamentary committees have a restricted role in law-making. In India, average turnover of committee members is high i.e. 33 percent. This deters committee members from developing specialized knowledge and expertise to make committees more effective. DRSCs have 45 members and a short lifespan (one year). The large size of the DRSC makes effective functioning difficult. Currently there are too many committees in Indian parliament to run efficiently and effectively. While India has significantly broadened committee involvement in various parliamentary businesses over the last decade, coordination mechanism is currently lacking. Committees operate in a fragmented manner. Very often, recommendations that are really important or of some consequence (as we have seen in the case of Bofors scandal, coffin scam, sleeping bags scam) were not accepted by the government. Ministries have rarely accepted the recommendations/observations of the committees when they relate to substantive issues like changing procedures, taking action against errant employees or disturbing the status quo.

In Bangladesh committees are beset with innumerous problems right from committee formation to acceptance and implementation of committee recommendations. Due to lack of consensus on the terms of references of committees between the two major parties, committees were formed belatedly, months or years after the start of new parliaments in the 1990s. Committees in the eighth JS had started working without the participation of the main opposition MPs. The opposition joined committee sessions three years after the start of the new parliament. Meetings are infrequently held and reports are seldom produced.

Some committee meetings were to be postponed due to quorum crisis. Burning issues have been dropped several times from the agenda of committee deliberation at the directive of higher government authorities. Moreover, the parliament secretariat is not in practice independent of the executive and is poorly resourced.

The domination of the ruling party is evident in the structural, functional arrangement and the real-world working of the committee system in Bangladesh. The frontiers (including the party chief/prime minister) of the ruling party have enormous influence from the formation of committee to the implementation of committee recommendations. Committees' role in securing executive accountability is half-heartedly confined to the initiation and the recommendation stages of their operations. At the implementation stage, their role to ensure executive accountability is virtually missing. A definite trend of degeneration of parliament and parliamentary committees is in sight in the current JS of Bangladesh.

From the experience of the functioning of committee system in Bangladesh for the last 15 years, it is evident that committees had been in operation amid periodic interruptions even when the major opposition parties had been boycotting the plenary sessions at times for years. Moreover, the relationships between the treasury bench and opposition members in the committees appeared less adverse. The prospect of committees seems promising in moderating the acrimonious relations between the two major political parties in Bangladesh, which for many is a key to the continuity of democratic governance in Bangladesh.

The semi-presidential system introduced in Sri Lanka in 1978 resulted in the emergence of a strong executive president and a weak parliament and parliamentary committee system. The provision of the president's power to dissolve parliament after one year of parliament's life at his/her will or convenience has undoubtedly made the parliament vulnerable to the president. Parliamentary committees in Sri Lanka are still at an incipient stage. The Sri Lankan parliament usually takes several months to constitute committees but it does not lead to any political stalemate between political parties. consultative committees are chaired by ministers. Key characteristics of Consultative committees in Sri Lanka can be compared with those of the pre-1990s departmental committees in Bangladesh and India. However, two significant financial committees – COPA and COPE – are chaired by the opposition MPs. The High Post Committee in the Sri Lankan parliament is unique in South Asia, in that it examines the suitability of high government officials.

In terms of ensuring government accountability, the role of committees in Sri Lanka is confined largely to the initiation and the recommendation stages with unknown implications at the implementation level. The High Post Committee has a useful symbolic effect on the behavior of high officials in the Sri Lankan government. Meetings were held irregularly and member attendance was poor. Sometimes committees suffered from quorum crisis also. The duration of committee deliberations was short. Committee reports were seldom produced.

Minutes are kept secret unless published. The decision of committees is not binding on the government agencies and no mechanisms and initiatives are in place to keep track of the implementation of committee recommendations.

All the respondents (100 percent, with mean score four) in three countries were of the view that a strong parliament is a prerequisite for a strong committee system and vice versa. They admit that within the Westminster parliamentary system, parliament is inherently weak vis-à-vis the executive and so is the parliamentary committee system. The parliament in India is a fairly functioning institution. Committees had performed well and still been in the process of evolution. Thus the parliamentary committee system has contributed substantially to transform the parliament as an institution to check the power of the executive.

Within the prevailing political context, parliament in Bangladesh is very weak vis-à-vis the executive and so is the parliamentary committee system. The parliament could not fare well due to frequent quorum crisis, prolonged boycott by the main opposition and the failure of the Speaker to conduct the sessions neutrally. Parliament in contemporary Bangladesh has lost its reputation as a prime political institution. It has become an institution of regime maintenance and largely failed to hold the executive accountable. Committees started well in the fifth JS and committees were formed immediately after the inauguration of the new parliament and the opposition continued to attend committee sessions despite boycotting the House. They apparently played some role in making the government behave. In the seventh JS, despite belated formation, committees were found assertive in holding the government accountable. However, the charms and efficacy of the committee system have been on wane since the start of the eighth JS and committees have been in the process of becoming a lackluster institution. Thus the parliamentary committee system fails to contribute significantly to transform the parliament as a strong institution to check the power of the executive and hold it to account. Within the prevailing semi-presidential system, the parliament of Sri Lanka is extremely weak vis-à-vis the executive and so is the parliamentary committee system. The committee system is in a formative stage and has a marginal role in making the government accountable.

The hypothesis that a strong parliament is a prerequisite for a strong committee system and vice versa and strong committee system is a prerequisite to call the government to account irrespective of whether the political system is parliamentary or presidential is well proved by the real-world functioning of parliament and parliamentary committees in all the three countries.

Democratic governance is a prerequisite for ensuring government accountability in any society. Whenever democracy gets a chance to thrive in any polity, some measures are usually put in place to make the rulers and administrators accountable. Immediately after independence in 1971, Bangladesh came across such an opportunity. But due to recurring military intervention in Bangladesh politics, political institutions including parliament could not flourish and had not been in active mode for a period of 15 years. The issue of ensuring accountability of politicians, administrators, and military rulers did not come to the limelight during these regimes. Consequently, no viable rules or instruments were devised to ensure executive accountability. During this time, Bangladesh experienced a presidential system of government with a powerful president having weak accountability devices. Parliaments came into being in highly rigged elections and thus the parliaments suffered from legitimacy and became rubber stamps in the hand of the executive to approve the policy decisions of the president. Accountability of government had been a peripheral issue in Bangladesh during the military and semi-military regimes. The president was simply replaced by a prime minister in a restored parliamentary system in 1991. The influence and experience of this prolonged misgovernance were so profoundly inculcated in the mind and thinking of the politicians and high officials in Bangladesh that it seemed difficult for them to delete their earlier experience from their memory and imbue them with new democratic values to account themselves to the stakeholders in a changed political environment. After the restoration of electoral democracy and the reintroduction of the parliamentary system of government in Bangladesh, parliament played more assertive role than before and parliamentary committees got activated and multiplied in volume and effectiveness which to some extent are said to have made some impacts on ensuring government accountability particularly at the initiation and recommendation stages of their involvement. Thus the country's checkered history of politics has profoundly influenced the under-institutionalization of parliament and parliamentary committees, which in turn has stood the way to exploit the full potential of committees and adversely affected the performance of these institutions to ensure executive accountability.

Except for a brief 18-month authoritarian interlude in 1975–1977, India has been a democracy since its independence from the British in 1947. The military has stayed away from politics and never hindered the democratic continuity. Likewise, India has demonstrated a remarkable ability to hold regular free and fair elections. Sri Lanka is one of South Asia's most established democracies. The military has never been deemed a serious threat to civilian government and has been kept on the periphery of the public policy-making arena. However, despite its democratic tradition, since 1971 Sri Lanka has been under emergency rule for longer than it has been under democratic rule. Democratically elected leaders had abused their power and used parliament to legitimate their decisions to materialize their personal and political interests.

Thus the foregoing discussion supports our hypothesis that the greater the stability and continuity of politics in any society, the more likely it is that the parliament and its committees are effective institutions of ensuring executive accountability.

State power is highly centralized rather than dispersed in the unitary state of Bangladesh. The president is a titular head of state and he performs according to the advices of the prime minister and plays into the hand of the ruling regime. All the major political institutions including the Speaker of the parliament have been politicized and used against the major opposition parties in the country. Main opposition parties have never been consulted by the incumbent government prior to appointing officials to major constitutional posts such as the CAG,

Chief Election Commissioner, Chairman of Public Service Commission, Chairman of Anti-Corruption Commission and so on. Major local government institutions have been dysfunctional for decades. Elections of local government bodies at the district and sub-district level did not take place for over 12 years. The parliament and parliamentary committees have been dominated and monopolized by the ruling government. No space has been left for the opposition political parties to participate and contribute to the governance system. The opposition is thus left out to the street to face and challenge the government.

Institutional arrangements are discernible in India which reflects dispersal of power among many political institutions and parties as well as the incumbent government's willingness to leave space for the opposition. Indian parliament is bicameral. To become law, legislation must pass each House and have the assent of the president. Coalition governments and fragmented parties since 1989 have weakened the executive and strengthened the power of the president and Supreme Court. India has an organized and integrated system of local government, having linkages from village to district/division levels. Elections of major local government institutions have taken place at regular intervals. There are many provincial parliaments (five have bicameral parliaments) in India which provides political space for different political parties to act and be accommodated within the governance system as a whole. In India, the prime minister is not leader of the House. The Speaker is usually elected on consensus among different political parties. Committee memberships and chairmanships are based on the proportional representation of parties in the House. Ministers who belong to the executive branch are kept excluded from committees and the neutrality and relative independence of committees as institutions of legislative branch has been maintained accordingly. Thus there remains enormous scope for the opposition political parties too to share the power through representations in different political institutions.

State power is highly centralized in the hands of the executive president in Sri Lanka. The president is all-powerful and can dissolve the parliament at will after one year of its life. All the major political institutions including the parliament (let alone parliamentary committees), the judiciary, the provincial parliaments and the local government units are made captive to the convenience of the president. However, elections of major local government institutions have taken place at regular intervals. There are nine elected provincial parliaments in Sri Lanka, which offer political space for different political parties to act and be accommodated within the governance system as a whole. In the absence of a second chamber, the attempt to promote substantial autonomy (by creating nine elected provincial parliaments) within a united country without regional representation (in the form of Senate or council of provinces) at the center did not produce any significant result.

Still within an executive dominated political framework, some institutional arrangements are in place in Sri Lanka which reflects dispersal of power as well as the incumbent government's willingness to leave space for the opposition. Instances are numerous. In Sri Lanka the prime minister is not leader of the

House. Currently, the Speaker and chairman of committees are from the opposition and the deputy Speaker is from the government. The High Post Committee which examines the suitability of high officials in Sri Lanka which was earlier headed by the prime minister is currently replaced by the Speaker. In terms of chairs and membership selection of committees the leader of the opposition is always consulted with. Chairmanships of COPA and COPE are from the opposition.

The hypothesis that the more governing power is diffused and shared between and among contending veto players regardless of the system of government, the more the system bears the potentials of having a strong parliament to hold the government to account gets its support from the preceding analysis.

The performance of committees is also influenced by the hierarchical nature of South Asian society. Culturally, a senior in a hierarchical society is assumed to be higher than a junior in terms of authority, status and social position. Consequently, devising mechanisms for ensuring the accountability of the senior or stronger group/patron is not strongly demanded. The hierarchical value of devising no strong/viable mechanism for ensuring accountability of the senior or stronger group is reflected in the formal arrangement of the committee system in Bangladesh, India and Sri Lanka. Of course, the influence and impact of culture is variable on three countries. In Bangladesh, ministers have still memberships of departmental committees and opposition MPs are not given a single chair position in any committee including the PAC. Government's dominance from committee formation to implementation of committee recommendations is substantial. In Sri Lanka, ministers chair all consultative committees. Two influential financial committees are headed by senior opposition MPs and this has been a recent development. In India, committee memberships and chairs are distributed among the political parties based on their proportional strength in the House. The parliament and its committee system are fairly institutionalized and there is an integrated chain from committee formation to acceptance of recommendations. However, the issue of implementation of recommendations is left to the incumbent government to act on. Hence the implementation of recommendations is contingent upon the willingness of the government and the nature of the risk involved in implementing the same.

Although all the three countries belong to hierarchical societies, the degree of hierarchism is variable. According to Hofstede (2001), Bangladesh is more hierarchical than India. We have seen that accountability mechanisms and institutions are better placed and more functional in India than in Bangladesh. Parliament and parliamentary committees in India also fared better and played more a significant role in holding the government to account than their counterparts in Bangladesh. Thus the hypothesis that accountability is lacking more in hierarchical society than in individualistic/egalitarian society and it is easier for a legislature and its legislative committees to call the executive to account in a predominantly individualist/egalitarian society than a hierarchical/fatalistic society has been partially proved.

Democracy that is a prerequisite for holding the government accountable requires a solid foundation to get its roots firmly entrenched in any society first so that it can move forward without much difficulty. Apart from Bangladesh's historical legacy of military rule and bureaucratic hegemony, which has a substantial impact on the working of democracy, the very foundation of democracy in Bangladesh is very unsteady and fragile. Free and fair election that is at the heart of democracy does not seem to be well placed in Bangladesh. The legitimacy and efficacy of elections under non-party caretaker government has already been subject to controversy. The losing political party has invariably termed the elections held under the caretaker governments largely rigged and reluctantly accepted the election results eventually amid enormous national and international pressure. Even the losing party has refused to attend the plenary session from the inaugural session of a new eighth JS elected in October 2001 and kept boycotting parliament for months. Elections under caretaker governments may be a temporary fix to deal with special situation i.e. transition from autocracy to democracy. Unfortunately the temporary fix has been repeatedly and regularly used in Bangladesh and, as a consequence, its efficacy is in decrease. The situation is different in India and Sri Lanka. Elections have been held under the incumbent government regularly and despite the allegation of vote riggings, losing political parties have conceded their defeats and accepted the election results. Thus the very foundation of democracy in India and Sri Lanka is well-rooted.

Until 1947, notwithstanding that Bangladesh was under British colonial rule, it did receive peripheral treatment from the British rulers. When India and Pakistan gained independence from the British, Bangladesh was attached to Pakistan from which it inherited military legacy and bureaucratic overdevelopment. Bangladesh took a prolonged 15 years to get out of the shadow of military regime. Moreover, unlike the Western world, electoral democracy precedes economic development and development of political institutions in Bangladesh that is causing problems for getting the root of democracy entrenched in Bangladesh. Democratic representative institutions evolved in the lowest and highest echelons (union council and parliament) of the political system without having any linkages in between (sub-district, district/divisional levels). Lack of interconnectedness between and among different tiers of government and piecemeal development of political institutions have marred the pace and maturity of democratic advancement in Bangladesh. The decline of parliament vis-à-vis the executive is linked to this historical development of politics in Bangladesh too.

India was the center of colonial rule in the Indian sub-continent and so received preferential treatment from the British. Moreover, the capability of India's leadership to continue, nurture and develop the political system inherited from the British colonial rulers has been remarkable. Democratic representative institutions blossomed in India in the lowest echelon of government i.e. in villages. There was an ascending order of local government from the village through block or sub-district, district to the state capital. This well-knit interconnectedness between and among different tiers of government from grassroots to center and institutionalized development of these political institutions have prompted the pace and maturity of democratic advancement in India.

The failure of Sri Lanka's leadership to continue, retain and develop the Westminster style political system (bicameral parliament and first-past-the post electoral system) inherited from the British colonial rulers and replace it with a semi-presidential system that does not suit the Sri Lankan condition for the pursuit of narrow political interest has proved to be ineffective and unproductive. Local government units in Sri Lanka are integrated. But its provincial legislatures have no second chamber in the form of Senate or councils of provinces to accommodate regional representation.

Understanding between the ruling and opposition parties lies at the heart of a functioning democracy that has been unfortunately on the wane in Sri Lanka over the course of time. This adverse relations between the two major parties revolves around the two leaders which is turning from bad to worse. Some respondents attribute this troubled relationship between the two to the hereditary democracy (the two leaders coming from two distinguished families whose ancestors alternated power) in Sri Lanka. The lack of bipartisanship in Sri Lankan militarized politics is a serious obstacle for parliament (its committees) to carry out its legislative and oversight functions and also to the present military conflict being brought to an end.

The race for power between the two major parties has been too stiff to allow the parliament to run and complete its full term let alone be a policy contributor in Bangladesh. In the political arena, the two major parties have hardly been seen compromising on significant national issues. The relationship between the ruling party and the opposition is characterized by a high degree of animosity and conflict. The two major parties abhor and demonize each other and the chiefs of these parties have not even been in talking terms with each other since the restoration of democratic governance in Bangladesh in 1991. Some respondents attribute this troubled relationship between the two to the hereditary democracy (the two leaders coming from two distinguished families whose ancestors alternated power) in Bangladesh. The opposition is seldom allowed to ventilate their grievances and opinion in the plenary sessions, which in turn provoke them to stage frequent walkouts or boycott the JS, and organize street protests.

Understanding between the ruling and opposition parties has been fortunately in existence in India for long. This working relationship between the two major parties has been sustained and carried forward by the two leaders of the two major parties. This has added value to making parliamentary democracy work in India. The emergence of bipartisanship (two major parties and coalitions) in Indian politics has become a blessing for parliament (its committees) to carry out its legislative and oversight functions too.

Thus the current state of securing executive accountability by parliamentary committees in Bangladesh, India and Sri Lanka hinges upon the prevailing macro-political context of the country and the institutional rules of the committee system, originating mainly from the political system and shaped in part by the prevailing hierarchical culture of the region.

Appendix

A1.1 Questionnaire survey: results of the questionnaire survey/interview of the perception of selected MPs on the role of parliament and parliamentary committees in holding the government accountable (Bangladesh, India and Sri Lanka)

Statement	*MPs' opinion*					
	Agree completely (%)[a]			*Mean score*		
	BAN	*IND*	*SL*	*BAN*	*IND*	*SL*
Context						
Institutionally, committees are much weaker in parliamentary systems than in presidential systems.	7	8	8	0.5	0.7	0.5
Upper house committees without government majorities can act more independently of government influence and make genuine and demanding scrutiny of government policy and actions.	20	100	70	1	4	3
Lack of party control over committee members is one of the most important aspects of committee strength in constraining/influencing the executive.	80	85	90	3.5	3.6	3.7
A strong but disciplined opposition is at the heart of a strong parliament and parliamentary committee system.	100	100	100	4	4	4
An anti-defection law is a threat to autonomy of an mp and a constraint to effective committee functioning.	40	35	40	2.5	1.9	2.6
A strong parliament is a prerequisite for a strong committee system and vice versa.	90	100	100	3.9	4	4
Structure						
The formation of committees immediately after the commencement of a new parliament is a sine qua non for the effective functioning of the committee system and calling the government to account.	90	85	91	3.9	3.5	3.8
The term of committees should be coterminous with the life span of each house to help members develop specialized knowledge conducive to active committee performance.	85	90	80	3.7	3.7	3.5
Departmentally related standing committees should parallel the structure of government ministries for effective functioning.	54	20	51	2.2	1.5	2.5
Committees should be small (composed of 10–20 members) in order to break down political division and enhance committee specialization.	80	70	91	3.5	3	3.8

Self-selection based on individual expertise and interest rather than government/party choice should be a key criterion in the selection of committee members.	64	70	60	2.3	2.9	2.2
The composition of the committees (including the chairmanship) should be based on the proportional strength of political parties in the parliament.	50	90	30	2.1	3.8	2.1
To secure executive accountability, ministers should not be allowed to serve even as members of parliamentary committees.	30	90	23	1.8	3.9	2.1
Senior members of the opposition should be appointed chairs of financial committees to secure the financial accountability and transparency of the government.	100	40	100	4	1.8	4
It is imperative to constitute a liaison committee comprised of the chairmen of departmentally related standing committees to ensure proper coordination and avoid overlapping functions.	95	90	96	3.9	3.5	3.9
Procedures						
Committee's ability to set its agenda is a crucial source of committee power to constrain/influence government.	60	70	59	2.3	3.1	2.2
Committee deliberation on legislative bills should take place prior to plenary consideration of bills, which tends to increase the influence of committees in determining outcomes.	32	20	42	1.5	1	2
Committee meetings should be closed in order to foster inter-party compromise and relax party discipline.	91	70	93	3.8	3.1	3.8
Public hearings on legislative bills and any other oversight issues can provide valuable information essential to ensure executive accountability.	90	90	95	3.7	3.6	3.9
Committees should possess the right to send for persons (including common public, civil servants and ministers), papers and records, and can punish those who fail to comply with its call.	60	70	80	2.5	3	3.3
Functions						
Committees should have exclusive jurisdiction over legislation as well as oversight of the executive.	60	55	75	2.3	2.2	3.1
Committee reports should be presented to the parliament regularly for deliberation on specific days in each session.	70	80	60	3.5	3.6	3.0
Minority members in a committee should be allowed to present their own reports which provide some political space for them and indicate that committees are not dominated by the government.	40	30	45	1.9	1.6	2.1

continued

A1.1 Continued

Statement	MPs' opinion					
	Agree completely (%)[a]			*Mean score*		
	BAN	*IND*	*SL*	*BAN*	*IND*	*SL*
Recommendations should be mandatory rather than advisory to get the maximum benefits from committee operations to hold the government to account.	45	30	60	2.2	1.5	3
To monitor the state of implementation of recommendations, an "action-taken sub-committee" of each committee should be formed, and in cases of ministries' failure to comply with the recommendations, they should submit an explanatory note to the committee immediately.	78	100	100	3.1	4	4
Resources						
Well paid full-time professional and experienced legislators coupled with low turnover of committee membership can help active and powerful parliamentary committees to emerge.	90	95	80	3.5	3.8	3.2
Committees should be backed up by a separate parliamentary secretariat and provided with a healthy budget, a sufficient number of specialized/competent staffers and adequate logistic support (including computer and internet access facilities, legislative database, developed library and research support, training program for committee members and staff, etc.) for their effective functioning.	77	60	64	3.1	3	3
Committees should be able to benefit from the expertise and knowledge of external experts who are relatively independent of executive influence.	100	100	100	4	4	4

Note

For each statement, there was a four-point answer scale (1–4) ranging from agree completely, agree partly, disagree partly, neither agree nor disagree to disagree completely. The higher the mean and percentage scores, the higher the statements by the respondents.

a Only percentage distribution for category agree completely is presented here.

A 2.1 Numerical strength of government and opposition in *Jatiya Sangsads*

JS/year elected	*Ruling party*	*Main opposition*	*Percentage of MPs*			*Total MPs**	*Tenure (in months)*	
			Government	*Opposition (including independents)*			*Normal*	*Actual*
First (1973)	AL	–	97.78	2.22	315	60	32	
Second (1979)	BNP	AL	75.15	24.85	330	60	36	
Third (1986)	JP	AL	62.42	37.58	330	60	17	
Fifth (1991)	BNP	AL	50.91	49.09	330	60	56	
Seventh (1996)	AL	BNP	52.7	46.97	330	60	60	
Eighth (2001)	BNP	AL	73.33	26.67	300	60	60	

Source: Rashid 1997; Ahmed 1998a; Bangladesh Election Commission, 2001.

Notes

*Sixth JS was very short-lived. It lasted for 11 days only (from March 19 TO March 30, 1996). One session was held only to pass the Non-Government Caretaker Government Bill in the House.

A2.2 Data on legislation in Bangladesh

JS	*Total bills passed*	*Government bills (% of total)*	*Ordinance-turned bills passed (% of total bills passed)*	*Bills scrutinized by committees*	*Private members' bills passed*
First	154	100	83 (53.3%)	3 (2%)	0
Second	65	97	15 (23%)	29 (44%)	2
Third	39	97.4	14 (36%)	–	1
Fourth	142	100	89 (62.7%)	–	0
Fifth	173	99.4	60 (34.7%)	8 (4.6%)	–
Sixth	1	100	0	0	0
Seventh	190	99.5	5 (2.6%)	190 (100%)	1
Eighth	72 (as of July 2003)	100	3 (4%)	4	1

Source: (Halim 1998: 233–235); Ahmed (2002: 85), *Independent* May 19, 2003.

A2.3 Structure of parliamentary committees

Nature of committees	*Number of committees formed (from the first JS to eighth JS)**						
	First JS	*Second JS*	*Third JS*	*Fourth JS*	*Fifth JS*	*Seventh JS*	*Eighth JS*
Standing committees							
Departmentally-related committees	–	36	–	32	35	35	39
Financial committees	3	3	–	3	3	3	3
Investigative committees	2	2	1	2	2	2	2
Scrutinizing committees	1	1	–	1	1	1	1
House committees	3	3	2	3	3	3	3
Service committees	2	2	1	2	2	2	2
Ad hoc committees							
Committees on bills (select and special)	3	3	–	–	5	1	
Special committee	–	1	2	1	2	1	
Total	14	51	6	44	53	48	50

Source: BJS (1973–1975; 1979–1982; 1987; 1988–1990; 1991–1995; 1996–2001; 2001–).

Note
*The 6th JS which only survived for a few days did not constitute any committee.

A3.1 Basic structure of parliamentary committees in the Indian parliament

Serial No.	*Committee*	*Membership*			*Mode of appointment*		*Tenure*
		LS	*RS*	*Total*	*Members*	*Chairmen*	
Joint committee (LS + RS)							
1–17	DRSCS (11 of LS and 6 of RS)	30	15	45	Nominated	Nominated	Not exceeding one year
18	Committee on the Welfare of Scheduled Castes And Scheduled Tribes	20	10	30	Elected	Nominated	Not exceeding one year
19	Committee on Empowerment of Women	20	10	30	Nominated	Nominated	Not exceeding one year
20	Public Accounts Committee	15	07	22	Elected	Nominated	Not exceeding one year
21	Committee on Public Undertakings	15	07	22	Elected	Nominated	Not exceeding one year
22	Joint committee on Offices of Profit	–	–	–	Elected	Elected by the committee	Duration of LS
23	Joint committee on Salaries and Allowances of MPs	10	05	15	Nominated	Nominated	One year
24	Library Committee	06	03	09	Nominated	Nominated	Not exceeding one year
Single House committees of Lok Sabha/Rajya Sabha							
25–26	Business Advisory Committee	15	11	–	Nominated	Speaker LS/chair RS	Until reconstituted (no fixed term)
27–28	Rules Committee	15	16	–	Nominated	Speaker LS/chair RS	Until reconstituted
29–30	General Purpose Committee	See note 3	See note 3	–	Nominated	Speaker LS/chair RS	See note 3
31–32	Committee of Privileges	15	10	–	Nominated	Nominated	Until reconstituted
33–34	Committee on Petitions	15	10	–	Nominated	Nominated	Until reconstituted
35–36	Committee on Government Assurances	15	10	–	Nominated	Nominated	Not exceeding one year in case of LS/until reconstituted RS
37–38	Committee on Subordinate Legislation	15	15	–	Nominated	Nominated	Not exceeding one year in case of LS/until reconstituted RS

39–40	Committee on Papers Laid on the Table	15	10	–	Nominated	Nominated	Not exceeding one year in case of LS/until reconstituted RS
41–42	House Committee	12	7	–	–	–	–
Standing committees only in Lok Sabha							
43	Committee on Estimates	30	–	–	Elected	Nominated	Not exceeding one year
44	Committee on Absence of Members from the sittings of the House	15	–	–	Nominated	Nominated	Not exceeding one year
45	Committee on Private Members' Bills and Resolution	15	–	–	Nominated	Nominated	Not exceeding one year
Standing committees only in Rajya Sabha							
46	Ethics Committee	10	–	–	Nominated	Nominated	Until reconstituted
47	Committee on Provision of computers for members	7	–	–	Nominated	Deputy Chair of RS	Until reconstituted
48	Committee on Members of Parliament Local Area Development Scheme	10	–	–	Nominated	Deputy Chair of RS	Until reconstituted

Source: Malhotra (2003: 23–24).

A3.2 Comparative accounts of bills introduced in the 13th *Lok Sabha* and bills referred to committees

No. of sessions	*Bill pending at the end of last session*	*Bills introduced*	*Bills passed*	*Bills referred to SCS*	*Bills reported by SCS*	*Bills referred to JCS*
First	0	8	4	0	0	0
Second	4	14	21	9	0	2
Third	8	26	27	7	5	0
Fourth	14	14	20	1	9	0
Fifth	18	20	17	3	4	0
Sixth	27	12	17	0	2	0
Seventh	28	24	35	16	8	0
Eighth	31	10	11	1	10	0
Ninth	36	31	38	8	8	0
Tenth	37	10	12	0	2	0
11th	43	17	37	4	14	0
12th	30	27	26	12	3	0
13th	34	15	11	12	6	0

Source: Calculated and compiled by the author from *Lok Sabha* Secretariat (1999–2004) "Resume of Parliament".

A3.3 Reports presented by DRSCS of *Lok Sabha* (April 8, 1993–December 31, 2002)

Committee	*Reports*					*ATRS*					*Grand total*
	DG	*B*	*P*	*AR/S*	*Total*	*DG*	*B*	*P*	*AR/S*	*Total*	
Agriculture	46	5	2	9	62	46	–	–	8	54	116
Information Technology	29	7	–	24	60	24	–	–	15	39	99
Defense	11	3	–	13	27	10	–	–	8	18	45
Energy	37	6	–	17	60	32	–	–	14	46	106
External affairs	10	1	–	4	15	9	–	–	4	13	28
Finance	30	21	–	2	53	29	–	–	4	33	86
Food, Civil Supplies and	22	3	–	6	31	20	–	–	5	25	56
Public Labor and Welfare	24	20	–	3	47	21	–	–	3	24	71
Petroleum and Chemicals	28	1	1	17	47	24	–	–	19	43	90
Railways	9	–	–	16	25	10	–	4	11	25	50
Urban and Rural Development	40	8	1	9	58	34	–	1	12	47	105
Total	286	75	4	120	485	259	–	5	103	367	852

Source: Malhotra (2003: 37).

Notes

Abbreviations: ATRS stands for action-taken report; DG for demands for grants; B for bills; P for policies and AR/S for annual reports/subjects.

A3.4 Activities of three financial committees in *Lok Sabha*

Lok Sabha	*Number of sittings*	*Duration hours/minutes*	*Reports presented*
First (1952–1957)	–	–	–
Second	508	1223:00	187
Third	836	2244:00	213
Fourth	650	1366:00	326
Fifth	1138	2678:00	454
Sixth	425	848:00	249
Seventh	1140	2244:20	421
Eighth	549	1209:00	406
Ninth	103	237:00	67
Tenth	401	774:40	230
11th	112	194:55	45
12th	56	87:30	22
13th	102	145:40	139

Source: Malhotra (2002: 769).

A3.5 Statements showing analysis of action taken by the government on recommendations made by all 11 DRSCS in the *Lok Sabha* from 1993–2002

	1994–1995	*1995–1996*	*1996–1997*	*1997–1998**	*1998–1999*	*1999–2000*	*2001*	*2002*	*Average per year*
Total number of recommendations made by the committees	393	1352	654	156	1497	1308	1070	1126	
Total number of recommendations accepted by the government	222.5 (56.62%)	827 (66.72%)	370 (56.58%)	82 (52.56%)	875 (58.45%)	666 (50.92%)	505 (47.20%)	562 (49.91%)	54.87%
Total number of recommendations which the committees did not pursue in view of government replies	54 (13.74%)	191 (14.03%)	95 (14.52%)	34 (21.79%)	200 (13.36%)	287 (21.94%)	201 (18.78%)	176 (15.63%)	16.72%
Total number of recommendations in respect of which replies of government have not been accepted by committee	90.5 (23.03%)	217 (15.93%)	125 (19.11%)	28 (17.95%)	236 (15.76%)	208 (15.90%)	195 (18.22%)	208 (18.74%)	
Total number of recommendations in respect of which final replies of government were awaited	26 (6.61%)	127 (9.32%)	64 (9.70%)	12 (7.70%)	186 (12.43%)	147 (11.24%)	169 (15.80%)	180 (15.98%)	

Source: compiled and calculated by the author from Kesavan (2003: 168–173); Indian *Lok Sabha* (2001, 2003, 2003a).

Note

The table depicts the analysis of action taken by government on the recommendations made by the committees in their earlier reports of which action-taken reports were presented during different year.

A3.6 Acceptance of PAC recommendations by government (1981–1999)

Lok Sabha	*Year*	*Total number of recommendations*	*Total number of recommendations accepted by government*	*Percentages of recommendations accepted by government*
Seventh	1981	558	313	56.09
	1982	820	483	58.90
	1983	612	412	66.72
	1984	646	431	66.51
Eighth	1985	91	59	64.84
	1986	666	407	61.11
	1987	346	198	57.23
	1988	274	177	64.60
	1989	97	49	50.52
Ninth	1990	207	112	54.11
	1991	385	220	57.14
Tenth	1992	278	163	58.63
	1993	229	129	56.33
	1994	206	132	64.08
	1995	268	164	61.19
	1996	110	70	63.64
11th	1997	156	106	67.95
12th	1998	75	45	60
13th	1999	88	39	44.32
Total	1980–1999	6112	3709	60.68

Source: adapted from Malhotra (2000: 182).

A3.7 Format of action-taken report

Parts	*Contents*
Chapter I	Reports.
Chapter II	Recommendations which have been accepted by the government.
Chapter III	Recommendations which the committee does not want to pursue in view of government's replies.
Chapter IV	Recommendations in respect of which replies of government have not accepted by the committee.
Chapter V	Recommendations in respect of which final replies of government have not yet been received.

Source: Nair (2003: 164–165).

A3.8 Number and duration of sittings of DRSCS of *Lok Sabha*

Committee	*Number and duration (in parenthesis in hours and minutes) of sittings*									
	1993–1994	*1994–1995*	*1995–1996*	*1996–1997*	*1997–1998*	*1998–1999*	*1999–2000*	*2001*	*2002*	*Average*
Agriculture	38 (66)	30 (35)	12 (16)	33 (49)	07 (11)	30 (66)	22 (35)	24 (39)	23 (38)	24 (39)
Information Technology	23 (46)	31 (63)	25 (29)	46 (163)	08 (14)	40 (68)	39 (69)	60 (104)	54 (84)	36 (71)
Defense	18 (30)	10 (19)	12 (22)	20 (36)	03 (05)	20 (49)	15 (33)	11 (19)	14 (39)	14 (29)
Energy	55 (92)	48 (67)	23 (16)	39 (60)	10 (12)	36 (55)	31 (50)	34 (49)	21 (39)	33 (49)
External Affairs	30 (66)	21 (44)	32 (44)	15 (30)	06 (08)	24 (48)	28 (42)	25 (36)	16 (26)	22 (38)
Finance	24 (57)	19 (36)	24 (37)	28 (78)	16 (43)	36 (112)	27 (74)	30 (58)	23 (41)	25 (60)
Food, Civil Supplies and Public Distribution	27 (59)	13 (29)	20 (39)	12 (23)	02 (03)	26 (52)	15 (30)	14 (35)	10 (13)	15 (31)
Labor and Welfare	18 (36)	17 (33)	25 (52)	17 (35)	06 (08)	17 (38)	14 (22)	15 (26)	15 (24)	16 (30)
Petroleum and Chemicals	42 (112)	25 (43)	23 (34)	18 (20)	07 (11)	25 (38)	36 (48)	37 (42)	29 (44)	27 (44)
Railways	61 (75)	22 (28)	21 (34)	74 (125)	11 (19)	40 (78)	27 (45)	20 (31)	20 (30)	33 (52)
Urban and Rural Development	50 (84)	35 (64)	41 (70)	54 (102)	15 (23)	48 (82)	27 (33)	29 (50)	24 (35)	36 (60)
Total	386 (723)	271 (461)	258 (513)	356 (791)	91 (157)	342 (686)	281 (476)	299 (489)	249 (413)	281 (523)

Source: Malhotra (2003: 39).

Notes

1 Introduction

1 The 13th amendment of Bangladeshs constitution provides that the incumbent government will hand over power to a non-partisan caretaker government (NCG) headed by a former Chief Justice three months before each parliamentary election is due. The head of the NCG is supported by a council of advisors consisting of eminent professionals on the basis of political consensus. Its prime task is to conduct the national parliamentary election and handover the power to the newly elected government.

2 Concepts, theories and methods

1 Seventh JS 1996–2001, eighth JS 2001–, 13th *Lok Sabha* 1999–2004, fifth parliament of Sri Lanka (December, 2002-February, 2004).

5 Parliamentary control and government accountability in Bangladesh: the role of parliamentary committees

1 CAG is a constitutional body responsible for auditing all public sector agencies and reporting the findings to the parliament.
2 Under the Rules of Business, the CAG is placed as a subordinate office of the Ministry of Finance. Most administrative matters including such important ones as budget and selection of personnel require approval from the Ministries of Finance and Establishment.
3 In matured democracies like the UK, Australia and India usually senior opposition members chair the financial committees.
4 For instance copies of the MIG purchase/contract at the cost of US$124 million was not made available to the members of Standing Committee on Ministry of Defense. Again the DGDP (Director General of Defense Purchase) brought to another committee meeting on the Ministry of Defense a copy of specifications of Korean frigate purchase at the cost of US$100 million that was not discussed due to time constraints who took the copy back saying it was secret.
5 BDT (Bangladesh Taka) is the currency of Bangladesh; US$ (US dollars) is the currency of the USA.
6 The Official Secrets Act of 1923 and the Government Servants Conduct Rules of 1979 bind the civil servant to an oath of secrecy even forbidding them to pass some official information to other government departments unless empowered by the government.
7 Chairing of the PAC and some important committees by opposition MPs, exclusion of ministers from departmentally-related committee membership, constitution of committees immediately after the inauguration of a new parliament on the basis of consensus among the major parties, regular holding of committee meetings and production of

reports, committee involvement in budget before plenary deliberation are some of the features which are missing in committee system in Bangladesh.

6 Parliamentary control and government accountability in India: the role of parliamentary committees

1 By one estimate, the time lost due to disruptions in the *Lok Sabha* cost taxpayers Rs75 million in just one session (*Business Standard*, April 28, 2001).
2 In the 14th *Lok Sabha*, the total number DRSCs has been increased from 17 to 24, 16 will be managed by the *Lok Sabha* secretariat and the remaining eight will be serviced by the *Rajya Sabha* secretariat. However, the size of the committee has been reduced from 45 to 30 now. This is a major structural change of the DRSCs since their introduction in 1993.
3 Sharing committee chairmanship with the opposition on the basis of party representation in the House, exclusion of ministers from committee chairmanship/membership, regular holding of committee meetings and production of reports, committee involvement in bill scrutiny and budget discussion before plenary deliberation and the presence of a strong PAC are some of the features which are present in committee system in India.

7 Parliamentary control and government accountability in Sri Lanka: the role of parliamentary committees

1 Between 1978 and 1988, the United Nationalist Party (UNP) government rammed through no fewer than 16 constitutional amendments, many of which were blatantly partisan or even whimsical in nature. The most egregious was the Fourth Amendment, which allowed the ruling party to hold a fraudulent referendum in December 1982 in place of scheduled parliamentary elections. This stunt enabled the party to use a simple electoral majority to extend its two-thirds parliamentary majority for another term.
2 Sharing committee chairmanship with the opposition on the basis of party representation in the House, exclusion of Ministers from consultative committee chairmanship/membership, regular holding of committee meetings and production of reports, committee involvement in bill scrutiny and budget discussion before plenary deliberation and the presence of a strong PAC are some of the features which are missing in the committee system in Sri Lanka.

Bibliography

Aberbach, J.D. (1979), "Congress in Congressional Oversight", *American Behavioral Scientist*, 22: 439–515.

Adonis, A. (1990), *Parliament Today*. Manchester: Manchester University Press.

Agh, A. (1998), "Changing Parliamentary Committees in Changing East-Central Europe: Parliamentary Committees as Central Sites of Policy Making", in L.D. Longley and R.H. Davidson (eds), *The New Role of Parliamentary Committees*. London: Frank Cass, 84–100.

Ahmed, N. (1997a), "Parliamentary Opposition in Bangladesh: A Study of its Role in Fifth Parliament", *Party Politics*, 3(2): 147–168.

—— (1997b), "Parliament-Executive Relations in Bangladesh", *The Journal of Legislative Studies*, 3(4): 70–91.

—— (1998a), "Reforming the Parliament in Bangladesh: Structural Constrains and Political Dilemmas", *Commonwealth and Comparative Politics*, 36(1): 68–91.

—— (1998b), "In Search of Institutionalization: Parliament in Bangladesh", *The Journal of Legislative Studies*, 4(4): 35–65.

—— (2000), "Committees in the Bangladesh Parliament: A Study in Comparison", *Asian Profile*, 28(6): 499–508.

—— (2001a), "Parliamentary Committees and Parliamentary Government in Bangladesh", *Contemporary South Asia*, 10(1): 11–36.

—— (2001b), "Development and Working of Parliaments in South Asia", *Asian Journal of Political Science*, 9(1): 18–48.

—— (2001c), *Parliament and Public Spending in Bangladesh: Limits of Control*. Dhaka: Bangladesh Institute of Parliamentary Studies.

—— (2002), *The Parliament of Bangladesh*. Aldershot: Ashgate Publishing Limited.

—— (2003), "From Monopoly to Competition: Party Politics in the Bangladesh Parliament (1973–2001)", *Pacific Affairs*, 76(1): 55–77.

Ahmed, N. and Ahmed, A. (1996), "The Quest for Accountability: Parliament and Public Administration in Bangladesh", *Asian Journal of Public Administration*, 18(1): 70–95.

Ahmed, N. and Khan, S. (1995), "The Development of Parliamentary Oversight in Bangladesh: A Research Note", *Legislative Studies Quarterly*, 20(4): 577–583.

Agor, W.H. (1970), "The Senate in the Chilean Political System", in A. Kornberg and L. Musolf (eds), *Legislature in Developmental Perspective*. Durham: Duke University Press.

Aminuzzaman, S. (1993), "Institutional Processes and Practices of Administrative Accountability: Role of *Jatiya Sangsad* (Parliament) in Bangladesh", *South Asian Studies*, 10(2): 44–61.

Arthur, J. (1991), *Democracy: Theory and Practice*. Andover, Hants: International Thomson Publishing Ltd.

Ashraf, A. (1999), "Parliamentary Finance Committees in Bangladesh", paper presented to a Conference on Comparative Constitutional Law: Parliamentary Committee System, organized by Bangladesh Jatiya Sangsad and Institute of Parliamentary Studies, Dhaka, May 27–28.

Asian Wall Street Journal (2005), January 4, 2005.

Austen-Smith, D. and Banks, J.S. (1988), "Elections, Coalitions and Legislative Outcomes", *American Political Science Review*, 82: 405–423.

Bach, S. (2000), "Incentives and Opportunities for Oversight: Comparative Implications of the American Congressional Experience", paper presented at the 2000 World Congress of International Political science, Quebec, Canada, August.

Baerwald, H. (1979), "Committees in Japanese Diet", in J.D. Lees and M. Shaw (eds), *Committees in Legislatures*. Durham: Duke University Press.

Baker, R.S. (2000), "Government Accountability and its Limits", *Issues of Democracy, IIP Electronic Journals*, 5(2): 6–12.

Bale, T. (1997), "Towards a Cultural Theory of Parliamentary Party Groups", *The Journal of Legislative Studies*, 3(4): 25–43.

Ball, A.R. and Peters, B.G. (2000), *Modern Politics and Government*. Houndmills, Basingstoke: Macmillan Press.

Bangladesh Election Commission [BEC] (2001), *Parliament Elections 2001 Results*. Dhaka: Election Commission Secretariat.

Bangladesh *Jatiya Sangsad* [BJS] (1991), *Sangsad Bulletin*, on first, second third and 17th session of fifth parliament. Dhaka: Bangladesh Parliament secretariat.

—— (1996), *Sangsad Bulletin*, on first, second and eighth session of seventh parliament. Dhaka: Bangladesh Parliament secretariat.

—— (1997), *The Rules of Procedure of Parliament of the People's Republic of Bangladesh* (as modified up to June 10). Dhaka: Bangladesh Parliament secretariat.

—— (1997–1999), *The Proceedings (1st to 10th meeting) of Committee on Public Undertakings*. Dhaka: Bangladesh Parliament secretariat.

—— (1997–1999a), *The Proceedings (1st to 21st meeting) of Committee on Estimates in the 7th JS*. Dhaka: Bangladesh Parliament secretariat.

—— (1997–1999b), *The Proceedings of (1st to 13th) the Meeting of Standing Committee on Ministry of Establishment*. Dhaka: Bangladesh Parliament secretariat.

—— (1997–1999c), *The Proceedings (1st to 14th meeting) of Standing Committee on Ministry on Agriculture*. Dhaka: Bangladesh Parliament secretariat.

—— (1998), *Third Report of Public Accounts Committee* in the seventh JS. Dhaka: Bangladesh Parliament secretariat.

—— (1999), Proceedings of a Conference on Comparative Constitutional Law: Parliamentary Committee System, organized by Bangladesh Jatiya Sangsad and Institute of Parliamentary Studies, Dhaka, May 27–28.

—— (2001), *Fourth Report of Public Accounts Committee* in the seventh JS. Dhaka: Bangladesh Parliament secretariat.

—— (2001a), *Fifth Report of Public Accounts Committee* in the seventh JS. Dhaka: Bangladesh Parliament secretariat.

—— (2001b), *First Report of the Standing Committee on Ministry of Defence* in the seventh JS. Dhaka: Bangladesh Parliament secretariat.

Barnhart, G. (1999), *Parliamentary Committees: Enhancing Democratic Governance: A Report of the Commonwealth Parliamentary Association, Study Group on Parliamentary Committees and Committee Systems*. London: Cavendish.

Bartolini, S. (1993), "Of time and Comparative Research", *Journal of Theoretical Politics*, 5: 131–167.

Baxter, C., Malik, Y.K., Kennedy, C.H. and Oberst, A.R.C. (2002), *Government and Politics in South Asia*. Boulder: Westview.

Behn, R.D. (2001), *Rethinking Democratic Accountability*. Washington, D.C.: Brookings Institution Press.

Benda, S.R. (1997), "Committees in Legislature: A Division of Labor", in L. Longly and A. Agh (eds), *Working Paper on Comparative Legislative Studies Part-2: The Changing Role of Parliamentary Committees*. Appleton: Research Committee of Legislative Specialists, International Political Science Association, 17–50.

Berman, H.J. (1983), *Law and Revolution: The Formation of the Western Legal Tradition*. Cambridge: Harvard University Press.

Beyme, K.V. (1993), "Parliamentary Crisis and How to Strengthen Democracy", in Douglas Greenberg (ed.), *Constitutionalism and Democracy: Transitions in the Contemporary World: The American Council of Learned Societies Comparative Constitutionalism Papers*. New York: Oxford University Press, 275–286.

Bhardwaj, R.C. (1995), "Parliamentary Partners: Departmentally-related Standing Committees in India", *The Parliamentarian*, 76(3): 313–319.

—— (1998), "India", in George Thomas Kurian (ed.), *World Encyclopedia of Parliaments and Legislatures* Vol. 1.Washington, D.C.: Congressional Quarterly Inc., 318–333.

Blondel, J. (1969–1970), "Comparative Legislative Behavior", *Government and Opposition*, 5: 67–85.

—— (1973), *Comparative Legislatures*. Englewood Cliffs: Prentice-Hall.

—— (1995), *Comparative Government*. London: Prentice-Hall/Harvester Wheatsheaf.

Bobbio, N. (translated by Peter Kennealy) (1989), *Democracy and Dictatorship: The Nature and Limits of State Power*. Cambridge: Polity Press.

Bosso, C.J., Portz, J.H. and Tolly, M.C. (2000), *American Government: Conflict, Compromise, and Citizenship*. Boulder: Westview Press.

Brazier, A. (2000), *Systematic Scrutiny: Reforming the Select Committees*. London: Hansard Society.

Business Standard (2001), April 28 (an English daily in India).

Cain, B.E, Ferejohn, J. and Fiorina, M. (1987), *The Personal Vote: Constituency Service and Electoral Independence*. Cambridge: Harvard University Press.

Cameron, W. (2004), "Public Accountability: Effectiveness, Equity, Ethics", *Australian Journal of Public Administration*, 63(4): 59–67.

Campbell, C. and Davidson, R.H. (1998), "US Congressional Committees: Changing Legislative Workshops", in L.D. Longley and R.H. Davidson (eds), *The New Role of Parliamentary Committees*. London and Portland: Frank Cass, 124–142.

Carey, J.M. (2002), "Parties, Coalitions and the Chilean Congress in the 1990s", in M. Scott and B. Nacif (eds), *Legislative Politics in Latin America*. New York: Cambridge University Press, 222–253.

Center for Applied Policy Research [CAP] (2005), Bertelsmann Transformation Index 2005. Munich: CAP.

Central Intelligence Agency [CIA] (2004), *The World Fact Book*. Washington, D.C.: Directorate of Intelligence.

Choudhury, D. (1994), *Constitutional Development in Bangladesh: Stresses and Strains*. Karachi: Oxford University Press.

Christensen, T. and Peters, B.G. (1999), *Structure, Culture and Governance: A Comparison of Norway and The United States*. Lanham: Rowman & Littlefield Publishers, Inc.

Collier, D. (1993), "The Comparative Method", in A. Finiftner (ed.), *Political Science: The State of Discipline*. Washington, D.C.: APSA.

Commonwealth Policy Studies Unit [CPSU] (2002), *Parliamentary Oversight of the Security Sector*. London: Institute of Commonwealth Studies.

Comptroller and Auditor General [CAG] (1997), *Annual Report* of the Office of Comptroller and Auditor General, Bangladesh. Dhaka: Office of CAG.

—— (1998), *Annual Report* of the Office of Comptroller and Auditor General, Bangladesh. Dhaka: Office of CAG.

—— (1999), *Annual Report* of the Office of Comptroller and Auditor General, Bangladesh. Dhaka: Office of CAG.

Copeland, G.W. and Patterson, S.C. (1998), "Parliaments and Legislatures", in G.T. Kurian (ed.), *World Encyclopedia of Parliaments and Legislatures* Vol. 2.Washington, D.C.: Congressional Quarterly Inc., xix–xxxi.

Coughlin, R.M. and Lockhart, C. (1998), "Group-Grid Theory and Political Ideology: A Consideration of their Relative Strength and Weaknesses for Explaining the Structure of Mass Beliefs Systems", *Journal of Theoretical Politics*, 10(1): 33–58.

Cowley, P. (ed.) (1997), *Conscience and Parliament*. London: Frank Cass.

Cowley, P. and Norton, P. (1996), "Are Conservative MPs Revolting?", *Centre for Legislative Studies Research*, Paper 2/96. Hull: University of Hull.

Cox, G.W. (1997), *Making Votes Count: Strategic Coordination in the World's Electoral Systems*. Cambridge: Cambridge University Press.

—— (2000), "On the Effects of Legislative Rules", *Legislative Studies Quarterly*, 25(2): 169–192.

Cox, G.W. and Shugart, M.S. (1996), "Strategic Voting under Proportional Representation", *Journal of Law, Economics and Organization*, 12(2): 299–324.

Coyle, D.J. and Ellis, R.J. (eds) (1994), *Politics, Policy and Culture*. Boulder: Westview.

Cremin, M. (1993), "The Setting-Up of the Departmental Select Committee after the 1992 Election", *Parliamentary Affairs*, 46(3): 192–202.

Crossman, R.H.S. (1985), "Prime Ministerial Government", in Anthony King (ed.), *The British Prime Minister*. Basingstoke: Macmillan.

Daily Observer (2005) October 16.

—— (2006), March 1.

Daily Financial Express (1996), August 22.

Daily Star (1999), September 29, October 23, November 29 (an English daily in Bangladesh).

—— (2000), April 4, 11, August 6, November 5.

—— (2003), August 1, September 29, October 27.

—— (2004), April 5.

Damgaard, E. (1992), *Parliamentary Change in Nordic Countries*. Oslo: Scandinavian University Press.

—— (1995), "How Parties Control Committee Members", in H. Doring (ed.), *Parliaments and Majority Rule in Western Europe*. Frankfurt Campus Verlag, New York: St. Martin's Press, 308–325.

Dawson, R. (1970), *The Government of Canada*. Toronto: University of Toronto Press.

Day, P. and Klein, R. (1987), *Accountabilities: Five Public Services*. London: Tavistock.

Deener, D. (1956), "Judicial Review in Modern Constitutional Systems", *The American Political Science Review*, 46(4): 1079–1099.

Deering, C.J. and Smith, S.S. (1997), *Committees in Congress*. Washington, D.C.: Congressional Quarterly Inc.

Denzin, N.K. (1978), *Sociological Methods: A Source Book*. New York: McGraw-Hill.

Derbyshire, J.D. and Derbyshire, I. (1999), *Political Systems of the World* (Vol. 1), Oxford: Helicon Publishing Ltd.

—— (2000), *Encyclopaedia of World Political Systems (Vol. 1)*. Armonk: M.E. Sharpe.

DeVotta, N. (2002), "South Asia Faces the Future: Liberalism and Ethnic Conflict in Sri Lanka", *Journal of Democracy*, 13(1): 84–98.

Diamond, L. (1997), *The End of Third Wave and the Global Future of Democracy*. Political Science Series, 45. Vienna: Institute for Advanced Studies.

Dickerson, M.O. and Flanagan, T. (1998), *An Introduction to Government and Politics: A Conceptual Approach*. Toronto, Albany: ITP Nelson.

Dodd, L.C. and Schott, R.L. (1979), *Congress and the Administrative State*. New York: Wiley.

Dogan, M. and Kazancigil, A. (1994), "Introduction: Strategies in Comparative Research", in M. Dogan, and A. Kazancigil (eds), *Comparing Nations: Concepts, Strategies, Substance*. Oxford and Cambridge: Blackwell, 1–13.

Döring, H. (ed.) (1995), *Parliaments and Majority Rule in Western Europe*. New York: St. Martin's Press.

Douglas, M. (1982), *In the Active Voice*. London: Routledge and Kegan Paul.

—— (1992), *Risk and Blame: Essays in Cultural Theory*. London: Routledge.

Drewry, G. (ed.) (1985), *The New Select Committees*. Oxford: Clarendon Press.

Duverger, M. (1964), *Political Parties*. London: Methuen.

Dwivedi, O.P. and Jabbra, J.G. (1989), "Public Service Responsibility and Accountability", in, J.G. Jabbra and O.P. Dwivedi (eds), *Public Service Accountability: A Comparative Perspective*. Hartfort: Kumarian Press, 1–16.

Economist (2003), September 5.

Edelman, M. and Zelniker, S. (1973), "Information Utilization in the Knesset: The Question of Legislative Autonomy", paper presented at the ninth world Congress of the International Political Science Association.

Elazar, D.J. (1995), "Federalism", in S.M. Lipset (ed.), *The Encyclopaedia of Democracy (Vol. 2)*. London: Routledge, 472–482.

Ellis, R.J. and Thompson, M. (eds) (1997), *Culture Matters: Essays in Honor of Aaron Wildavsky*. Boulder: Westview.

Enskat, M, Mitra, S.K. and Singh, B. (2001), "India", in D. Nohlen, F. Grotz and C. Hartmann (eds), *Elections in Asia and the Pacific: A Data Handbook*, Vol. 1. Oxford: Oxford University Press, 559–584.

European Institute of Public Administration [EIPA]. (2000), *Governance by Committee: The Role of Committees in European Policy-making and Policy Implementation* (Research Paper-00/GHA). Maastricht: EIPA.

Evans, C.L. (1999), "Legislative Structure: Rules, Precedents and Jurisdictions", *Legislative Studies Quarterly*, 24: 605–642.

Evans, D.H. (2001), "Bangladesh: An Unsteady Democracy", in A. Shastri and A.J. Wilson (eds), *The Post-colonial States of South Asia: Democracy, Development and Identity*. London: Curzon Press, 69–87.

Evans, G. (1982), "Scrutiny of Executive by Parliamentary Committees", in J.R. Nethercote (ed.), *Parliament and Bureaucracy*. Sydney: Hale & Iremonger, 78–92.

Faure, A.M. (1994), "Some Methodological Problems in Comparative Politics", *Journal of Theoretical Politics*, 6: 307–322.

Feigenbaum, H., Samuels, R. and Weaver, R.K. (1993), "Innovation, Coordination, and Implementation in Energy Policy", in R. Kent Weaver and Bert A. Rockman (eds), *Do Institutions Matter?: Government Capabilities in the United States and Abroad.* Washington, D.C.: Brookings Institution, 42–109.

Fenno, R.F. (1973), *Congressmen in Committees.* Boston: Little, Brown.

Fiorina, M.P. (1977), *Congress: The Keystone of Washington Establishment.* New Haven: Yale University Press.

Flinders, M. (2001), *The Politics of Accountability in the Modern State.* Aldershot: Ashgate.

Foweraker, J. (2001), "Transformation, Transition, Consolidation: Democratization in Latin America", in K. Nash and A. Scott (eds), *The Blackwell Companion to Political Sociology.* Oxford: Blackwell Publisher.

Francis, W.L. (1989), *The Legislative Committee Game: A Comparative Analysis of Fifty States.* Columbus: Ohio State University Press.

Franks, C.E.S. (1987), *The Parliament of Canada.* Toronto: University of Toronto Press.

Freedom House (2005), *Freedom in the World, 2005.* Washington, D.C.: Freedom House.

Frendreis, J.P. (1983), "Explanation of Variation and Detection of Covariation: The Purpose and Logic of Comparative Analysis", *Comparative Political Studies*, 16: 255–273.

Froman Jr., Lewis A. (1968), "Organization Theory and the Explanation of Important Characteristics of Congress", *The American Political Science Review*, 62(2): 518–526.

Gallagher, M. *et al.* (1992), *Representative Government in Western Europe.* New York: McGraw-Hill.

George, B. and Graham, A. (1994), "Defense Committees in Democratic and Democratizing Legislatures", paper presented at the Workshop of Parliamentary Scholars and Parliamentarians, Berlin, August, 19–20.

Gerlich, P. (1973), "The Institutionalization of European Parliament", in A. Kornberg (ed.), *Legislatures in Comparative Perspective.* New York: David Mckay.

Gladdish, K. (1991), *Governing from the Center: Politics and Policy-Making in the Netherlands.* Dekalb: Northern Illinois University Press.

Government of India (2001), *A Consultation Paper on Efficacy of Public Audit System in India-C& AG-Reforming the Institution.* New Delhi: Ministry of Law Affairs.

Government of the People's Republic of Bangladesh [GOPRB]. (1996), *The Constitution of the People's Republic of Bangladesh* (as modified up to March 25, 1996), Dhaka: Bangladesh Government Press.

Greenwood, J. and Thomas, C.S. (1998), "Regulating Lobbying in the Western World", *Parliamentary Affairs*, 51(4): 487–499.

Gregory, D. (1999), "Style over Substance? Labor and the Reform of Parliament", *Renewal*, 7(3): 42–50.

Grendstad, G. (1995), "Party Fellowship and Leadership in Norway: A Political Cultural Approach", *Party Politics*, 1(2): 221–243.

Grendstad, G. and Selle, P. (1995), "Cultural Theory and the New Institutionalism", *Journal of Theoretical Politics*, 7(1): 5–27.

Griffith, J.A.G, Ryle, M. and Wheeler-Booth, M.A.J. (1989), *Parliament: Functions, Practice and Procedures.* London: Sweet and Maxwell.

Groseclose, T. and King, D.C. (2001), "Committee Theories Reconsidered", in L.C. Dodd and B.I. Oppenheimer (eds), *Congress Reconsidered.* Washington, D.C.: CQ Press, 191–216.

Hague, R., Harrop, M. and Breslin, S. (1992), *Political Science: A Comparative Introduction.* New York: St. Martin's Press.

—— (1993), *Comparative Government and Politics: An Introduction.* Basingstoke: Macmillan.
Halim, M.A. (1998), *Constitution, Constitutional Law and Politics: Bangladesh Perspective.* Dhaka: Khan, Y.A.
Hall, P.A. (1986), *Governing the Economy: The Politics of State Interventions in Britain and France.* Oxford: Oxford University Press.
Hall, P.A. and Taylor, R.C.R. (1996), "Political Science and Three New Institutionalism", *Political Studies*, 44: 952–973.
Hamilton, L. (1999), "Assessing the Effectiveness of Congressional Oversight", Heritage Foundation Symposium, December 3, 1999, Washington, D.C.: The Heritage Foundation.
Handy, C.B. (1993), *Understanding Organizations.* London: Penguin Books.
Hanson, A.H. and Walles, M. (1975), *Governing Britain.* Glasgow: Fontana.
Harris, J.P. (1964), *Congressional Control of Administration.* Washington, D.C.: The Brookings Institution.
Hartz, L. (1955), *The Liberal Tradition in America.* New York: Harcourt, Brace and Company.
Hazan, R.Y. (2001), *Reforming Parliamentary Committees: Israel in Comparative Perspective.* Columbus: Ohio State University Press.
Herath, R.B. (2002), *Sri Lankan Ethnic Crisis: Towards a Resolution.* Victoria: Trafford Publishing.
Hibbing, J.R. (1988), "Legislative Institutionalization with Illustrations from British House of Commons", *American Journal of Political Science*, 32: 681–712.
Hindu (1995), International Edition May 18 (an English daily in India).
—— (1998), International Edition October 3.
—— (2001), International Edition, December 3.
Hofstede, G.H. (1991), *Cultures and Organizations: Software of the Mind.* New York: McGraw-Hill.
—— (2001), *Culture's Consequences: Comparing Values, Behaviors, Institutions, and Organizations across Nations.* Thousand Oaks: Sage Publications.
Hood, C. (1996), "Control over Bureaucracy: Cultural Theory and Institutional Variety", *Journal of Public Policy*, 15(3): 207–230.
—— (1998), *The Art of the State: Culture, Rhetoric and Public Management.* New York: Clarendon Press.
Huber, J. (1996), "The Vote of Confidence in Parliamentary Democracies", *American Political Science Review*, 90: 269–282.
Huntington, S.P. (1965), "Political Development and Political Decay", *World Politics*, 17: 386–430.
Huq, M.M. (1989), "Criticisms on Public Corporations in Bangladesh First Parliament; the Case of Debates on Budgets", *Journal of Local Government*, 18(2): 35–60.
Immergut, E. (1998), "The Theoretical Core of the New Institutionalism", *Politics and Society*, 26: 5–34.
Independent (2003), May 19. (an English daily in Bangladesh).
Indian *Lok Sabha* (1997), *Fifty Years of Indian Parliamentary Democracy.* New Delhi: *Lok Sabha* Secretariat.
—— (1998), *Rules of Procedures and Conduct of Business in Lok Sabha.* New Delhi: *Lok Sabha* Secretariat.
—— (2000), *First Report of COPU on Action Taken by Government on the Recommendations Contained in the 2nd Report of the COPU (12th Lok Sabha) Regarding*

Follow-up Action of the Reports of CAG of India (Commercial). New Delhi: *Lok Sabha* Secretariat.
—— (2001), *Departmentally-Related Standing Committees (1999–2000): A Review*. New Delhi: *Lok Sabha* Secretariat.
—— (2003), *Departmentally-Related Standing Committees (2001): A Review*. New Delhi: *Lok Sabha* Secretariat.
—— (2003a), *Departmentally-Related Standing Committees (2002): A Review*. New Delhi: *Lok Sabha* Secretariat.
—— (2003b), *Forty-sixth Report of PAC on Procurement of Defective Sleeping Bags*. New Delhi: *Lok Sabha* Secretariat.
—— (2003c), *Fifty-fourth Report of PAC on Review of Procurement for Operation Vijay (Army)*. New Delhi: *Lok Sabha* Secretariat.
—— (2003d), *Nineteenth Report of Standing Committee on Defense*. New Delhi: *Lok Sabha* Secretariat.
—— (2003e), *Twenty First Report of Standing Committee on Defense*. New Delhi: *Lok Sabha* Secretariat.
—— (2004), Reports of PAC (first to 63rd 1999–2004), in the 13th *Lok Sabha*, New Delhi: *Lok Sabha* Secretariat.
—— (2004a), Reports of COPA (first to 57th 1999–2004), in the 13th *Lok Sabha*, New Delhi: *Lok Sabha* Secretariat.
—— (2004b), Reports of COE (first to 19th 1999–2004), in the 13th *Lok Sabha*, New Delhi: *Lok Sabha* Secretariat.
—— (2004c), Reports of Standing Committee on Agriculture (46th–50th), in the 13th *Lok Sabha*, New Delhi: *Lok Sabha* Secretariat.
—— (2004d), Resume of Work of 13th *Lok Sabha* (1999–2004). New Delhi: *Lok Sabha* Secretariat.
Indian *Rajya Sabha* (2001), *Administrative Report of 2000* (Committee Section). New Delhi: *Rajya Sabha* Secretariat.
—— (2002), *Annual Report of 2001* (Committee Section) New Delhi: *Rajya Sabha* Secretariat.
—— (2003), *Annual Report of 2002* (Committee Section) New Delhi: *Rajya Sabha* Secretariat.
—— (2003a), 84th Report of Standing Committee on Home Affairs. New Delhi: *Rajya Sabha* Secretariat.
—— (2004), *Annual Report of 2003* (Committee Section) New Delhi: *Rajya Sabha* Secretariat.
Inter-Parliamentary Union [IPU] (1986), *Parliaments of the World: A Comparative Reference Compendium*. Aldershot, Hants: Gower.
Jaensch, D. (1994), *Power Politics: Australia's Party System*. Sydney: Allen and Unwin.
Jain, R.B. (1988), "Public Service Accountability in India", in J.G. Jabbra and O.P. Dwivedi (eds), *Public Service Accountability: A Comparative Perspective*. Hartfort: Kumarian Press, 122–135.
—— (1991), "Electronics Policy and the Indian Parliament", in David M. Olsen (ed.), *Legislatures in the Policy Process; The Dilemmas of Economic Policy*, Cambridge: Cambridge University Press, 1–21.
—— (1998), "Political Control of Bureaucracy in India", *Indian Journal of Public Administration*, 44(1): 1–16.
Jamil, I. (1998), *Administrative Culture in Public Administration: Five Essays on Bangladesh*. Bergen: Los-Sentret. Rapport 9801.

Jensen, L. (1998), "Cultural Theory and Democratizing Functional Domains: The Case of Danish Housing", *Public Administration*, 76: 117–139.

Jensen, J.L. and Rodgers, R. (2001), "Cumulating the Intellectual Gold of Case Study Research", *Public Administration Review*, 61(2): 236–246.

Jillson, C. (2002), *American Government: Political Change and Institutional Development*. Belmont: Wadsworth/Thomson Learning.

Judge, D. (1993), *The Parliamentary State*. London: Sage.

Kapur, D. and Mehta, P. (2002), "The Indian Parliament as an Institution of Accountability", report prepared for the Inter-Parliamentary Union, May 2002.

Kashyap, S.C. (ed.) (1973), *Parliamentary Committees in India*. New Delhi: Institute of Constitutional and Parliamentary Studies.

—— (1979) "Committees in the Indian *Lok Sabha*", in J.D. Lees and M. Shaw (eds), *Committees in Legislatures: A Comparative Analysis*. Oxford: Martin Robertson, 288–326.

—— (1997), "Parliament: Changing Face and Functions", in V.N. Narayan and S. Joyti (eds), *India at 50: Bliss of Hope and Burden of Reality*. New Delhi: Sterling.

—— (2000), "Institutions of Governance: the Parliament, the Government and the Judiciary", in V.A.P. Panandikar (ed.), *Problems of Governance in South Asia*. New Delhi: Konark Publishers Pvt. Ltd., 89–154.

Kesavan, K.V. (ed.) (2003), *Parliamentary Committees in Japan and India: Functions and Relevance*. New Delhi: Manak Publications Pvt. Ltd.

Khalequzzaman, M. (1999), "A Paper on the Committee System in Bangladesh", paper presented to a Conference on Comparative Constitutional Law: Parliamentary Committee System, organized by Bangladesh Jatiya Sangsad and Institute of Parliamentary Studies, Dhaka, May 27–28.

Khalidkar, R.K. (1979), "Parliamentary Committees: Case for Wider Powers", in S.C. Kashyap (ed.), *Parliamentary Committees in India*. New Delhi: The Institute of Constitutional and Parliamentary Studies, 8–13.

Kiewiet, D.R., Lowenberg, G. and Squire, P. (2002), "The Implications of the Study of the US Congress for Comparative Legislative Research", in G. Lowenberg, P. Squire and D.R. Kiewiet (eds), *Legislatures: Comparative Perspectives on Representative Assemblies*. Ann Arbor: University of Michigan Press, 3–22.

King, D. (1995), *Turf Wars: How Congressional Committees Claim Jurisdiction*. Chicago: University of Chicago Press.

Klitgaard, R.E. (1988), *Controlling Corruption*. Berkeley: University of California Press.

Knight, J. (1992), *Institutions and Social Conflict*. Cambridge: Cambridge University Press.

Kolobov, O.A. (1994), "Interest Groups in the Legislative Structures of Power: The Case of Russia", in Lawrence D. Longley (ed.), *Working Papers on Comparative Legislative Studies*. Appleton, Wisconsin: Research Committee of Legislative Specialists, International Political Science Association, Lawrence University.

Kothari, R. (1964), "The Congress System in India", *Asian Survey*, 4(12): 1161–1173.

Kornberg, A. (1970), "Parliament in Canadian Society", in A. Kornberg and L. Musolf (ed.), *Legislature in Developmental Perspective*, Durham: Duke University Press.

Krafchik, W. and Wehner, J. (1998), "The Role of Parliament in the Budget Process", *South African Journal of Economics*, 66(4): 512–541.

Krasner, S. (1984), "Approaches to the State: Alternative Conceptions and Historical Dynamics", *Comparative Politics*, 16: 223–246.

Kurian, G.T. (1998), "Sri Lanka", in G.T. Kurian (ed.), *World Encyclopaedia of Parliaments and Legislatures*, Vo. 1.Washington, D.C.: Congressional Quarterly Inc., 318–333.

Landman, T. (2000), *Issues and Methods in Comparative Politics: An Introduction.* London and New York: Routledge.

Lane, J.E. and Ersson, S.O. (1997), "Is Federalism Superior?", in A. Stennunenberg, F. Van Vught (eds), *Political Institutions and Public Policy*. Dordrecht: Kluwer Academic Publishers.

—— (2000), *The New Institutional Politics: Performances and Outcomes.* London: Routledge.

Lees, J.D. (1977), "Legislatures and Oversight: A Review Article on a Neglected Area of Research", *Legislative Studies Quarterly*, 2(May): 193–208.

Lees, J.D. and Shaw, M. (eds) (1979) *Committees in Legislature: A Comparative Analysis*. Oxford: Martin Robertson.

Leonard, D. and Herman, V. (1972), *The Backbencher and Parliament.* London: St. Martin's Press.

Lijphart, A. (1971), *World Politics: The Writings of Theorists and Practitioners, Classical and Modern.* Boston: Allyn and Bacon.

—— (1984) *Electoral Systems and Party Systems.* New York: Oxford University Press.

—— (1991), "Foreword: Cameral Change and Institutional Conservatism", in L.D. Longley and D.M. Olson (eds), *Two into One: The politics and Processes of National Legislative Cameral Change*. Boulder: Westview Press, ix–xii.

—— (1994), *Electoral Systems and Party Systems: A Study of Twenty-seven Democracies, 1945–1990.* Oxford: Oxford University Press.

—— (1996), "The Puzzle of Indian Democracy: A Consociational Interpretation", *American Political Science Review*, 90(2): 258–268.

—— (1999), *Patterns of Democracy: Government Forms and Performance in Thirty-six Countries*. New Haven: Yale University Press.

—— (2002), "Foreword", in J. Woldendrop, H. Keman and I. Budge (eds), *Parliamentary Government in 48 Democracies* (1945–1998). Dordrecht: Kluwer Publishers, vii–viii.

Linz, J.J. and Valenzuela, A. (1994), *The Failure of Presidential Democracy*. Baltimore: Johns Hopkins University Press.

Lipset, S.M. (1959), "Some Social Requisite of Democracy", *American Political Science Review*, 53(1): 69–105.

Lockhart, C. (1999), "Cultural Contribution to Explaining Institutional Form, Political Change and Rational Decisions", *Comparative Political Studies*, 32(7): 862–893.

Loewenberg, G. and Patterson, S.C. (1979), *Comparing Legislatures*. Boston: Little, Brown.

Longley, L.D. (1996), "Parliaments as Changing Institutions and as Agent of Regime Change: Evolving Perspectives and a New Research Framework", *Journal of Legislative Studies*, 2(2): 21–43.

Longley, L.D. and Davidson, R.H. (1998), "Parliamentary Committees: Changing Perspective on Changing Institutions", *Journal of Legislative Studies*, 4(1): 1–15.

Longley, L.D. and Olson, D.M. (1991), "The Politics and Processes of National Legislative Cameral Change", in Lawrence D. Longley and D.M. Olson (eds), *Two into One: The Politics and Processes of National Legislative Cameral Change*. Boulder: Westview Press, 1–41.

Lowndes, V. (1996, "Varieties of New Institutionalism: A Critical Appraisal", *Public Administration*, 74: 181–197.

—— (2002), "Institutionalism", in David March and Gerry Stoker (eds), *Theory and Methods in Political Science*. Hampshire and New York: Palgrave Macmillan.

McCubbins, M.D. and Rosenbluth, F.M. (1995), "Party Provision for Personal Politics: Dividing the Vote in Japan", in P.F. Cowhey and M.D. McCubbins (eds), *Structure and Policy in Japan and the United States*. Cambridge: Cambridge University Press.

Mackie, T.T. and Hogwood, B.W. (1955), *Unlocking the Cabinet: Cabinet Structures in Comparative Perspectives*. London and Beverly Hills: Sage Publications.

McSweeney, D. and Owens, J. (eds) (1998), *Republican Takeover on Capitol Hill*. New York: Macmillan.

Maheshwari, S.P. (1968), "Informal Consultative Committees of Parliament", *Journal of Constitutional and Parliamentary Studies*, 2: 27–53.

Malhotra, B.K. (2002), "Parliamentary Committees – Impact of Recommendations", in G.C. Malhotra (ed.), *Fifty Years of Indian Parliament*. New Delhi: *Lok Sabha* Secretariat, 395–401.

Malhotra, G.C. (1993), "India's Departmentally-Related Committee System", The *Parliamentarian*, 74(7): 165–175.

—— (2000), "Ensuring Executive Accountability: India's Public Accounts Committee", *The Parliamentarian*, 81: 179–186.

—— (2001), "Safeguarding Democracy: Role of Opposition in Indian Parliament", *The Journal of Parliamentary Information*, 47(2): 141–184.

—— (2002), "The Changing Profile of *Lok Sabha* – A Socio-economic Study of Members", in G.C. Malhotra (ed.), *Fifty Years of Indian Parliament*. New Delhi: *Lok Sabha* Secretariat, 101–133.

—— (2003), *Parliamentary Committees with Special References to Departmentally-Related Committees*. New Delhi: Bureau of Parliamentary Studies and Training.

Maniruzzaman, T. (1992), "The Fall of the Military Dictator: 1991 Elections and the Prospect of the Civilian Rule in Bangladesh", *Pacific Affairs*, 65(2): 203–223.

March, G.J. and Olsen, J.P. (1984), "The New Institutionalism: Organizational Factors in Political Life", *American Political Science Review*, 78: 734–749.

—— (1989), *Rediscovering Institutions*. New York: Free Press.

—— (1993) "Institutional Perspectives on Governance", Bergen: LOS-senter. Notat 93/15.

—— (1995), *Democratic Governance*. New York: Free Press.

—— (1996), "Institutional Perspectives on Political Institutions", *Governance: An International Journal of Policy and Administration*, 9(3): 247–264.

Marsh, D. and Read, M. (1988), *Private Members Bills*. Cambridge: Cambridge University Press.

Martin, K. (1982), "Parliament, Information and Intelligence", in J.R. Nethercote (ed.), *Parliament and Bureaucracy*. Sydney: Hale & Iremonger, 227–237.

Mathur, B.P. (2002), "PAC-Strengthening Parliamentary Financial Control", in G.C. Malhotra (ed.), *Fifty Years of Indian Parliament*. New Delhi: *Lok Sabha* Secretariat, 421–438.

Mattson, I. and Strøm, K. (1995), "Parliamentary Committees", in Herbert Döring (ed.), *Parliaments and Majority Rule in Western Europe*. Frankfurt: Campus Verlag, New York: St. Martin's Press, 249–307.

Mayhew, D.E. (1974), *Congress: The Electoral Connection*. New Haven: Yale University Press.

Meny, Y. (1993), *Government and Politics in Western Europe: Britain, France, Italy, Germany*. Oxford: Oxford University Press.

Merkel, W. (1998), "The Consolidation of Post-Autocratic Democracies: A Multi-level Model", *Democratization*, (5)3: 33–68.

Mezey, M.L. (1979), *Comparative Legislatures*. Durham: Duke University Press.

—— (1985), "Third World Legislatures", in G. Loewenberg, S.C. Patterson and M.E. Jewell (eds), *Handbook of Legislative Research*. Cambridge: Harvard University Press.

—— (1991), "Parliaments and Public Policy: An Assessment", in D.M. Olsen (eds), *Legislature in the Policy Process; The Dilemmas of Economic Policy*. Cambridge: Cambridge University Press, 201–216.

—— (1993), "Legislatures: Individual Purposes and Institutional Performance", in A.W. Finifter (ed.), *Political Science: The State of Discipline II*. Washington, D.C.: The American Political Science Association, 335–364.

—— (1994), "New Perspective on Parliamentary System: A Review Article", *Legislative Studies Quarterly*, 19(3): 429–441.

—— (1998), "Executive–Legislative Relations", in G.T. Kurian (ed.), *World Encyclopedia of Parliaments and Legislatures*. Vol. 2. Washington, DC: Congressional Quarterly Inc.

Miller, D. (1993), "Deliberative Democracy and Social Choice", in D. Held (ed.), *Prospect for Democracy*. Stanford: Stanford University Press.

Mills, John Stuart ([1943] 1967), *A System of Logic, Ratiocinative and Inductive*. Toronto: University of Toronto Press.

Mukhopadhyay, P.K. (2002), "Parliamentary Control over Public Purse in India", *Journal of Management and Training*, April 2002–December 2002, 1–10.

Mulgan, R. (1989), *Democracy and Power in New Zealand*. Auckland: Oxford University Press.

—— (2000), "Accountability: An Ever-expanding Concept", *Public Administration*, 78(3): 555–573.

Muttemwar, V. (2002), "Role of Parliamentary Committees in Strengthening Accountability Mechanism", in G.C. Malhotra (ed.), *Fifty Years of Indian Parliament*. New Delhi: *Lok Sabha* Secretariat, 402–405.

Nair, M.R. (2003), "Financial Committees of Parliament", in *Parliamentary Committees in Japan and India: Their Functions and Relevance*. New Delhi: Manak Publications Pvt. Ltd, 150–176.

National Commission to Review the Working of the Constitution [NCRWC] (2001), *Effectiveness of Public Audit System in India: Reforming the Institution of the Comptroller and Auditor General (CAG)*, New Delhi: Ministry of Parliamentary Affairs.

National Endowment for Democracy [NED] (1997), *Democracy in South Asia*, Washington, D.C.: Ned.

Nolan, L. (1996), First Radcliff Lecture, Warwick University, July 11.

Norton, P. (1975), *Dissension in the House of Commons 1945–74*. London: Macmillan.

—— (1979), "The Organization of Parliamentary Parties", in S.A. Walkland (ed.), *The House Of Commons in the Twentieth Century*. Oxford: Oxford University Press.

—— (1980), *Dissension in the House of Commons 1974–79*. Oxford: Oxford University Press.

—— (1981), *The Commons in Perspective*. Oxford: Martin Robertson.

—— (1984), "Parliament and Policy in Britain: The House of Commons as a Policy Influencer", *Teaching Politics*, 13: 198–202.

—— (1990) (ed.), *Legislatures*. Oxford: Oxford University Press.

—— (1990a), "Parliament: A Framework for Analysis", in P. Norton (ed.), *Parliaments in Western Europe*. London and Portland: Frank Cass, 1–9.

—— (1990b), "Parliament in the United Kingdom: Balancing Effectiveness and Consent", in P. Norton (ed.), *Parliaments in Western Europe*. London and Portland: Frank. Cass, 10–31.

—— (1990c), "Conclusion: Legislatures in Perspective", in Philip Norton (ed.), *Parliaments in Western Europe*. London and Portland: Frank Cass, 143–152.

—— (1993), *Does Parliament Matter?* London: Hemel Hempstead, Harvester Wheatsheaf.

—— (1994), "The Legislative Powers of Parliaments", in C. Flinterman, A.W. Herings and L. Waddington (eds), *The Evolving Role of Parliaments in Europe*. Antwerpen: Maklu Uitgevers, Baden-Baden: Nomos Verlag, 15–35.

—— (1994a), "Representation of Interests: The Case of British House of Commons", in S.C. Patterson and G.W. Copeland (eds), *Parliaments in the Modern World: Changing Institutions*. Ann Arbor: University of Michigan Press, 13–28.

—— (1994b), "The Parliamentary Party and Party Committees", in A. Seldon and S. Ball (eds), *The Conservative Party in the Twentieth Century*. Oxford: Oxford University Press, 97–144.

—— (1997), "Legislatures in Perspective", in P. Norton (ed.), *Parliaments in Western Europe (second edition)*. London: Frank Cass.

—— (1997a), "Parliamentary Oversight", in P. Dunleavy, A. Gamble, I. Holliday and G. Peele (eds), *Developments in British Politics 5*. Basingstoke, Hampshire: Macmillan, 155–176.

—— (1998), "Introduction: The Institutions of Parliaments", in P. Norton (ed.), *Parliaments and Governments in Western Europe*. London Frank Cass, 1–15.

—— (1998a), "Conclusion: Do Parliaments Make a Difference", in P. Norton (ed.), *Parliaments and Governments in Western Europe*. London: Frank Cass, 190–208.

—— (1999), "Conclusion: Making Sense of Diversity", in P. Norton and N. Ahmed (eds), *Parliaments in Asia*. London: Frank Cass, 139–191.

—— (2000), "Reforming Parliament in the UK: The Report of the Commission to Strengthen Parliament", *The Journal of Legislative Studies*, Vol. 6(3): 1–14.

—— (2001), "Playing by the Rules: The Constraining Hands of Parliamentary Procedure", *Journal of Legislative Studies*, 7(3): 13–33.

Norton, P. and Ahmed, N. (1999), "Legislatures in Asia: Exploring Diversity", in P. Norton and N. Ahmed (eds), *Parliaments in Asia*. London: Frank Cass, 1–12.

Norton, P. and Olson, D.M. (1997), "Parliaments in Adolescence", in D.M. Olsen and P. Norton (eds), *The New Parliaments of Central and Eastern Europe*. London and Portland: Frank Cass, 231–243.

Oberst, R.C. (1985), "Legislative Behavior and Ethnicity in a Third World Democracy-Sri Lanka", *Pacific Affairs*, 58(2): 265–286.

O'Donnel, G. (1997), "Illusion about Consolidation", in L. Diamond, M.F. Plattner, Y. Chu and H. Tien (eds), *Consolidating the Third Wave Democracies: Themes and Perspective*. Baltimore and London: Johns Hopkins University Press.

Oleszek, W.J. (1996), *Congressional Procedures and the Policy Process*. Washington, D.C.: CQ Press.

Olson, M. (1982), *The Rise and Decline of Nations: Economic Growth, Stagnation and Social Rigidities*. New Haven: Yale University Press.

Olson, D.M. (1994), *Democratic Legislative Institutions: A Comparative View*. Armonk: M.E. Sharpe.

Olson, D.M. and Longley, L.D. (1991), "Conclusions: Cameral Change Politics and Processes in the Three Nations and Beyond", in L.D. Longley and D.M. Olson (eds), *Two into One: The Politics and Processes of National Legislative Ccameral Change*. Boulder: Westview Press, 203–232.

Olson, D.M. and M.L. Mezey (1991), "Parliaments and Public Policy", in D.M. Olson (ed.), *Legislatures in the Policy Process: The Dilemmas of Economic Policy*. Cambridge: Cambridge University Press, 1–21.

Olson, D.M. and P. Norton. (1996), "Legislatures in Democratic Transition", in D.M. Olson and P. Norton (eds), *The New Parliaments of Central and Eastern Europe*. London and Portland: Frank Cass, 1–15.

Olson, D.M. and Crowther, W.E. (1998), "Committees in New and Established Democracies", paper presented to an International Conference on Committees in New and Established Democracies. University of North Carolina Greensboro, May 30–June 2.

Opello, W.C., Jr. (1986), "Portugal's Parliament: An Organizational Analysis of Legislative Performance", *Legislative Studies Quarterly*, 11: 291–320.

Ornstein, N.J. (1981) (eds), *The Role of the Legislature in Western Democracies*. Washington, D.C.: American Enterprise Institute for Public Policy Research.

Overseas Development Assistance [ODA] (1993), "Good Government", Technical Note No. 10, London: ODA.

Packenham, R.A. (1970), "Legislatures and Political Development", in A. Kornberg and L. Musolf (eds), *Legislatures in Developmental Perspective*. Durham: Duke University Press.

Palmer, G. (1992), *New Zealand's Constitution in Crisis*. Auckland: Oxford University Press.

Parliament of Sri Lanka (1993), *Standing Order of the Parliament of the Democratic Socialist Republic of Sri Lanka*. Colombo: The Parliament Secretariat.

—— (1995), *Report of the Committee on Public Accounts*, Parliamentary series No. 13. Colombo: The Parliament Secretariat.

—— (2003), *Minutes of Committee on Public Accounts of 1st and 2nd session of the 5th Parliament*. Colombo: The Parliament Secretariat.

—— (2003a), *Minutes of Committee on Public Enterprises of 1st and 2nd session of the 5th Parliament*. Colombo: The Parliament Secretariat.

—— (2003b), *Minutes of the Committee on High Post of the 1st session of 5th Parliament (Vols 1–3), Parliament of Sri Lanka*. Colombo: The Parliament Secretariat.

—— (2003c), *Minutes of the Consultative Committee on Ministry of Defense of the 5th Parliament*. Colombo: The Parliament Secretariat.

—— (2003d), *Minutes of the Consultative Committee on Public Administration, Management and Reform of the 5th Parliament*. Colombo: The Parliament Secretariat.

—— (2004), *Bills Register/Acts Register*. Parliament Secretariat, Sri Lanka (2000–2004) Colombo: The Parliament Secretariat.

Patterson, S.C. (1995), "Legislative Institutions and Institutionalism in the United States", *The Journal of Legislative Studies*, 1(4): 10–29.

Patterson, S.C. and Copeland, G.W. (1994), "Parliaments in the Twenty-first Century", in G.W. Copeland and S.C. Patterson (eds), *Parliaments in the Modern World: Changing Institutions*. Ann Arbor: The University of Michigan Press, 1–11.

Patzelt, W.J. (1994), "A Framework for Comparative Parliamentary Research in Central and Eastern Europe", in L.D. Longley (ed.), *Working Paper on Comparative Legislative Studies Part-1: The Role of Legislature and Parliaments in Democratizing and Newly Democratic Regimes*. Appleton: Research Committee of Legislative Specialists, International Political Science Association, 431–444.

Paul, S. (1991), "Accountability in Public Service: Exit, Voice and Capture", Policy Research and External Affairs Working Papers WPS 614. Washington, D.C.: World Bank.

Pennings, P. (2003), "Beyond Dichotomous Explanations: Explaining Constitutional Control of the Executive with Fuzzy-sets", *European Journal of Political Research*, 42: 541–567.

Perera, J. (2000), "Tribute: A Lasting Contribution", *Frontline*, 17(4) (February19-March 3), 1–4.
Perera, N.M. (1958), "Financial Procedure in the House of Representatives", *Ceylon Journal of Historical and Social Studies*, 1: 25–35.
Peters, B.G. (1991), *European Politics Reconsidered*. New York: Holmes and Meier.
—— (1995), *The Politics of Bureaucracy*. New York: Longman.
—— (1998), *Comparative Politics: Theory and Methods*. Houndmills: Macmillan.
—— (1999), *Institutional Theory in Political Science: The New Institutionalism*. London and New York: Pinter.
Phandis, U. (1989), "Sri Lanka", in L. Diamond, J. Linz and S. Lipset (eds), *Democracy in Developing Countries: Asia*. Boulder: Lynne Rienner Publishers.
Pollitt, C. (1999), "Accountability and Democracy: Answering to Political Authority and Citizen's Need", paper presented to the International Institute of Administrative Sciences Conference, Civil Service College Sunningdale, May 12–15, 1999.
Polsby, N.W. (1968), "The Institutionalization of US House of Representatives", *American Political Science Review*, 62(1): 144–168.
—— (1975), "Legislatures", in F.I. Greenstein and N.W. Polsby (eds), *Handbook of Political Science*, Vol. 5. Reading: Addition-Wesley, 257–319.
Powell, G.B. (2000), *Elections as Instruments of Democracy: Majoritarian and Proportional Visions*. New Haven: Yale University Press.
Prathom Alo (2004), January 8 (a vernacular daily in Bangladesh).
Przeworski, A. and Tuene, H. (1970), *The Logic of Comparative Social Enquiry*. New York: John Wiley.
Przeworski, A, Alvarez, M., Chebub, J.A. and Limongi, F. (1996), "What Makes Democracies Endure?", *Journal of Democracy*, 7(1): 39–55.
Putnam, R.D. (1993), *Making Democracy Work: Civil Traditions in Modern Italy*. Princeton: Princeton University Press.
Pyper, R. (1996) (ed.), *Aspects of Accountability in the British System of Government*. Merseyside, England: Tudor Business Publication.
Quirk, B. (1997), "Accountable to Everyone: Post Modern Pressures on Public Managers", *Public Administration*, 75: 569–586.
Radin, B.A. and Boase, J.P. (2000), "Federalism, Political Structure, and Public Policy in the United States and Canada", *Journal of Comparative Policy Analysis*, 2(1): 65–89.
Rae, D.W. (1971), *The Political Consequences of Electoral Laws*. New Haven: Yale University Press.
Ragin, C.C. (1987), *The Comparative Method: Moving Beyond Qualitative and Quantitative Strategies*. Berkeley: University of California Press Limited.
—— (1992), "Introduction: Cases of what is a Case", in C.C. Ragin and H.S. Becker (eds), *What is a Case? Exploring the Foundation of Social Enquiry*. Cambridge: Cambridge University Press, 1–17.
Rahman, M.T. (2000), "The Role of Parliamentary Committees in Ensuring Bureaucratic Accountability in Bangladesh", unpublished MPhil Thesis. Bergen: University of Bergen.
Ramacharyulu, P.P.K. (2003), "Parliamentary Committees and Executive Accountability: A Case Study of Departmentally-Related Standing Committees in India", in K.V. Kesavan (ed.), *Parliamentary Committees in Japan and India: Their Functions and Relevance*. New Delhi: Manak Publications Pvt. Ltd, 133–149.
Rasch, B.E. (2000), "Parliamentary Floor Voting Procedures and Agenda Setting in Europe", *Legislative Studies Quarterly*, 25(1): 3–23.
Rashid, A. (1997), *Pramanno Sangsad* (in Bengali). Dhaka: Tatthya Seba.

—— (2002), *A Study on 8th Jatiya Sangsad*. Dhaka: Tatthya Seba.

Rashid, H. (2003), "Parliamentary Control and Financial Accountability in Bangladesh: The Role of Public Accounts Committee of Jatiya Sangsad", paper presented to a Seminar on Parliamentary Control and Financial Accountability in Bangladesh: The Role of Financial Committees jointly organized by Parliament of Bangladesh and UNDP, Dhaka, December 15.

Rawlings, H. (1986), "Judicial Review and the Control of Government", *Public Administration*, 64(2): 135–146.

Rayner, S. and Melone, E.L. (1998), *Human Choice and Climate Change*. Columbus, Ohio: Battele Press.

Rhodes, R. (1997), *Understanding Governance*. Buckingham: Open University Press.

Riggs, F.W. (1964), *Administration in Developing Countries: The Theory of Prismatic Society*. Boston: Houghton Mifflin.

—— (1975), *Legislative Origins: A Comparative and Contextual Approach*. International Studies Association, Occasional Paper No. 7. Pittsburgh: International Studies Association.

Riker, W.H. (1975), "Federalism", in F.I. Greenstein and N.W. Polsby (eds), *Handbook of Political Science, 5: Governmental Institutions and Processes*. Reading: Addison-Wesley, 5: 93–172.

—— (1982), *Liberalism Against Populism: A Confrontation between the Theory of Democracy and the Theory of Social Choice*. San Francisco: W.H. Freeman.

Rockman, B.A. (1985), "Legislative-executive Relations", in G. Loewenberg, S.C. Patterson and M.E. Jewell (eds), *Handbook of Legislative Research*. Cambridge: Harvard University Press.

Rommetvedt, H. (1998), "Norwegian Parliamentary Committees: Performance, Structural Change and External Relations", *The Journal of Legislative Studies*, 4(1): 60–84.

Romzek, B.S. (2000), "Accountability of Congressional Staff", *Journal of Public Administration Research and Theory*, 10(2): 413–446.

—— (2000a), "Dynamics of Public Sector Accountability in an Era of Reform", *International Review of Administrative Sciences*, 66(1): 21–44.

Romzek, B.S. and Dubnick, M.J. (1987), "Accountability in the Public Sector: Lessons from the Challenger Tragedy", *Public Administration Review*, 47(3): 227–238.

—— (2000), "Accountability", in J.M. Shafritz (ed.), *Defining Public Administration: Selections from the International Encyclopedia of Public Policy and Administration*. Boulder: Westview Press, 382–396.

Romzek, B.S. and Ingraham, P.W. (2000), "Cross Pressures of Accountability: Initiative, Command and Failure in the Ron Brown Plane Crash", *Public Administration Review*, 60(3): 240–253.

Rose, R. (1984), "The Use of Laws as a Policy Resource", in R. Rose (ed.), *Understanding Big Government: The Programme Approach*. London: Sage Publications, 63–92.

Rosen, B. (1989), *Holding Government Bureaucracies Accountable*. New York: Praeger.

—— (1998), *Holding Government Bureaucracies Accountable*. 3rd edn. Westport. Conn.: Praeger.

Rubinoff, A.G. (1996), "India's Subject-based Parliamentary Standing Committees", *Asian Survey*, 36(7): 723–738.

—— (1999), "The Decline of India's Parliament", in P. Norton and N. Ahmed (eds), *Parliaments in Asia*. London and Portland: Frank Cass, 13–33.

Rueschemeyer, D., Stephens, E. and Stephens, J.D. (1992), *Capitalistic Development and Democracy*. Cambridge: Polity Press.

Rush, M. (1998), "Lobbying", in T. Kurian (ed.), *World Encyclopaedia of Parliaments and Legislatures*. Washington, D.C.: Congressional Quarterly Inc, 810–815.

Russell, M. (2000), *Reforming the House of Lords: Lessons from Overseas*. Oxford: Oxford University Press.

Ryle, M. (1988), "Where have we got to?", in M. Ryle and P.G. Richards (eds), *The Commons under Scrutiny*. London: Routledge, 229–241.

Saloma, J.S. (1969), *Congress and the New Politics*. Boston: Little, Brown and Company.

Sartori, G. (1970), "Concept Misinformation in Comparative Politics", *American Political Science Review*, 64: 1033–1053.

—— (1991), "Comparing and Miscomparing", *Journal of Theoretical Politics*, 3(3): 243–257.

—— (1994), "Compare Why and How: Comparing, Miscomparing and Comparative Method", in M. Dogan and A. Kazancigil (eds), *Comparing Nations: Concepts, Strategies and Substance*. Oxford and Cambridge: Blackwell, 14–34.

—— (1994a), *Comparative Constitutional Engineering: An Inquiry into Structures, Incentives, and Outcomes*. New York: New York University Press.

Schlesinger, J.A. (1991), *Political Parties and the Winning of Office*. Ann Arbor: University of Michigan Press.

Schuttermeyer, S.S. (1994), "Hierarchy and Efficiency in the Bundestag: The German Answer for Institutionalizing Parliament", in S.C. Patterson and G.W. Copeland (eds), *Parliament in the Modern World: Changing Institutions*. Ann Arbor: University of Michigan Press.

Schwarz, J.E. (1980), "Exploring a New Role in Policy-making: The British House of Commons in the 1970s", *American Political Science Review*, 74: 23–37.

Scott, W.R. (1995), *Institutions and Organizations*. London: Sage Publications.

Selznick, P. (1957), *Leadership in Organizations*. New York: Russel Sage.

—— (1996), "Institutionalism 'Old' and 'New'", *Administrative Science Quarterly*, 41(2): 270–277.

Sharma, S.D. (2003), "India's Democratic Resilience", *Harvard Asia Pacific Review*, 7(1): 77–80.

Shastri, A. and Wilson, A.J. (2001), *Post-colonial States of South Asia: Democracy, Identity, Development, and Security*. Richmond: Curzon.

Shastri, S. (1998), "Department Related Standing Committees in the Indian Parliament", *Indian Journal of Public Administration*, 44(2): 184–200.

Shaw, M. (1979), "Conclusion", in J.D. Lees and M. Shaw (eds), *Committees in Legislatures*. Durham: Duke University Press, 361–431.

—— (1998), "Parliamentary Committees: A Global Perspective", in L.D. Longley and R.H. Davidson (eds), *The New Role of Parliamentary Committees*. London: Frank Cass, 225–251.

—— (1998a), "Legislative Committees", in G.T. Kurian (ed.), *World Encyclopedia of Parliaments and Legislatures*, Vol. 2. Washington, D.C.: Congressional Quarterly Inc., 786–796.

Shekar, B. (2003), "Departmentally-Related Standing Committees in the India", in K.V. Kesavan (ed.), *Parliamentary Committees in Japan and India: Their Functions and Relevance*. New Delhi: Manak Publications Pvt. Ltd, 88–105.

Shell, D.R. (1998), "Second Chambers", in G.T. Kurian (ed.), *World Encyclopedia of Parliaments and Legislatures*, Vol. 2. Washington, D.C.: Congressional Quarterly Inc., 845–852.

Shepsle, K.A. and Weingast, Barry R. (1987), "The Institutional Foundations of Committee Power", *American Political Science Review*, 81(1): 85–104.

Shrivastava, M.P. and Shrivastava, K.P. (1999), *Parliament and Financial Committees*. New Delhi: Anmol Publications Pvt. Ltd.

Shugart, M.S. and Carey, J.M. (1992), *President and Assemblies: Constitutional Design and Electoral Dynamics*. New York: Cambridge University Press.

Shugart, M.S. and Haggard, S. (2001), "Institutions and Public Policy in Presidential Systems", in S. Haggard and M.D. McCubbins (eds), *Presidents, Parliaments and Policy*. Cambridge and New York: Cambridge University Press, 64–102.

Shugart, M.S. and Mainwaring, S. (1997), "Conclusion: Varieties of Presidentialism", in S. Mainwaring and S. Matthew (eds), *Presidentialism and Democracy in Latin America*. Cambridge: Cambridge University Press.

Silva, K.M.D. (2000), "The Working of Democracy in South Asia", in V.A.P. Panandiker (ed.), *Problems of Governance in South Asia*. Delhi: Konark Publishers Pvt. Ltd., 47–88.

Simms, H. (ed.) (1980), *Towards a Science of the Singular*. Norwich: Centre for Applied Research in Education, University of East Anglia.

Simms, M. (1999), "Models of Political Accountability and Concepts of Australian Government", *Australian Journal of Public Administration*, 58(1): 34–38.

Singhvi, L.M. (1970), "Parliament in the Indian Political System", in A. Kornberg and L. Musolf (eds), *Legislature in Developmental Perspective*, Durham: Duke University Press.

—— (1979), "Key Role of Standing Committees: Agenda for Reform", in S.C. Kashyap (ed.), *Parliamentary Committees in India*. New Delhi: The Institute of Constitutional and Parliamentary Studies, 1–7.

Smith, B. (1996), *Understanding Third World Politics*. London: Macmillan.

Smith, G. (1980), Politics in Western Europe. London: Heinemann.

Sobhan, R. (1998), *Crisis in Governance: A Review of Bangladesh's Development, 1997*. Dhaka: Center for Policy Dialogue and University Press Limited.

Squire, P. (1992), "The Theory of Legislative Institutionalization and the California Assembly", *The Journal of Politics*, 54(4): 1026–1054.

Stake, R.E. (1995), *The Art of Case Study Research*. Thousand Oaks: Sage Publications.

Stepan, A. and Skatch, C. (1993), "Constitutional Frameworks and Democratic Consolidation: Parliamentarianism versus Presidentialism", *World Politics*, 46: 1–22.

Strøm, K. (1990), *Minority Government and Majority Rule*. New York: Cambridge University Press.

—— (1998), "Parliamentary Committees in European Democracies", *Journal of Legislative Studies*, 4(1): 20–59.

Supakar, S. (1979), "Committees in Indian Parliamentary System", in S.C. Kashyap (ed.), *Parliamentary Committees in India*. New Delhi: The Institute of Constitutional and Parliamentary Studies, 14–17.

Suri, P. (1979), *Growth of Committee Systems in the Central Legislatures of India 1920–1947*. New Delhi: Associated Publishing Co.

Taagepera, R. (1998), "How Electoral Systems Matter for Democratization", *Democratization*, (5)4: 68–92.

Taagepera, R. and Shugart, M.S. (1989), *Seats and Votes: The Effects and Determinants of Electoral Systems*. New Haven: Yale University Press.

Tayeb, M.H. (1988), *Organizations and National Culture: A Comparative Analysis*. London: Sage.

Taylor, M. and Herman, V. (1971), "Party Systems and Government Stability", *American Political Science Review*, 65: 28–37.

Telegraph (2004), March 3 (an English-language daily in India).

Thompson, M. (1996), *Inherent Rationality*. Bergen: LOS Center. Report 9608.

Thompson, M., Ellis, R.J. and Wildavsky, A. (eds) (1990), *Cultural Theory*. Boulder: Westview Press.

Thompson, M., Grendstad, D. and Selle, P. (eds) (1999), *Cultural Theory as Political Science*. London: Routledge.

Transparency International [TI] (2004a), National Integrity Systems – Transparency International, Country Study Report – India 2003. Berlin: Transparency International Secretariat.

—— (2004b), National Integrity Systems – Transparency International, Country Study Report – Sri Lanka 2003. Berlin: Transparency International Secretariat.

—— (2005), *Corruption Perception Index (CPI)*. Berlin: Transparency International Secretariat.

Transparency International Bangladesh [TIB] (2002), Annual Report. Dhaka: TIB.

—— (2003), *Parliament Watch*, (1–6 session), Eighth JS. Dhaka: TIB.

—— (2004), *Parliament Watch*, (7–10 session), Eighth JS. Dhaka: TIB.

—— (2004), *Parliament Watch*, (11–14 session), Eighth JS. Dhaka: TIB.

Truman, D.B. (1981), *The Governmental Process: Political Interests and Public Opinion*. Westport: Greenwood Press.

—— (1995), "Bicameral Negotiations: The Navette System in France", *British Journal of Political Science*, 25(1): 101–129.

Tsebelis, G. (2002), *Veto Players: How Political Institutions Work*. New York: Russell Sage.

Tsebelis, G. and Money, J. (1997), *Bicameralism, Political Economy of Institutions and Decision*. Cambridge: Cambridge University Press.

Turner, M. and Hulme, D. (1997), *Governance, Administration and Development: Making the State Work*. London: Macmillan.

Uhr, J. (1982), "Parliament and Public Administration", in J.R. Nethercote (ed.), *Parliament and Bureaucracy*. Sydney: Hale & Iremonger, 26–66.

—— (1997), Keeping Government Honest: Preconditions of Parliamentary Effectiveness'. Paper on Parliament No. 29. Canberra: The Department of Senate, Parliament House, 51–64.

—— (1998), *Deliberative Democracy in Australia: The Changing Place of Parliament*. Cambridge: Cambridge University Press.

—— (1999), "Three Accountability Anxieties: A Conclusion to the Symposium", *Australian Journal of Public Administration*, 58(1): 98–101.

Ullah, A. (1992), *Members of the Fifth Jatiya Sangsad*. A documentary (in Bengali). Dhaka: Suchayan Prakashan.

Unekis, J.K (1998), "Dealing with the Loyal Opposition in Democratic Parliaments: Lessons from the United States Congress", in L.D. Longley and D. Zajc (eds), *Working Papers on Comparative Legislative Studies iii: The New Democratic Parliaments in the First Year*. Appleton, Wisconsin: Research Committee of Legislative Specialists, International Political Science Association, 195–206.

Unekis, J.K and Franke, J.L. (1997), "The Resurgence of Partisanship in the Committees of the US House of Representatives", in L.D. Longley and A. Agh (eds), *Working Papers on Comparative Legislative Studies ii: The Changing Role of Parliamentary Committees*. Appleton, Wisconsin: Research Committee of Legislative Specialists, International Political Science Association, 195–206.

United Nations Development Programme [UNDP] (1993), Governance, Public Sector Management and Human Development: A UNDP Strategy Paper. New York: UNDP.

—— (1999), The Constitution and its Relationship to the Legislature – UNDP short technical paper. New York: UNDP.

—— (2000), Legislature and Constituency Relations – A UNDP-MAGNET technical series publication. New York: UNDP.

—— (2004), Human Development Index. New York: UNDP.

United Nations Development Programme [UNDP] Bangladesh (2005), *Beyond Hartals: Towards Democratic Dialogue in Bangladesh*. Dhaka: UNDP.

Wagner, C. (2001), "Sri Lanka", in D. Nohlen, F. Grotzn and C. Hartmann (eds), *Elections in Asia and the Pacific: A Data Handbook.* Oxford: Oxford University Press, 697–713.

Walkland, S. (1983) "Parliamentary Reform, Party Realignment and Electoral Reform", in D. Judge (ed.), *The Politics of Parliamentary Reform*. London: Heinemann, 37–54.

Ward, V. (1998), "Towards a Theory of State–Non-state Actors: A Grid-group Cultural Approach", in J. Dominique, O. Andrew and V. Marco (eds), *Culture in World Politics*. London: Macmillan, 206–244.

Warnapala, W.A.W. (1980), "Sri Lanka's New Constitution", *Asian Survey*, 20(9): 922–930.

—— (2003), "Parliamentary Oversight Committees", *The Island*, October 15.

—— (2004), *Parliament and Accountability in Sri Lanka.* Colombo: Godage International Publishers (Pvt.) Ltd.

Weaver, R.K. and Rockman, B.A. (1993), "Assessing the Effects of Institutions", in R.K. Weaver and B.A. Rockman (eds), *Do Institutions Matter?* Washington, D.C.: Brookings Institute Press, 1–41.

Weiner, M. (1980), *India at the Polls, 1980.* Washington, D.C.: American Enterprise Institute.

Welikala, A. (2002), *Parliamentary Committee Systems*. Colombo: Center for Policy Alternative.

Wheare, K.C. (1955), *Government by Committee*. Oxford: Clarendon Press.

Wijesekera, P. (2002), *Parliamentary Practice in Sri Lanka.* Colombo: Parliament Secretariat.

Wildavsky, A. (1987), "Choosing Preferences by Constructing Institutions: A Cultural Theory of Preferences Formation", *American Political Science Review*, 81(1): 3–21.

Wilson, A.J. (1979), *Politics in Sri Lanka, 1947–1979*. London: Macmillan.

—— (1980), *The Gaullist System in Asia: The Constitution of Sri Lanka, 1978*. London: Macmillan.

Wilson, J.Q. and DiIulio, J.J. (1995), *American Government: Institutions and Policies*. Lexington, Massachusetts: D.C. Heath.

Wiltshire, K. (1982), "Staffing and Appropriation of Parliament", in J.R. Nethercote (ed.), *Parliament and Bureaucracy*. Sydney: Hale & Iremonger, 302–318.

Winetrobe, B.K. (2000), *Shifting Control? Aspects of the Parliamentary-Executive Relationships*. Research Paper-00/92. London: Parliament and Constitution Centre.

Wolf, A. (2000), "Symposium on Accountability in Public Administration: Reconciling, Democracy, Efficiency and Ethics", *International Review of Administrative Sciences*, 66(1): 15–20.

Wood, B.D. and Walterman, R.W. (1994), *Bureaucratic Dynamics: The Role of Bureaucracy in a Democracy*. Boulder: Westview.

World Bank, The. (1991), *Proceedings of the World Bank Annual Conference on Development Economics*. Washington, D.C.: The World Bank.

—— (1994), *Governance: The World Bank's Experience.* Washington, D.C.: The World Bank.

—— (1996), *Bangladesh: Government that Works: Reforming the Public Sector*. Dhaka: University Press Ltd.

—— (2002), *Taming Leviathan: Reforming Governance in Bangladesh – An Institutional Review*. Washington, D.C.: The World Bank.

—— (2003), *Sri Lanka – Country Financial Accountability Assessment* (CFAA), Final Report, Washington, D.C.: The World Bank.

—— (2004), *World Development Indicators Database*. Washington, D.C.: The World Bank.

Yin, R.K. (1994), *Case Study Research: Design and Methods*. London: Sage Publications.

Zellick, G. (1986), "Government Beyond the Law", *Public Law*, 283–308.

Index